Vincent Gasnier

"It always gives me great pleasure when I can pass on what I have learnt from tasting many of the world's finest–and not so fine–wines in a simple, easily-assimilated form. So I was delighted when Dorling Kindersley invited me to provide lists of the Top 10 Wines of the US and Canada, category by category. Obviously there was not room to include every deserving wine, but the lists have been devised to cover a broad range. They naturally feature many well-known labels from major producers, but they also contain names that may be unfamiliar to many readers, from the fabulous–and, in many cases, fabulously expensive–wines of the Napa Valley to the country's best-kept secrets, with remarkably good-value wines from lesser-known wine areas, produced by talented, up-and-coming winemakers."

Vincent Gasnier
London, May 2006

TOP 10 Selections

No hierarchy of quality is implied by the order in which the wines appear in the Top 10 lists. The 10 selections are of roughly equal merit.

Fine Red Wines of the USA *p27*
Best Napa Producers *p33*
Great California Chardonnays *p36*
Best-Kept Secrets of California Wine *p39*
Magnificent Merlots *p41*
Great California Cabernet Sauvignons *p43*
Zinfandel Producers *p50*
Good Wines for Everyday Drinking *p53*
Best Sparkling Wine Houses *p60*
Sustainably Farmed or Organic Wines *p62*
Wines for Celebrations *p66*
Fine White Wines of the USA *p70*
Best Rosé (Blush) Producers *p72*
Exceptional California Syrah Wines *p77*
Fabulous Dessert Wines *p80*
Great Riesling Makers *p85*
Best Wineries in the Pacific Northwest *p96*
Outstanding Pinot Noir Wines *p103*
Fabulous Fortified Wines *p109*
Best Canadian Reds *p128*
Best Canadian Whites *p130*

About Vincent Gasnier

A young French sommelier, now working in Britain, Vincent Gasnier has enjoyed a rapid rise to preeminence in his profession. In 1994–5, while working at the Restaurant Laurent in Paris, he was promoted to Sommelier under Philippe Bourguignon, regarded as one of the best sommeliers in France. In 1997, at the age of 22, he qualified as Master Sommelier: the youngest person in the world to achieve this distinction. After a period as Chef-Sommelier at the Hotel du Vin, Winchester, he set up a consultancy business of his own, offering advice on wine purchase, cellar management, VIP wine events, and exclusive wine tours. He shares his expertise with many distinguished clients, including the Houses of Parliament in London. He is a wine judge and has appeared on TV and in various wine magazines.

For more on Vincent Gasnier, check **www.vincentgasnier.co.uk**

Old versus New Wines

Today, wine is said to come from the Old World or the New. The classic regions of France, Italy, and Spain are at the core of the Old World. The New World comprises the southern hemisphere and North America. Until recently it was relatively easy to pick up a glass of wine and identify, with a small sniff and a sip, whether it was from the New World or the Old. A New World wine would have all the rich fruit flavors and aromas that reflect warm-climate vineyards. An Old World example would be rather more subtle with delicate, complex aromas and leaner flavors. Today, however, improved techniques mean that an Old World wine can taste every bit as luscious and ripe as a New World version. Meanwhile, the New World uses such Old World techniques as barrel-fermenting, wild yeasts, and lees-stirring to create more complexity.

Estate versus Branded Wines

Techniques in the winery are now so advanced that, with recourse to appropriate grapes, a winemaker has many options. The art of making the mass-production wines is to make each batch and vintage the same so that the brand is reliable and affordable. Estate wines, by contrast, are a true reflection of their land and culture. These are the wines that evoke passionate discussion, genuine loyalty—and a hugely variable price range. They are also the wines that can undergo near-miraculous flavor transformations when laid down to age.

Trends in Wine Consumption

The traditional wine-drinking countries of France, Italy, and Spain have actually seen a slump in consumption over the last 30 years. There are several reasons for this. In the first place, because water quality has improved, wine is no longer needed as a general beverage, and it is perceived as an impediment to work performance. There has also been a decline in café drinking. In an effort to combat the ever-growing European "wine lake," wine is thus produced in smaller quantities and to a higher standard (and price) in these countries. It is no longer regarded as a drink for quaffing, but for sipping and enjoying.

In the English-speaking world, the picture is quite different; wine consumption in the UK for example has risen by over 500 percent since 1970. The surge in wine's popularity is a direct result of the huge quantities of affordable ripe-fruited New World wines flooding onto the market and the advent of "branded" wines. Wine is no longer the preserve of a privileged elite.

There is a general belief that wine is part of healthy living. Wine's benefits as a sociable beverage, a health-giver, and as an all-around focus of interest suggest it will be part of culture for years to come.

Domaine Drouhin vineyard, Oregon

32° and 51° in the northern hemisphere, and 28° and 42° in the southern. Wine is made in virtually all the parts of the world with a suitable climate—from Chile to New Zealand and South Africa to China.

Mediterranean Europe is the Old World heartland of viticulture, enjoying around 240 hours of sunshine a month, temperatures averaging 62.5°F (17°C) in the growing season, annual rainfall of about in 23.5 in (600 mm), and a crisp coldness to the winters, which allows the vines a period of dormancy. The classic regions of Bordeaux, Burgundy, the Rhône Valley, Rioja, and Tuscany benefit from these ideal conditions, and their wines and their *terroirs* have developed as global benchmarks.

It is the pursuit of new *terroir* that has led growers to venture into the New World. California has proved easy territory, where grapes grow prolifically in the heat with little effort. But producers have found that the best wines come from vineyards where the heat is tempered by the soothing effects of water—a lake, river, or coastline location—or the cooling influence of altitude. The Great Lakes and Pacific Northwest are proving themselves in this respect. When vines have to work that bit harder to survive, grapes tend to develop more refined flavors.

What is Terroir?

In every vineyard, a unique combination of climate, topography, and soil type shapes the character of the vines that grow there. Rich soils can lead to excessive leaf growth and mediocre fruit. Soils of low fertility are therefore better. Soil structure is considered even more important than chemical makeup, with good drainage being essential. The grapes that the vines yield and, in turn, the wine made from these grapes reflect aspects of this distinct place. The French word *terroir*, literally meaning "soil," is used to describe not only the soil, but the entire environment in which the vine grows. Find the right *terroir* and the resulting wines will have the most harmonious composition with acidity, sweetness, fruit flavors, and tannins, all poised to perfection. With the wrong *terroir*, the harvest will all too often fail.

For more general information about wine, including styles, tasting terminology, and a glossary **See pp. 136–153**

The World of Wine

Wine is as simple or as complex as you wish: on one level it can be an immediate sensory pleasure, or, at a deeper level, the embodiment of a piece of land and a moment in time. Wine is a pure reflection of its terroir (see box opposite)*, and no other product expresses its cultural and geographical origins in quite the same way. Each harvest yields wines that are the culmination of different climatic and human processes, so no two wines are ever identical.*

Origins and Cultural Significance of Wine

Wine is thought to have originated in the Caucasus mountains of Georgia and it has formed part of world culture since historical records began. In ancient Greece and Rome the god Dionysus (or Bacchus) embodied the spirit of celebration with wine. Firmly established in the Mediterranean way of life, wine subsequently became an important part of the Christian religion. Indeed, medieval monasteries did much to advance the quality of wine, improving vine cultivation and developing new techniques in their cellars.

In the 16th century, Europeans ventured into the Americas and other parts of the New World, taking their religion and their vines with them. Being clean and safer to drink than water, wine became as much a part of North American daily life for slaking thirst as it was a sacramental tradition. Meanwhile, wine trading in Europe burgeoned, bottle-making techniques were perfected, sparkling winemaking evolved, and the wines of Bordeaux, Burgundy, Germany, and Portugal became prized and imitated around the world.

Today, more than ever, wine is a part of everyday life, both as a celebratory drink and a versatile partner to food. Aside from the relaxing effects of alcohol, wine continues to fascinate with its ever-changing character, so inextricably linked to the land, people, and culture that created it.

The Expanding World of Wine

The world now has over 20 million acres (8 million ha) under vine, producing about 240 billion gallons (300 million hectoliters) of wine each year. Vineyards lie between

Vineyards at Paraiso Springs, Monterey, California

Left **Okanagan vineyard, Canada** Center **Bedell Cellars label** Right **Beringer label**

Contents

THE WORLD OF WINE 4

Vincent Gasnier 7

Index of Top 10 Lists 7

INTRODUCING THE WINES OF THE US 10

Grape Varieties in the US 14

Influential Winemakers 16

Wine Laws and AVAs in the US 18

Reading a US Wine Label 19

CALIFORNIA 22

North Coast California 26

Napa Valley 30

Sonoma 48

Mendocino & Lake County 58

Central & Southern California 66

PACIFIC NORTHWEST 90

Washington 94

Oregon 97

ATLANTIC NORTHEAST 112

New York State 116

OTHER WINE REGIONS OF THE US 124

CANADA 128

REFERENCE 135

Wine Styles 136

Tasting Wine 138

Wine and Food Matching 142

Storing and Serving 146

Glossary 148

Index 154

Acknowledgments 160

Navarro vineyards in Mendocino

Key to Symbols

- soil types
- red grape varieties
- white grape varieties
- wine styles
- contact details
- open to the public
- not open to the public
- ★ notable wine brands or varietals

WINES OF THE US

Introducing the Wines of the US 10–13

Grape Varieties in the US 14–15

Influential Winemakers 16–17

Wine Laws and AVAs 18

Reading a US Wine Label 19

Introducing the Wines of the US

The US is blessed with a wide variety of growing regions suitable for winemaking, ranging from the sun-drenched slopes of California to the cooler, Burgundian climes of Oregon and the frosty Finger Lakes of New York State. Each region has its own captivating set of wine styles.

Early Years

The first North American wines were made in the 16th century by settlers on the East Coast. The settlers used the native *Vitis labrusca* vines that they found growing in abundance in the wild *(see p. 14)*. Wines made from *labrusca* have a very distinctive aroma and flavor not generally enjoyed by European palates. "They be fatte, and the juyce thicke. Neither doth the taste so well please when they are made into wine," wrote one Captain John Smith in 1606.

Subsequent waves of settlers from France, Italy, and other parts of Europe brought *Vitis vinifera* vines with them—the traditional varieties for winemaking—and tried to grow them in the American colonies on the East Coast. But however hard they tried, they could not succeed in keeping the *vinifera* vines alive. Unbeknownst to them at the time, they were experiencing the first ravages of the bug phylloxera *(see box opposite)*, which is endemic on the East Coast. The phylloxera insects, so tiny that they weren't even spotted by the early colonists, were attacking the European vines without mercy, killing them off at the roots.

The situation was different on the West Coast, which did not have the phylloxera problem at the time of the early colonization of the Americas. When the pioneering Spanish missionaries arrived in the California region in the 18th century they brought *Vitis vinifera* cuttings to plant at their missions for the purpose of making Communion wines. These vines thrived throughout California, arriving in Sonoma by 1805. And so, by the mid-19th century, America had two distinct wine industries—that of the East Coast,

Vineyard belonging to Navarro, North Coast California

Preceding pages **Autumnal view of a Silverado Trail vineyard in Yountville, Napa Valley**

still producing poor-quality, cloying wines from *labrusca* grapes, and that of the West Coast, where the red wines from the Napa Valley were already recognized as high quality and a viable alternative to wines imported from France. Indeed, by the mid-to-late 19th century, the California wine industry enjoyed such a good reputation that some of the great French wine areas, including Champagne, formed syndicates to protect themselves from the perceived threat to their markets.

Two disasters then struck. The first was the global spread of phylloxera in the late 19th century, accidentally taken over to Europe and across to the West Coast by traders. The second—even more damaging to the US wine industry—was Prohibition in 1920–33 *(see p. 119)*. The official ban on alcohol in these years saw most of the vineyards of California abandoned or neglected, and wineries closed down, although some survived by producing sacramental wines or grape juice.

After Prohibition came one of the worst economic depressions in American history, followed by World War II. Little wonder, then, that by the end of the war, the US wine industry was completely out of touch with European progress. Cheap, fortified wines were being produced in California, and only a handful of fine red wines existed. Eastern states such as New York were churning out poor sparkling wines and sweet reds from inferior *labrusca* varieties.

Modern History

New influences came to the fore in the 1960s, with mentors such as André Tchelitscheff and Robert Mondavi *(see pp. 16–17)* guiding the way. Mondavi built the first new winery in the Napa Valley since Prohibition. Others soon followed, and quality-conscious wineries were established in other California regions such as Sonoma and Santa Cruz. In the 1970s the potential of southern regions such as Monterey and Santa Barbara County began to be tapped, and it was also at this time that Oregon, in the north, gained recognition as a place for cool-climate viticulture, including outstanding Pinot Noir *(see p. 99)*. In the 1980s, the real potential for wines made from Bordeaux and Rhône varieties was identified in Washington State.

Despite problems such as a new outbreak of phylloxera in the 1980s, the US has never looked back. Quality and prices reach exceptional heights in California. States such as Ohio, Michigan, New York, and Virginia, have shown that they too are capable of producing great wines.

The Phylloxera Bug

Phylloxera vastatrix is a tiny aphid native to North America, which likes to eat vine roots. While native American vines have a natural resistance to this parasite, the European vines *(Vitis vinifera)* traditionally used in winemaking can be badly damaged. The bug was accidentally exported to Europe in the 1860s and wiped out swathes of vineyards in France, until in the 1880s French wine yields had almost halved. It then swept through other countries, including Australia, while at the same time *vinifera* varieties planted in North America were dying. The solution, developed in the 1870s by botanist Jules-Emile Planchon and entomologist Charles Riley, was to graft together the phylloxera-resistant roots of American vines with the fruit-bearing shoots of European vines. This is still the practice today in many parts of the US.

Viticulture and Vinification

Pioneering winemakers *(see pp. 16–17)* and innovative vineyard and winery practices have characterized the post-Prohibition wine industry in the US. A key force has been the University of California Davis, which has a faculty dedicated to the analysis of winemaking in California, including the suitability of vine varieties to different soils and mesoclimates in all the winemaking areas of the state. Utilizing the results of these studies, California vineyard owners have introduced new trellis systems to keep their vines cooler during long hot summer days, and instigated mist irrigation systems that water and cool the plants in summer and also protect them against frost in winter.

The university has also developed mechanical methods for pruning and harvesting, and the process of cold fermentation, which allows winemakers in hot areas to produce elegant, fragrant wines normally only possible in cooler climates. Meanwhile, in the cooler wine areas of Washington and Oregon, facilities such as the Prosser research station *(see box p. 90)* and a marriage of Old World and New World techniques has further helped to shape the modern face of US viticulture and winemaking.

The US Wine Industry Today

In terms of volume, the US is the fourth-largest wine-producing country in the world (behind France, Italy, and Spain). The state of California alone is responsible for about 94 percent of the US's wine output. In terms of national wine consumption, the US comes third (after Italy and France). However, in contrast to the European countries where the majority of the population are wine drinkers, just eight percent of US citizens consume 80 percent of all the country's wine.

Another way in which the US's wine industry contrasts with the European wine industries is the absence of regulation governing the standard of wines and their labeling *(see pp. 18–19)*.

The wine industry's dependence on market forces means that occasionally the US over- or underproduces. This occurred in 2003, when there was a major glut, and tens of thousands of acres of vines were pulled up in

Vineyard and school house in St. Helena, Napa Valley

Wine Regions

California dominates the US's wine industry, but there are significant wine-producing areas in almost all states. Of most viticultural significance are Washington and Oregon in the northwest and New York State in the east. Many other states have been dogged by a poor reputation, but Michigan, Ohio, and Virginia are steadily making improvements to the quality of their wines.

California. Such periods of instability tend to be short-lived, however, and many industry experts believe that the lack of government interference makes for a culture of free enterprise that is beneficial to both product quality and consumer satisfaction.

Big Players

Although there are thousands of wineries in the US, the market is dominated by a handful of large producers. Ernest & Julio Gallo *(see p. 83)* was the biggest wine producer for decades, accounting for about 30 percent of the entire market. Mondavi *(see p. 43)* has been another giant, along with the international wine group Beringer Blass, which is now owned by the Australian beer group Foster's. The Canadian-owned Vincor group, Anglo-Spanish Allied-Domecq, Diageo (UK), The Wine Group (San Francisco), and Jackson Wine Estate also account for many leading US wineries. Very recently, however, an unprecedented series of seismic corporate takeovers has resulted in a company called Constellation Brands becoming the largest wine producer in not only the US but also the world.

The World's Largest Wine Company

The story of Constellation Brands began in 1945, when Canandaigua Industries Co. was founded on the East Coast, selling bulk wine to bottlers. By the 1970s the company was thriving, with sales from Scuppernong wine (a native grape), the Wild Irish Rose brand, and J. Roget Champagne. Acquisitions in the 1990s included Paul Masson, Taylor, and Inglenook. In 2000 the company became Constellation Brands. A year later it formed a partnership with the Australian wine group BRL Hardy, another drinks giant.

In 2004, Constellation bought BRL Hardy, putting itself ahead of Gallo. Within months it also bought up Mondavi. In 2006 Constellation restructured into several divisions: Icon Estates, in the Napa Valley, has the Robert Mondavi winery, Columbia winery, Ravenswood, and other leading fine wines. Centerra and North Lake Wines in New York State have most of the others.

Sales in 60 countries total $4 billion a year; whether this behemoth will rest on its laurels or expand further is uncertain.

Grape Varieties in the US

North America has many native vines that early settlers used to make wines, and for years the bulk of the American wine industry was based on these. Vitis vinifera *varieties were brought over from Europe in the 19th century, which supplemented the native varieties first in California, and later in other parts of the US. The leading varieties today all have a European heritage.*

Native Varieties
Vitis labrusca (fox grape) varieties grow wild in the eastern US and Canada and are still used for table wines and grape juice. The pink-skinned Catawba was one of the first *labrusca* varieties to be produced as wine on a commercial scale, from 1802. The best-known *labrusca* variety is Concord, a red grape with the classically "foxy" taste of *labrusca*, which was introduced in 1854. Niagara is a white variety related to Concord. Ives and Campbell (red), Diamond, Norton, and Delaware (white) are among other *labrusca* hybrids. *Labrusca* was the mainstay of the wine industry in New York State right up until the 1970s.

The southeastern US is home to *Vitis rotundifolia*, better known as Muscadine (not to be confused with Muscatel), and sometimes called Scuppernong. Muscadines have a "musky" rather than "foxy" taste and have been cultivated since the 16th century for American port and dessert wines. *Vitis riparia*, commonly known as the river bank grape or frost grape, is sometimes used for wine.

Today, the US's native varieties are produced in small quantities as wines; their main purpose is in grape breeding progams. Their phylloxera-resistant rootstock is used for grafting *(see p. 11)*, and their hardy genes are crossed with European vines to create hybrids.

Leading Red Grape Varieties

California's leading reds are usually made in a rich, almost burly, fruit-driven style with high alcohol, which is a consequence of the balmy California climate. Reds from the Pacific Northwest and Atlantic Northeast often show balance rather than power.

Cabernet Sauvignon
Worldwide, more quality wines are made from Cabernet Sauvignon than any other red variety. The grape orginated in Bordeaux in France, where it is blended with Merlot and Cabernet Franc. In the US it has been very successful in the Napa Valley, both in full-bodied, ageworthy, blends and as a varietal in its own right, bursting with ripe fruit.

Cabernet Sauvignon

Zinfandel
The California classic *(see above)* varies from light pink blush (rosé) to powerful, alcoholic reds, with juicy berry flavors and soft tannins.

Merlot
Used in blends in Bordeaux, Merlot is more common as a varietal in the US. Soft tannins and juicy flavors are typical of Californian Merlot. Some can age well.

Pinot Noir
A fickle Burgundy grape that demands a cool climate and low yields, Pinot Noir is the mainstay of Oregon where it makes wonderful medium-bodied wines with perfumed aromas that evolve with age.

Syrah
A complex and ageworthy Rhône variety (known as Shiraz in Australia) that has gained ground in California.

For more on wine styles **See pp. 136–137**

Zinfandel

Though Zinfandel is sometimes regarded as a native variety, it has a European heritage *(see p. 51)* and is similar to (probably the same as) Italian Primitivo. It has been cultivated in California since the 19th century. As the focus of winemaking shifted to classic European varieties in the 1970s, Zinfandel lost much of its status and was close to extinction by the mid-1980s. However, it was saved by the invention of blush (rosé) wine and is currently enjoying a surge in popularity in both blush and red styles. Some of the best Zinfandel wines today are made from vines that are many decades old. For the Top 10 best Zinfandel producers, *see p. 50.*

Classic European Varieties

Cabernet Sauvignon is by far the most important red variety in California, accounting for almost one-quarter of all red grapes in the state. For some years Merlot has been been neck and neck with Zinfandel in second place. Merlot's popularity peaked in the late 1990s, but many weak, overcropped wines have marred its reputation. Pinot Noir, meanwhile, has made great strides in cool regions such as Oregon, and Syrah seems to be thriving everywhere. Other red varieties hailing from Europe include Grenache, Cabernet Franc, and Gamay; there are dozens more.

Classic red varieties are more widely planted than white varieties in a ratio of roughly 60:40. Of the white grapes, Chardonnay is overwhelmingly the first choice, accounting for at least 80 percent. Rich and opulent, its popularity shows little sign of diminishing in the US. Other white grapes such as Viognier, Roussanne, Pinot Gris, and Riesling produce some excellent wines, in much smaller quantities. Only Sauvignon Blanc (often called Fumé Blanc) is a viable alternative to Chardonnay in terms of quantity.

Leading White Grape Varieties

Chardonnay is a relatively easy vine to cultivate and is the favorite white variety in the US by far. Unfortunately, much of this production is bland, but there are still many winemakers who can tease out the best in this versatile grape and other whites.

Chardonnay
This is generally a full-bodied, dry wine, but its flavor varies from crisp and steely to intense and tropical depending on *terroir* and production method. In the warmth of California, it has a tendency to develop overly high levels of sugar when left too long to ripen, at the expense of acidity.
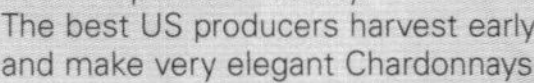
The best US producers harvest early and make very elegant Chardonnays.

Chardonnay grapes

Riesling
Typically produces a light, fragrant wine, with lively acidity, aromatic flavors, and relatively low alcohol levels. A typical grape of Germany, it is gaining ground in the Pacific Northwest.

Pinot Gris
Known as Pinot Grigio in Italy, this full-bodied, deep-colored white grape has subtle flavors of honey, smoke, and spice.

Sauvignon Blanc / Fumé Blanc
A dry, crisp, and intensely aromatic variety with a firm streak of acidity, Sauvignon Blanc is often aged in oak and called Fumé Blanc in California.

Viognier
A few US producers are making top-quality dry white wines from this full-bodied, Rhône variety with its aromas of apricots and musk.

Influential Winemakers

Prohibition in the 1920s shattered the North American wine industry. Many wineries closed, and by the time the ban on alcohol was lifted, in 1933, there was an acute shortage of modern equipment and trained winemakers in the US. Thus, it was just a handful of enthusiasts–led by Beaulieu Vineyards and winemaker André Tchelitscheff–who initiated the industry's revival and became heroes of the winemaking world. Tchelitscheff influenced generations of winemakers, who put California firmly back on the international stage.

André Tchelitscheff (1901–94)

Russian-born, French-trained enologist Tchelitscheff was hired in 1938 to revamp the corroded Napa Valley winery at Beaulieu Vineyard *(see p. 36)*. Beaulieu had survived Prohibition by supplying wine for liturgical purposes. Moreover, it was one of the few California estates with substantial plantings of mature Cabernet Sauvignon vines.

Tchelitscheff overhauled the winery and produced a series of famous Cabernets, known as the Georges de Latour Private Reserve. His main achievement was to recognize the importance of viticultural practices such as frost protection, temperature controlled techniques of fermentation, and malolactic fermentation. He imparted his knowledge to countless US winemakers, who collectively improved the overall quality of California wine.

Martin Ray (1905–76)

Martin Ray bought Paul Masson's winery in 1936, sold it to Seagram in 1943, then established his own vineyards and winery at Mount Eden, over 2,000 ft (600 m) up in the Santa Cruz Mountains. Even though US wine law allows a varietal wine to include up to 25 percent of another grape, Ray insisted that his wines be 100 percent single varietals. He campaigned against the use of chemical additives and concentrates, which were widely used by other wineries at the time. He believed that California should adopt European viticultural and winemaking practices, a view widely accepted today, but regarded as eccentric in the 1950s.

Robert Mondavi (1913–)

Born in Minnesota, Mondavi came from a wine-producing family of Italian descent, but his visits to Europe persuaded him that quality throughout California needed to be improved so that the wines could rival European models. His family did not agree, so after a bitter dispute he set up his own winery in Napa Valley *(see p. 43)*. Within a few years he was making some of California's most sophisticated wines. His passion for

Robert Mondavi in his world-famous winery

excellence has been inspirational to other winemakers, and he has been unstintingly generous in sharing the results of his research into techniques such as oak-aging. He also strongly believes in educating consumers on the virtues of responsible wine consumption as a life-enhancing experience. By 2006, Mondavi, though age 93, was still an energetic international crusader for the value of wine, food, and the arts. The US practice of labeling wines varietally—an idea that is now even filtering into the Old World—has largely arisen through Mondavi's influence.

Warren Winiarski (1928–)
In 1970, Winiarski, a thoughtful political scientist from Chicago, left for California, took a lowly job as a cellarhand at Mondavi, and eventually acquired vineyards and a winery in Napa's Stags Leap district. His Cabernet Sauvignon soundly beat the grandest French opposition at the famous "Judgment of Paris" tasting *(see p. 44)* in 1976. Winiarski continues to produce impeccable Cabernets, which demonstrate that although Napa wines have their own character, they have won the right to be regarded alongside the greatest wines of France.

Paul Draper (1936–)
Paul Draper has been the winemaker at Ridge Vineyards *(see p. 80)* in Santa Cruz since 1969. His achievement has been twofold; he created an American wine classic in his long-lived Monte Bello Cabernet Sauvignon; and he has demonstrated that Zinfandel can be more than a brawny, rustic red wine, and that it can take its place among the world's most desirable reds. For over 35 years he has shown that old-vine Zinfandel can produce simply delicious wines that are stylistically unique to California.

David Lett (1940–)
The great American winemakers are not confined to California. If it weren't for David Lett's conviction that Pinot Noir was better suited to Oregon than California, Oregon might have remained a viticultural backwater. The Pinots he made in the 1970s triumphed when blind-tasted alongside Burgundies *(see p. 99)*, and Oregon has gone from strength to strength.

Randall Grahm (1953–)
Randall Grahm of Bonny Doon Vineyard *(see p. 81)* in Santa Cruz has the most original and inventive mind of any American winemaker. In the early 1980s, he attempted a revolution by turning his back on the ubiquitous Cabernet and Chardonnay to focus instead on Mediterranean varieties, primarily from the Rhône, and somewhat unfashionable grapes such as Riesling. He is an amazingly gifted publicist for the like-minded group known as the Rhône Rangers *(see p. 75)*, and has persuaded drinkers worldwide to reevaluate the potential of California wine.

Helen Turley (1946–)
Helen Turley is a consultant winemaker who has established the dominant style for top-flight California wine since the early 1990s: made from ultraripe grapes, with richness of oaky flavor compensating for low acidity and high alcohol, and bottled without filtration. Turley is the best known of the growing band of consultants who have become important in the US as wealthy patrons have taken to setting up vineyards and wineries without any personal experience.

Wine Laws and AVAs in the US

The US's official wine regions are called AVAs (American Viticultural Areas). Wine labels can include an AVA name if at least 85 percent of the wine comes from that area. However, the usage of AVA names is not a strict appellation system–it is not comparable to the French AOC or Italian DOC classifications.

The AVA System

The original system of wine appellations in the US was based simply on political boundaries such as counties or states—"Napa" meant Napa County. In 1978, however, the government's Bureau of Alcohol, Firearms, and Tobacco (BATF) published its first laws and regulations for a system of Viticultural Areas (AVAs) based on geographical and climatic considerations. This supplemented the political appellations rather than superseded them.

By 2006 there were more than 160 AVAs in the US, almost 100 of them in California, with the number growing each year. In many cases, wine growers themselves petition for official AVA status. Some AVAs embrace entire counties; others may encompass fewer than 250 acres (100 ha). Sub-AVAs exist within larger ones, and their boundaries can overlap. Green Valley AVA, for example, is an enclave within Russian River Valley AVA, which is within Sonoma AVA, which itself is within North Coast California AVA.

Generic appellations for whole states and the word "American" are also recognized *(see opposite).*

Alcohol Warnings in the US

One legacy of the temperance movement in the US is that alcohol is perceived in a more negative light here in comparison with attitudes in other wine-drinking countries. US wine labels must by law include a government health warning issued by the Surgeon General, stating "women should not drink alcoholic beverages during pregnancy because of the risk of birth defects," and "consumption of alcoholic beverages impairs your ability to drive a car or operate machinery and may cause health problems." Wine producer websites require viewers to confirm that they are over the age of 21 before they can enter the site. A few counties, mainly in the South, are "dry" and do not permit the sale of alcohol.

Limitations of AVAs

AVAs differ fundamentally from the European appellation systems because they are simply geographical descriptors with no qualitative criteria. In France, an appellation such as "St.-Émilion Grand Cru" can be used only for wines sourced from a handful of venerable old vineyards and made in a highly specialized way. In the US, by contrast, there are no AVA rules governing the varieties grown, methods of training employed, yield allowed, or the style of wines produced.

On the one hand, this freedom can be a positive force for it allows enterprising wine producers to experiment in ways that Old-World producers are unable to. On the other hand, consumers have no indication of style and quality even when the label includes a famous name like "Oakville, Napa Valley." Furthermore, there are many semigeneric appellations, such as "American Burgundy" or "American Chianti," which are allowed by US Federal Law but have little in common with their European forebears *(see opposite).*

"Hock" or "rhine wine" are terms allowed under US Federal Law for light, dry, white wines

Reading a US Wine Label

Wine producers in the US like to name the grape variety (varietal) on their labels, but this is not always possible for blends. The AVA name or general appellation indicates which part of the US the wine originates from. If you are familiar with the US wine areas, this can give you an idea of whether you are looking at a cool-climate Oregon wine, for example, or a big, fruity California wine—but it is not an indicator of quality. "Estate Bottled" means that all the grapes come from the estate's vineyard, and the wine has been made and bottled on site.

The vintage indicates the year in which the grapes were harvested.

The producer or brand name can count for a lot in the US wine industry in the absence of any guarantee of quality from AVA names.

Varietal wines have the name of the grape written on the label. This is a key point of many wines in the US.

AVA name—Columbia Valley is the main AVA of Washington State.

Alcoholic strength must be stated by law.

General Appellations Permitted on US Wine Labels

GENERIC TERMS

county appellation The county name may be used on a label if at least 75 percent of the wine comes from the county indicated.

state appellation The state name may be used if at least 75 percent of the wine orginates from that state, except for California, which requires 100 percent.

multicounty / multistate appellations The percentage of wine from each county or state must be clearly indicated.

American (or USA) A description for blends or varietals from anywhere in the US. Labels are not allowed to carry a vintage.

SEMIGENERIC TERMS

The following terms have no legal definition on American wine labels but are allowed under US Federal Law when qualified with their true place of origin, such as "California Champagne." Such wines bear no resemblance to French chablis, Italian chianti, Spanish sherry, etc.

burgundy Used loosely in the US for basic red wines, usually full-bodied and dark in color

chablis Blended white table wine

champagne Sparkling wine

chianti Medium-bodied, basic red wines

claret Basic, light red wine

madeira Any fortified wine of 17–24 percent, usually a sweet blend of American sherry and angelica.

malaga Similar to madeira, but usually made from Concord grapes

marsala Fortified wine, often amber or brown and flavored with herbs

moselle Light-bodied white wine, often Chenin Blanc and Riesling.

port Fortified wines made from various grape varieties, sometimes Portuguese (Tinta port). Some American ports are very good.

sauterne(s) Sweet wines.

sherry Sweet, fortified, oxidated wines.

"Burgundy" and other semigeneric terms are allowed; the words "bordeaux," "rhône," and "liebfraumilch" are banned from labels

WINES OF CALIFORNIA

Introducing Californian Wines 22–23

North Coast California (including Napa Valley & Sonoma) 26–63

Central & Southern California 66–87

Introducing California Wines

CALIFORNIA *is the source of rich, hedonistic wines–a viticultural paradise that continues to build on its strengths. Today, this state is responsible for about 85 percent of the US's total wine production, and about 95 percent of the country's wine exports. California is a mecca for producers of Chardonnay and Cabernet Sauvignon, and its rich* terroir *is capable of supporting a wine collection as diverse as anything found in Europe.*

Wine Pioneers in California

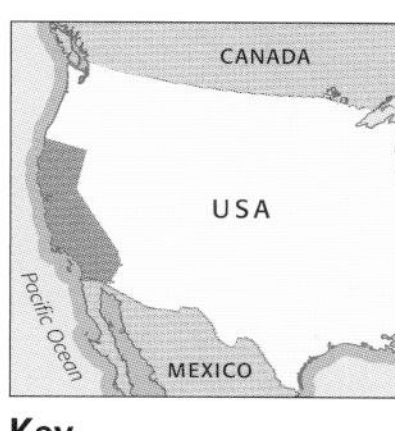

Key

California

The first people known to have planted vines in California were the Spanish missionaries, who arrived in 1769 *(see box opposite)*. By the mid-19th century, settlers from Italy and Germany were planting high on sun-drenched slopes in an attempt to reproduce their European landscape. One man in particular, Jean-Louis Vignes from Bordeaux, arrived in 1833. He established California's first commercial winery in Los Angeles and, in 1840, became the first person to export California wines. George Yount *(see p. 42)* was the first to plant vines in the Napa Valley. Another individual who had a huge impact on the fledgling industry was Agoston Haraszthy de Mokesa, a political exile from Hungary. In the 1850s Haraszthy imported 170 vine varieties from Europe and planted them over 570 acres (230 ha) near the town of Sonoma.

The success of his Buena Vista winery, coupled with Haraszthy's larger-than-life personality, drew the attention of the governor of California who, in 1861, asked Haraszthy to study the winemaking areas of Europe. Haraszthy visited every wine region in France, Germany, Italy, Spain, and Switzerland, interviewing thousands of grape growers and winemakers, and accumulating samples and reference material. He came back to California with an amazing number of cuttings—as many as 100,000—of 300 European *vinifera* varieties. By 1864 Buena Vista was described as "the largest wine-growing estate in the world." Haraszthy's legacy was to change the course of Californian viticulture.

Quady Winery, Central Valley

Developments in the 20th Century

The double blows of phylloxera *(see p. 11)* and Prohibition *(see p. 119)* devastated the wine industry in California, as elsewhere in the US. In the prosperous era after World War II, viticulture began to flourish again, though the industry remained small until the 1960s, when the real renaissance in California wines began. Robert Mondavi *(see p.16)* established his winery in the Napa Valley in 1966, and in the early 1970s two California wines scored a stunning victory over top French *cuvées* in the so-called "Judgment of Paris"

Preceding pages **Fall scene in the Napa Valley**

View over Byron vineyard and winery to the Sierra Madre Mountains in Santa Barbara

(see p. 44). The stage was set, and California winemakers have not looked back since then.

Wine Regions of California

California has a host of designated wine areas and subdistricts (AVAs). It also has five categories of climatic regions, graded from 1, the coolest, to 5, the hottest. Developed by the University of Davis, California, the climate system measures the amount of heat each region has in "degree days" each year, which helps growers to predict where different grape varieties will thrive.

The North Coast AVA of northern California is the most important region. It incorporates the richly endowed Napa Valley, which is mainly categorized as Region 2 on the climate scale, and is the most celebrated (but not the largest) of California's wine areas. Cabernet Sauvignons from the Napa Valley can attain the heights of wines from Bordeaux in France. Of the other key areas, neighboring Sonoma, most of which is also classified as Region 2, has a more diverse climate and range of grapes.

In Central California, Monterey is ideal for Chardonnay and Riesling, while Santa Barbara County (also Region 2) is showing potential for dazzling Chardonnay, Pinot Noir, and Syrah. Farther inland is the domain of brawny Zinfandels and fortified wines from the Sierra Foothills, and vast quantities of basic but drinkable wines from the blisteringly hot Central Valley (climate Region 5).

Today, California is home to at least 800 wineries stretching from Mendocino County in the North Coast AVA down to the Mexican border in Southern California.

The Father of Californian Wine

Father Junípero Serra (1713–84), a Franciscan friar born on the island of Mallorca in Spain, is regarded by many as the Father of Californian wine. He came to America in 1749, initially to Mexico City and the Baja Peninsula, and in 1769 accompanied Governor Gaspar de Portolà on an expedition to Nueva (New) California. When the party reached San Diego, Serra stayed on and founded a mission. Though Serra himself avoided rich food and wine, he planted a vineyard at San Diego to make sacramental wines for use in masses. The variety he planted came to be known as the Mission grape and was the main vine grown in California until about 1880.

NORTH COAST CALIFORNIA

Introduction
26–27

Wine Map of
North Coast California
28–29

Wine Areas of the
Napa Valley
30–33

A Wine Tour of the
Napa Valley
34–35

Major Producers
in the Napa Valley
36–45

Wine Areas of Sonoma
48–49

Major Producers
in Sonoma
50–55

Wine Areas of
Mendocino
& Lake County
58–59

Major Producers
in Mendocino
60–63

NORTH COAST CALIFORNIA

EXTENDING NORTH FROM SAN FRANCISCO to the top of Mendocino County, the North Coast region of California is about 95 miles (150 km) long and 50 miles (80 km) wide. Though designated an AVA (American Viticultural Area) in its own right, the North Coast is best known by the wine districts that lie within it, which are also AVAs. Foremost of these is the world-famous Napa Valley, followed by neighboring Sonoma. The county of Mendocino, along with Lake County, and portions of Marin and Solano counties also have their own AVAs.

The Napa Valley

The largest valley of Napa County is a relatively small wine area—just one-eighth of the size of Bordeaux in France—but it has become a household name in the wine-drinking world. The first vines were planted in the valley in 1838 by George Yount *(see p. 42)*. Napa's close proximity to San Francisco, where wine was a popular tipple in the gold-rush years of the mid-19th century, its varied soil, and favorable climate attracted a number of winemakers. By the 1880s about half the valley was taken up with vineyards.

Key

North Coast California AVA

The first commercial wineries included Charles Krug (1861), Schramsberg (1862), Beringer (1876), and Inglenook (1879). The companies lurched from problems of oversupply to phylloxera *(see p. 11)*, but managed to make reasonable wines up until 1920, when the enforcement of Prohibition in California saw most of the Napa vineyards abandoned.

After World War II, a dynamic trade organization, the Napa Valley Vintners, was formed with the goal of promoting Napa Valley wines at home and abroad. In 1966 Robert Mondavi *(see p. 16)*, who had been working for his family at the old Krug winery, broke away from the firm and chose Oakville in the Napa Valley to site a new winery, which was to become a groundbreaking establishment *(see p. 43)*. Mondavi was one of the first American winemakers to label his wines as varietals, and his eagerness to educate others about the best vinification and winemaking techniques raised standards in Napa and beyond.

In the 1970s, Mondavi's pupil Warren Winiarski *(see p. 17)* founded Stag's Leap *(p. 44)* in a fertile area of the valley southeast of Oakville. The high quality of a Cabernet Sauvignon from Stag's Leap—which beat the best of Bordeaux and Burgundy in a historic blind tasting in 1976—further helped to focus the wine world's attention on Napa.

Since the 1970s, almost every bit of spare land in the valley—about 37,000 acres (15,000 ha)—has come under vine. This is 11 percent of California's vineyards, but, due to low yields, only four percent of wine production. The wineries (260 by 2006) range from large corporations using high-tech methods of mass production to boutique wineries using modern techniques to create small quantities of world-class wines.

Preceding pages **Vineyard in the foothills of the Mayacamas Mountains, Knights Valley, Sonoma**

Joseph Phelps' estate in St. Helena, Napa Valley

Sonoma County

Vines were grown in Sonoma some 13 years before they were planted in Napa, but the county was quickly overshadowed by its sophisticated neighbor. It was not until 1969, when Russell Green took over the ailing Simi winery, that Sonoma proved itself capable of producing high-quality varietal wines. Sonoma winemakers changed their attitudes and methods, and new interlopers rapidly appeared on the scene. Piper-Heidsieck from Champagne, Spanish winemaker Torres, and Cava producer Freixenet were among those who moved in. By 1985 there were 93 wineries in Sonoma County; by 1995 the figure was 160. Today, Sonoma is one of the US's most important AVAs, producing wines to rival those of Napa.

Mendocino & Other Counties

For decades the main role of Mendocino, California's most northerly growing area, was to supply grapes to major producers based farther south, who found they could purchase first-rate grapes at attractive prices for generic wines. Robert Mondavi, Beringer, and Duckhorn have vineyards here. However, as Mendocino has gained renown, many smaller growers have arrived to establish their own wineries.

Lake County is set around the largest natural lake in California, and supplies mainly Cabernet Sauvignon and Sauvignon Blanc grapes to wineries elsewhere. Marin and Solano counties have a handful of vineyards and wineries, mostly producing Pinot Noir.

VINCENT GASNIER'S TOP 10 Fine Red Wines of the US

1. **Opus One** Napa Valley *p. 42*
2. **Dominus: Cabernet Sauvignon** Napa Valley *p. 39*
3. **Ridge Vineyards: Monte Bello** San Francisco Bay *p. 80*
4. **Kistler: Pinot Noir** Sonoma *p. 54*
5. **Williams Selyem: Pinot Noir** Sonoma *p. 55*
6. **Abreu: Cabernet Sauvignon** Napa Valley *p. 45*
7. **Caymus: Cabernet Sauvignon** Napa Valley *p. 37*
8. **Colgin** (various reds) Napa Valley *p. 37*
9. **Harlan Estate** (various reds) Napa Valley *p. 40*
10. **Domaine Drouhin: Pinot Noir** Willamette Valley *p. 107*

Wine Map of North Coast California

The North Coast AVAs are mostly coherent topographical entities with distinctive subregions. In Sonoma, however, the boundaries are more complicated, with subregions broken up into further overlapping subregions. Producer entries in this chapter are listed alphabetically under their main AVA–Napa Valley, Sonoma, or Mendocino. Sub-AVA names (for example, Stags Leap, Russian River Valley) are noted where relevant.

MAIN AVAs & MAJOR PRODUCERS

Napa Valley *pp. 30–33*

Araujo *p. 36*
Beaulieu Vineyard *p. 36*
Beringer *p. 36*
Caymus Vineyards *p. 37*
Chateau Montelena *p. 37*
Colgin *p. 37*
Cuvaison *p. 38*
Dolce Vineyard *p. 38*
Domaine Carneros *p. 38*
Domaine Chandon *p. 38*
Dominus *p. 39*
Duckhorn Vineyards *p. 39*
Far Niente *p. 40*
Frog's Leap *p. 40*
Harlan Estate *p. 40*
Heitz Cellar *p. 40*
Hendry *p. 41*
Joseph Phelps *p. 41*
Kongsgaard *p. 41*
Merryvale *p. 41*
Mumm Napa *p. 42*
Opus One *p. 42*
Patz & Hall *p. 42*
Robert Mondavi *p. 43*
Shafer *p. 44*
Spottswoode *p. 44*
Stag's Leap Wine Cellars *p. 44*
Z. D. Wines *p. 45*

Sonoma *pp. 48–9*

Arrowood *p. 50*
Chateau St. Jean *p. 50*
Cline *p. 50*
Clos du Bois *p. 51*
Ferrari-Carano *p. 51*
Gallo of Sonoma *p. 52*
Gary Farrell *p. 52*
Gloria Ferrer *p. 52*
Iron Horse *p. 52*
Kendall-Jackson *p. 53*
Kenwood *p. 53*
Kistler *p. 54*
Marimar Torres *p. 54*
Peter Michael *p. 54*
Ravenswood *p. 54*
Windsor Vineyards *p. 55*

Pruning vines in Beringer's vineyards, Napa Valley

Mendocino *pp. 58–9*

Fetzer *p. 60*
Greenwood Ridge *p. 60*
Handley Cellars *p. 61*
McDowell Valley Vineyards *p. 61*
Monte Volpe *p. 62*
Navarro *p. 62*
Roederer Estate *p. 62*
Scharffenberger Cellars *p. 63*

Lake County *p. 59*

Guenoc Estate *p. 63*

Good recent vintages in North Coast California include 1994, 1995, 1997, 1999, 2001, 2003, 2004, and 2005

Regional Information at a Glance

Latitude 38–40° N.

Altitude 65–2,300 ft (20–700 m). Valley floors in all counties are close to sea level, while Pacific ridgelands in Sonoma and Mendocino can be 2,000 ft (600 m). Spring Mountain vineyards are higher still.

Topography Vines are planted on the floors and lower slopes of valleys that run mostly from north to south. Napa is the major river of Napa Valley, and the Russian River flows through parts of Sonoma and Mendocino. Land close to the rivers tends to be too fertile for good viticulture, but benchlands may have ideal conditions.

Soil Extremely varied, with loam and clay dominating.

Climate Winters can be quite rainy; summers tend to be very hot; falls are usually balmy and dry.

Temperature July average is 72°F (22°C).

Rainfall Annual average is 37 in (950 mm).

Viticultural Hazards Spring frosts; drought; Pierce's Disease.

Gloria Ferrer wines, Sonoma

Wine Areas of the Napa Valley

The Napa Valley runs in an arc from Napa city at its southern end, following a northwest trajectory for about 30 miles (50 km) up to Calistoga. The floor of the valley is very flat and flanked by slopes leading up to the tree-covered mountains.

There are several fairly distinct climate zones. The southern end of the valley, including Carneros and up to Oakville, is the coolest zone because it is close to the Bay of San Francisco, where fog often rolls in from the sea. The middle of the valley, from Oakville up to St. Helena, has a warm spot around Calistoga. Vineyards on the valley floor have rich soil, average rainfall, a long hot ripening period, and suffer very little danger from frost. Vines growing on the slopes higher up experience cooler temperatures, different types of soil, and are at risk of frost. All these factors add up to wines with different characteristics in different parts of the valley, and there are a number of sub-AVAs in addition to the Napa Valley AVA. The most important of these are described on the next few pages. Throughout the valley, Cabernet Sauvignon is the red variety of grape that reigns supreme, combining opulent fruit with firm tannic structure and more power and flesh than Bordeaux wines. Merlot, Syrah, and Zinfandel are also excellent. Among the whites, Chardonnay is highly impressive. *gravel, loam, sand, silt, clay, volcanic, shale, tufa* *Cabernet Sauvignon, Syrah, Merlot, Pinot Noir, Sangiovese, Zinfandel* *Sauvignon Blanc, Chardonnay* *red, white, sparkling*

Frog's Leap label, Rutherford

Cult Napa Wines

Every year the press reports another astronomical price paid for a bottle of cult Napa Cabernet. In 2000, a magnum of 1996 Screaming Eagle fetched over $10,000 at a Napa charity auction. Most of the cult wines are produced in minute quantities by consultant winemakers hired at enormous salaries. These rich, oaky wines are awarded near-perfect scores by US wine critics, making them highly desirable—and scarcely obtainable. Most are of exceptionally high quality, even if they tend to come from the same mold: highly concentrated and steeped in new French oak. Much of the hype is due to the extravagance (and wealth) of North American wine collectors, who assemble every year at the Napa Valley Wine Auction to outbid each other on the valley's finest.

Rutherford

This is the historical core of the Napa Valley, where Inglenook, Beaulieu *(see p. 36)*, and other celebrated vineyards were planted in the 19th century. This AVA retains some of the most prized viticultural land in America and is home to some of California's top wineries. The wines are highly sought after and very expensive. Cabernet Sauvignon performs marvelously, giving sumptuous wines of great profundity and longevity: some Rutherford Cabernets from the 1940s and 50s are still very enjoyable.
It is thought that the secret to Rutherford's success lies in the gravelly loam soil and the well-drained benchlands at the foot of

By 2006 there were 14 sub-AVAs in the Napa Valley, though not all producers use the AVA names on their labels

the Mayacamas Mountains, west of the town of Rutherford. The vineyards that lie closer to the Napa River have richer soil and can be overproductive.

St. Helena & Calistoga

Immediately north of Rutherford, the St. Helena AVA stretches some way north of the little town of the same name. Like Rutherford, this is red wine territory, though some white grapes are also planted. St. Helena is slightly warmer than Rutherford, but is still capable of delivering Cabernet Sauvignon with striking elegance and richness. Many of Napa's old wineries are based here: among them, Beringer *(see p. 36)*, Charles Krug, and Freemark Abbey. The northern continuation of St. Helena is the hot area around Calistoga, which, though not officially an AVA, is known for its powerful reds from estates such as Chateau Montelena *(see p. 37)* and Araujo *(see p. 36)*.

Oakville

It was Robert Mondavi *(see pp. 16 & 43)* who put the Oakville AVA on the map when he built a Spanish-style winery here in the 1960s. The district is home to some of the valley's best-known vineyards: To-Kalon, largely owned by Mondavi, and Martha's Vineyard, which supplies grapes to Heitz *(see p. 40)* in the Napa Valley. These benchland sites are similar to the more celebrated examples within Rutherford. It is also where the vineyards of the Mondavi/Rothschild joint venture, Opus One *(see p. 42)*, are planted. Cabernet Sauvignon from Oakville often shows more spice, if less power, than that from Rutherford. The climate is slightly fresher here than farther north, so white grapes, especially Sauvignon Blanc and Chardonnay, can give exceptionally good results.

Yountville

The most southerly of the red-wine regions of Napa Valley, Yountville AVA is distinctly cooler than Oakville and the regions farther north. Dominus *(see p. 39)* is its best known winery, showing that muscular Bordeaux-style reds can be produced on its well-drained loamy soils.

Robert Mondavi's winery at Oakville

The verdant hills of Carneros, which has a rich history of Mexican settlers

Stags Leap

Lying to the east of Yountville and tucked against the Vaca mountain range, Stags Leap was put on the world wine map when a Cabernet Sauvignon from here won the historic 1976 "Judgment of Paris" *(see p. 44)*. It was awarded its own AVA in 1989, in recognition of its unique soils, which are distinctive and reddish in color, with volcanic subsoil and outcroppings on the slopes. The district is tiny 2,700 acres (1,093 ha), forming just one percent of the Napa Valley AVA, but it has become renowned in the wine world its elegant Cabernets.

Some highly regarded wineries here, including Shafer and Stag's Leap Wine Cellars *(see p. 44)*, claim that the stylish elegance of their wines can be attributed to the complex pattern of air flow over the hills and ridges of the western and southwestern vineyards, which funnels in cool air from San Pablo Bay during the afternoon and prevents the vines from becoming too hot and baked. As a consequence, the wines of this area are supple, yet have the structure to age well. Another theory is that the 1,150 ft (350 m) column of basalt rocks (the legendary "stag's leap") to the east of the district retain the heat of the afternoon sun and release the warmth slowly through the night to the benefit of the vineyards on the slopes below.

Howell Mountain & Atlas Peak

High up in the Vaca Range, Howell Mountain overlooks St. Helena; Atlas Peak is above Stags Leap. Their mesoclimate differs from the regions on the Napa Valley floor not only because their elevation is between 1,000 and 2,000 ft (300 m and 600 m) but also because they are above the fog that creeps in from the Bay of San Francisco. They lack the "air-conditioning" effect of the fog, and their nighttime temperatures are cooler. Howell Mountain is renowned for its Cabernets and Zinfandels, which emerge in a big, brawny style. They may lack elegance but make up for it with power and intensity. There is only one estate in the Atlas Peak AVA; it bears the name of the district and is owned by Tuscan producer

Antinori and partners. The Chiles Valley AVA is another growing region in these mountains, but it has very few vineyards of note.

Mount Veeder & Spring Mountain

These two AVAs are located up in the Mayacamas Mountains, hugging the border with Sonoma County. They face onto Howell Valley and Atlas Peak on the other side of Napa Valley, with similar elevation and fog-free conditions. Mount Veeder is planted with Cabernet, Merlot, and some Chardonnay. Its reds can be burly and tannic. The exceptionally beautiful Spring Mountain, with its eroded volcanic soils, produces wines that are slightly more supple than those from Mount Veeder. Spring Mountain's best-known wineries include Newton, Kennan, Cain, Togni, and Stony Hill.

Carneros

The grassy hills of the Carneros AVA, close to San Pablo Bay, comprise Napa's most southerly wine area, a district shared with Sonoma County. *Carneros* is Spanish for "sheep"—there were more sheep ranches than vineyards here until the 1980s. Far cooler than the valley floor because of its proximity to Pacific breezes and fog, Carneros is not suited to Cabernet Sauvignon, but Merlot and Syrah give good results in sheltered pockets. It is mostly planted with Chardonnay and Pinot Noir, which are vinified as still or sparkling wine. The French and Spanish sparkling wine houses Taittinger and Codorníu have set up estates in Carneros.

Best Napa Producers

1. **Araujo** *p. 36*
2. **Beaulieu** *p. 36*
3. **Dominus** *p. 39*
4. **Shafer** *p. 44*
5. **Opus One** *p. 42*
6. **Spottswoode** *p. 44*
7. **Stag's Leap Wine Cellars** *p. 44*
8. **Joseph Phelps** *p. 41*
9. **Chateau Montelena** *p. 37*
10. **Duckhorn** *p. 39*

Pinot Noir: The Heartbreak Grape

Admirers of this impossibly difficult grape love to debate over which California wine region produces the best Pinot Noir. There is no definitive answer, but the main contenders are generally thought to be Sonoma Coast *(see p. 49)*, Carneros *(above)*, which straddles Napa and Sonoma Counties, and the Russian River Valley *(p. 48)*. Sonoma Coast is too recently planted for anyone to be certain about its potential, but its Pinot Noirs can have exquisite perfume and considerable finesse and purity; Carneros, while fresh and fruity, is rarely complex or long-lived; and the Russian River Valley delivers more layered wines, with Burgundian nuances and an ability to age for the medium term. There are other areas of note from the Central and Southern regions, but it is the North Coast AVA that has the longest track record with the grape. California Pinot Noir rarely emulates Burgundy, but the combination of selected sites, good clones, and sensitive winemaking is beginning to produce some world-class wines.

Pinot Noir label

TOP 10 A Wine Tour of the Napa Valley

Thirty years ago, Napa Valley was a rural backwater. The celebrity of its vineyards and its proximity to San Francisco, however, have since combined to make it one of the greatest tourist attractions in the US. Visitors flock to the many hospitable tasting rooms, as well as to the fine delis and restaurants, country clubs, and luxurious inns. The most direct route follows the main highway, Highway 29. However, if this is overcrowded, take the alternative Silverado Trail, which has retained its charming rural character.

1 Copia

Napa's lavish center for wine, food, and the arts is located along the banks of the Napa River. The admission charge includes wine tuition, and the center hosts special exhibitions, dinners, blind tastings, and other events. ✆ *707 259 1600 • www.copia.org*

2 Napa Wine Train

The luxurious Napa Wine Train *(above)* offers the most effortless way to view the valley—at a price. The train takes a nonstop tour from Napa station to St. Helena and back. There are wine tastings and meals to entertain passengers during the three-hour ride. ✆ *707 253 2111 • www.winetrain.com*

3 Hess Collection

The early 20th-century Christian Brothers stone winery was leased by Swiss tycoon Donald Hess in 1986. There are wine tastings and tours of the winery as well as of Hess's remarkable contemporary art collection. ✆ *707 255 1144 • www.hesscollection.com*

4 Robert Mondavi

The Robert Mondavi winery *(right)* is not only a local landmark but it also offers the best and most detailed winery tours in the valley. Some focus on the technical aspects of winemaking, others on the complexities of wine tasting or food matching. Advanced booking is essential. *(See p. 43.)*

5 Old Inglenook

Filmmaker Francis Ford Coppola has bought some of Rutherford's most historic vineyards, and the former Inglenook winery, which he has converted into a museum devoted to the history of the estate. The museum also includes a collection of Coppola's movie memorabilia. ✆ *1 800 782 4266 • www.rubiconestate.com*

Visitors' Tips

Route *This 40-mile (65-km) tour begins in Napa and follows Highway 29 to Calistoga. For a circular route, return to Napa on the quieter Silverado Trail.*
Duration *It will take a full day, or for a more leisurely visit stop off overnight.*
Wineries *Most Napa wineries have a tasting room, and some have picnic tables where you can enjoy an alfresco lunch. Many producers make a small charge for tasting, refundable if you make a purchase.*
Hotels *Meadowood Resort in St. Helena is the ultimate in luxury and spaciousness.* ✆ *www.meadowood.com; Rancho Caymus in Rutherford has a cozy ambience and central location* ✆ *www.ranchocaymus.com; Inn at Southbridge in St. Helena is cheap, modern, comfortable, and functional.* ✆ *707 967 9400*

6 Tra Vigne Restaurant

This lofty, long-established restaurant in St. Helena is an excellent choice for lunch and dinner. Mediterranean-style cooking is accompanied by a good list of wines sold by the bottle and the glass. Prices are reasonable, and advance booking is essential. ✆ 703 963 4444 • *www.travignerestaurant.com*

7 Clos Pegase

When the architect Michael Graves won the competition to build this winery, some neighbors tried to block its construction. The Minoan-style structure *(above)*, surrounded by owner Jan Shrem's modern sculpture collection, was built in 1987. It is Napa's most controversial winery, both loved and loathed. Take one of the daily tours and decide for yourself. ✆ 707 942 4981 • *www.clospegase.com*

8 Sterling Vineyards

Sterling Vineyards' spectacular winery is based on the whitewashed buildings typical of the Greek islands. Access to the hilltop site is by a cable car, and tours and tastings of an excellent range of varietal wines are available daily. ✆ 1 800 726 6136 • *www.sterlingvineyards.com*

9 Calistoga

Calistoga's attractions include hot springs with therapeutic mud baths and the chance to enjoy a two-hour balloon ride *(above)* over the vineyards while enjoying a champagne breakfast. ✆ *www.caohwy.com/b/balloons.htm*

10 Silverado Trail

In 1858–75 there was a silver rush here, hence the name of the road. Robert Louis Stevenson wrote *Silverado Squatters* after staying at a nearby ghost town in 1880. The author and the period are the subject of a museum in St. Helena. ✆ *www.silveradomuseum.org*

Key

Tour route

Writing in 1883 after visiting the Napa Valley, Robert Louis Stevenson described the local wine as "better than a Beaujolais, and not unlike"

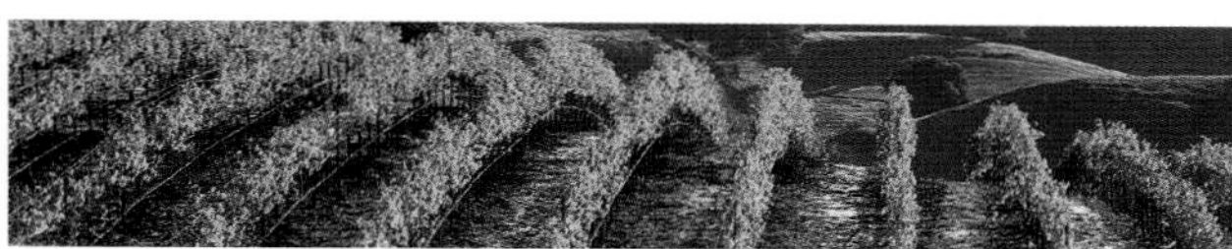

Rows of vines in fall, Carneros, Napa Valley

Major Producers in the Napa Valley

Araujo

Napa Valley / Calistoga

Known as the Eisele Vineyard in the 1970s and 80s, this estate was the source of outstanding Cabernet Sauvignon for Ridge *(see p. 80)* and Phelps *(p. 41)*. In the early 1990s it was bought by Bart and Daphne Araujo, who are typical of the new generation of rich entrepreneurs buying vineyards in Napa. Firmly stating their commitment to making superb wines from this exceptional site, the Araujos employ organic methods in the vineyard and have added Sauvignon Blanc and Syrah to the range. The wines are consistently outstanding, especially the reds, with typically Calistogan flavors of black currant, chocolate, and black olives. *2155 Pickett Rd., Calistoga • 707 942 6061 • www.araujoestatewines.com* ● *red, white* ★ *Eisele Vineyard: Cabernet Sauvignon, Syrah, Sauvignon Blanc, Viognier*

Beaulieu Vineyard

Napa Valley / Rutherford

This legendary property was founded by Frenchman Georges de Latour in 1899. An equally legendary winemaker, André Tchelitscheff *(see p. 16)*, crafted many magnificent Cabernets here in the 1950s and 60s. Quality plummeted in the 1970s, but today, under corporate giant Diageo, standards have improved again. The basic varietal ranges are correct if unexciting, but the Signet Collection offers Rhône-style blends and Sangiovese of real character. *1960 St. Helena Hwy, Rutherford • 707 967 5230 • www.bvwines.com* ○ *red, white, sparkling* ★ *Private Reserve Cabernet*

Beringer

Napa Valley / St. Helena, Yountville & other areas

Beringer's historic winery at St. Helena dates from the 1880s and is the oldest continuously

VINCENT GASNIER'S TOP 10 Great California Chardonnays

1. **Shafer: Red Shoulder Ranch Chardonnay** Napa Valley *p. 44*
2. **Far Niente** (various Chardonnays) Napa Valley *p. 40*
3. **Patz & Hall** (various Chardonnays) Napa Valley *p. 42*
4. **Stag's Leap Wine Cellars: Arcadia Vineyard Chardonnay** Napa Valley *p. 44*
5. **ZD Wines** (various Chardonnays) Napa Valley *p. 45*
6. **Cuvaison: Chardonnay Carneros** Napa Valley *p. 38*
7. **Blackjack Ranch** (various Chardonnays) Santa Barbara *p. 85*
8. **Au Bon Climat: Harmony Nuits-Blanches au Bouge** Santa Barbara *p. 84*
9. **Beringer: Sbragia Family Vineyards Chardonnay** Napa Valley *above*
10. **Chalk Hill: Estate Chardonnay** Sonoma *p. 55*

operating winery in the Napa Valley. The site has been owned by a succession of corporations, most recently the Australian Beringer Blass group. Although the company buys fruit from all over California, its biggest holdings are in Napa. Ed Sbragia has long been chief winemaker, giving a generous, oaky style for all the wines. The best are the Bordeaux-style blends known as Alluvium, and the Private Reserves, which have excellent aging capability. A curiosity here is Nightingale, a sweet wine made from Sauvignon Blanc and Semillon grapes that have been artificially induced with botrytis. *2000 Main St., St. Helena • 707 963 4812 • www.beringer.com* *red, white* ★ *North Coast Zinfandel, Private Reserve Merlot, Sbragia Family Vineyards*

Beringer's Nightingale

Caymus Vineyards
Napa Valley / Rutherford
Founded by Charlie Wagner in 1972 and now run by son Chuck, Caymus excels at Cabernet Sauvignon. The Wagners continually gauge the condition of the three soil types that make up their 62-acre (25-ha) estate and have figured out how to play each to its strengths. The combination of attention to detail and experience works: the Special Selection Cabernet Sauvignon is one of California's most applauded fine wines. Conundrum, a white blend developed by Caymus in the 1990s, is still owned as a brand by the Wagner family, but the Rutherford site is now dedicated to Cabernet. *Conn Creek Rd., Rutherford • 707 963 4202 • www.caymus.com* *red, white* ★ *Napa Valley Cabernet Sauvignon, Special Selection Cabernet Sauvignon*

Chateau Montelena
Napa Valley / Calistoga, Mount Veeder
This 19th-century winery was restored by James Barrett, whose son Bo has been winemaker since 1981. It was Chateau Montelena's 1973 Chardonnay that won top prize for whites at the historic "Judgment of Paris" tastings in 1976 *(see p. 44)*. The top wine today is the intense, magisterial Estate Cabernet Sauvignon, while the cheaper Calistoga Cuvée is made from bought-in grapes. The atypical Chardonnay sees hardly any new oak, and though austere when young, it can age well. *1429 Tubbs Lane, Calistoga • 707 942 5105 • www.montelena.com* *red, white* ★ *Calistoga Cuvee, Cabernet Sauvignon, Montelena Estate Zinfandel, Napa Valley Chardonnay*

Colgin
Napa Valley
Pity the recent convert to Ann Colgin's mail-order-only selection of reds, for there is usually a waiting list of 4,000 customers. Colgin's method of operation shows the kind of dedication necessary to become a major player in Californian wine. Regularly bringing in geologists to evaluate the condition of her *terroir*, Colgin then often sends for other teams to provide a second diagnosis. Married to this relentlessly scientific approach is a welcome dash of style, as evidenced by her penchant for commissioning cases designed by David Linley. *8700 Conn Creek Rd., Rutherford • 707 963 0999 • www.colgincellars.com* *red* ★ *IX Estate, Herb Lamb Vineyard Cabernet Sauvignon, Tychson Hill, Cariad Napa Valley Red Wine*

The Napa Playground

The Napa Valley has become something of a playground for the rich and famous; winery buildings of all shapes and styles vie with each other to be the biggest, best, or just most outlandish. In Calistoga, Clos Pegase boasts a Minoan-style villa, and Sterling Vineyards offers a cable-car ride up to its whitewashed Greek island-style buildings located high in the hills (see p. 35 for both). Robert Mondavi's 1960s-built Spanish Mission-style winery is located at Oakville, with the world-famous Opus One vineyard planted across from it (see pp. 42–3). In Rutherford, filmmaker Francis Ford Coppola bought the Old Inglenook winery (see p. 34) in 1975 and established his own wine labels. Now called Rubicon Estate (www.rubiconestate.com), the restored 19th-century chateau complex includes a museum with memorabilia from Coppola's movies, including his five Oscars.

Cuvaison

Napa Valley / Carneros & Mount Veeder

Jay Schuppert and Steven Rogstad attribute their estate's success to the Napa Valley morning fog (it keeps the grapes from heating up too quickly). All of Cuvaison's grapes are harvested by hand on its prime sites in Carneros and the Brandlin Ranch on Mount Veeder. The latter has a gravelly clay loam and is planted mainly with Cabernet Sauvignon. Chardonnay, grown on the hard clay soil at Carneros, is Cuvaison's main variety and is aged in French oak barrels. The winery also buys grapes from other vineyards in the Napa Valley. *4550 Silverado Trail North, Calistoga • 707 942 6266 • www.cuvaison.com* ☐ *red, white, dessert* ★ *Estate Selection Chardonnay, Pinot Noir, Napa Valley Carneros, Cuvaison BMV Zinfandel*

Dolce Vineyard

Napa Valley

Greg Allen made the right decision in 2000 when he chose between a career healing sports injuries and a job at Far Niente *(see p. 40)*. Within a year, Allen was promoted to winemaker at Far Niente's Dolce Vineyard at the base of the Vaca Mountains—claimed to be the only winery in North America that is devoted to a single late-harvest dessert wine. Inspired by the great Sauternes wines of France, Dolce is made with a blend of Semillon and Sauvignon Blanc grapes which are exposed to the beneficial *botrytis cinerea* mold, or "noble rot." Some years, 3,000 cases emerge from the winery, generally to great acclaim: other years, none at all. *Coombsville • 707 944 8868 • www.dolcewine.com* ● *dessert* ★ *Dolce vintage*

Domaine Carneros

Napa Valley / Carneros

Big names and a big investment: Claude Taittinger of the eponymous Champagne house built the landmark French-style château here in 1989. The winery in the grounds of the château is devoted to the production of sparkling wine, using exclusively Carneros grapes, and it maintains its supremacy by prioritizing quality over tonnage. Each spring sees the vineyards being combed for shoots that are deemed to be weak, which are then destroyed. *1240 Duhig Rd., Napa • 707 257 3020 • www.domaine.com* ☐ *sparkling* ★ *Brut Cuvee, Brut Rose*

Domaine Chandon

Napa Valley

Another global name, this facility, founded in 1973, was the brainchild of former French Resistance hero, Count Robert Jean de Vogué, the president of

For more on sparkling wines **See pp. 60–61**

Duckhorn's estate in St. Helena

the Moët & Chandon Champagne house. De Vogué identified Napa as one of several sites around the world that would be suitable for sparkling wine. The company has vineyards at Carneros, Mount Veeder, and Yountville, and employs modern sustainable farming practices. The sparkling wines are produced according to the *méthode traditionnelle* of Champagne. A few still wines are also now being released.
1 California Drive, Yountville • 707 944 8844 • www.chandon.com ☐ red, white, sparkling ★ Chandon Reserve Brut, Etoile Brut

Dominus
Napa Valley / Yountville
The modern winery at Dominus, designed by Swiss architects Herzog and de Meuron in 1997, stands in the middle of a historic vineyard, which in the 19th century was a source of Inglenook's legendary Cabernet. In 1982 the site was acquired by the Moueix family, owners of Château Pétrus in France. At first, the top wine from Dominus, made in Bordelais fashion, was tough, but the team soon adapted to Napa conditions and today the wine is better balanced, showing power and depth. The second wine, Napanook, is intended for earlier drinking.
2570 Napanook Rd., Yountville • 707 944 8954 • www.dominusestate.com ☐ red ★ Dominus, Napanook

Duckhorn Vineyards
Napa Valley & other areas
Long before Merlot became fashionable in California, Dan Duckhorn was producing rich, powerful examples with imposing tannic structure. He also invented a style he calls Paraduxx, an appealing blend of Zinfandel, Cabernet, and Merlot. From his land in Mendocino comes a fine Pinot Noir, called Goldeneye.
1000 Lodi Lane, St. Helena • 707 963 7108 • www.duckhornvineyards.com ■ red, white ★ Paraduxx, Three Palms Vineyard Napa Merlot, Napa Cabernet Sauvignon

VINCENT GASNIER'S TOP 10

Best-Kept Secrets of California Wine

1. **Etude: Pinot Gris** (white) Napa Valley *p. 45*
2. **Spottswoode: Sauvignon Blanc** (white) Napa Valley *p. 44*
3. **Cline** (red, white & sparkling) Sonoma *p. 50*
4. **Clos du Bois** (red, white & rosé) Sonoma *p. 51*
5. **Walter Hansel: Pinot Noir** (red) Santa Rosa *p. 87*
6. **Cakebread Cellars: Cabernet Sauvignon** (red) Napa Valley *p. 45*
7. **Heitz Cellar: Cabernet Sauvignon** (red) Napa Valley *p. 40*
8. **Far Niente: Cabernet Sauvignon** (red) Napa Valley *p. 40*
9. **Joseph Phelps** (red, white & rosé) Napa Valley *p. 41*
10. **Havens** (red) Napa Valley *p. 45*

Far Niente
Napa Valley
One of California's oldest wineries, Far Niente (Italian for "doing nothing") was founded in 1885 by a certain John Benson. The winery flourished until Prohibition, but was then abandoned and not resurrected until 1979. Current winemaker Stephanie Putnam originally planned to join the FBI; these days she enforces a policy of small-yield excellence at Larry Maguire's 250-acre (101-ha) estate. There are just two wines, a Chardonnay and a Cabernet Sauvignon. Both are pricey, attract rave reviews, and sell fast. *1350 Acacia Drive, Oakville • 707 944 2861 • www.farniente.com* *red, white* ★ *Estate Bottled Chardonnay, Cabernet*

Frog's Leap
Napa Valley / Rutherford
John Williams at Frog's Leap turns out elegant Sauvignon Blanc, Cabernet Sauvignon, and Zinfandel, as well as a Cabernet Sauvignon-Cabernet Franc blend called Rutherford. The wines are often undervalued because Williams aims for style and balance rather than power and overt oakiness. The result is a range of eminently drinkable, as well as serious, wines that are made from organic grapes. *8815 Conn Creek Rd., Rutherford • 707 963 4704 • www.frogsleap.com* *red, white* ★ *Cabernet Sauvignon, Zinfandel, Rutherford*

The Oldest Wine of California

In 1998 a very old bottle of wine was unearthed in a cellar in Marin County. Complete with a sepia-tone artwork of a hammock piled up with clusters of grapes, the wine was a Sweet Muscat of 1886, made by the original Far Niente winery *(above)*. This is the oldest known intact bottle of California wine in existence, and it is preserved unopened. A century after that wine was produced, Far Niente's sister, Dolce Vineyard *(see p. 38)*, released its first vintage (1985) of dessert wine, which was soon declared by critics as one of the best sweet wines ever made in California.

Harlan Estate
Napa Valley
Bill Harlan's approach shows the single-minded pursuit of greatness that characterizes many Napa producers. He spent 20 years choosing his estate—240 acres (97 ha) in the western hills of Oakville. Next came a meticulously researched grape selection, which resulted in clones of Cabernet Sauvignon, Merlot, Carnet Franc, and Petit Verdot. He and his winemaker, Bob Levy, are now awash with plaudits. *1551 Oakville Grade, Oakville • 707 944 1441 • www.harlanestate.com* *red* ★ *Harlan Estate, The Maiden*

Heitz Cellar
Napa Valley
Opened by Joe and Alice Heitz in 1961, Heitz may appear unglitzy in comparison with its Napa colleagues, but it consistently produces the goods. Another Heitz, the appropriately named Avid, keeps a hawklike watch over the maximum amount of time that the Cabernet Sauvignons and Chardonnays can withstand oak-aging. Avid takes calculated risks, and the results are some of the finest Cabernets in the world. These allow Heitz to be as fearless about its pricing as it is about its production. *500 Taplin Road, St. Helena • 707 963 3542 • www.heitzcellar.com* *red, white, rose, fortified* ★ *Martha's Vineyard, Trailside Vineyard, Chardonnay Cellar Selection*

Hendry

Napa Valley

The "Block" that appears in the names of Hendry's products refers to the scientific way in which ex-physicist George Hendry works his vineyard. Using soil type, exposure, and clone and root stock as definition criteria, Hendry has split his 117 acres (47 ha) into 49 blocks, each of which is regarded as an ongoing grape-growing experiment. This commitment means that Hendry's wines will change far more rapidly than their competitors. So far, though, results have been superb, especially the Hendry Block 20 Chardonnay. *3104 Redwood Road • 707 226 8320 • www.hendrywines.com* *red, white, rosé ★ Block 20 Chardonnay, Block 28 Zinfandel*

VINCENT GASNIER'S TOP 10 Magnificent Merlots

1. **Duckhorn** Napa Valley *p. 39*
2. **Merryvale** Napa Valley *below*
3. **Blackjack Ranch** Santa Barbara *p. 85*
4. **Arrowood** Sonoma *p. 50*
5. **Flora Springs** Napa Valley *p. 45*
6. **Switchback Ridge** Napa Valley *p. 45*
7. **Owen Roe** Oregon *www.owenroe.com*
8. **Havens** Napa Valley *p. 45*
9. **Lewis Cellars** Napa Valley *p. 45*
10. **Neyers Vineyards** Napa Valley *p. 45*

Joseph Phelps

Napa Valley

Established in 1972, Joseph Phelps made its name with sweet Rieslings and was one of the first producers of Syrah in California. Although the company has a fine reputation for Cabernet and its prestigious Insignia, winemaker Craig Williams has continued to develop Rhône-style wines including an excellent Viognier, a juicy blend called Le Mistral, and a delicious Grenache rosé. *200 Taplin Rd., St. Helena • 707 963 2745 • www.jpvwines.com* *by appt* *red, white, rosé ★ Viognier, Syrah*

Kongsgaard

Napa Valley

John Kongsgaard began making wine under his own label in 1996, determined to keep production limited to ensure that everything could be handmade. To this end, he has restricted himself to four wines: a Chardonnay blend from various sites in the Napa Valley; a single-vineyard Chardonnay called "The Judge"; a Viognier and Roussanne blend; and Syrah from Carneros. Kongsgaard sees winemaking as a highly aesthetic process, the enhancement of which has seen violinist Isaac Stern and others performing concerts in the winery itself. *4050 Spring Mountain Road, Oakville • 707 963 4512 • www.kongsgaardwine.com* *white, red ★ Napa Valley Chardonnay The Judge*

Merryvale

Napa Valley / Oakville, Rutherford & other areas

Now owned by Californian and Swiss partners, Merryvale has benefited from top winemakers and the advice of consultant Michel Rolland. Substantial volumes of wine are made here, all to a high standard. The top ranges—Reserve and Prestige—are outstanding, but Profile, an elegant Bordeaux-style blend aged in new oak, is usually the best. *1000 Main St., St. Helena • 707 963 7777 • www.merryvale.com* *red, white, fortified ★ Silhouette Chardonnay, Carneros Merlot, Profile*

Merryvale occupies the site of the first winery to be built in the Napa Valley after the repeal of Prohibition in 1933

George Yount: The Napa Pioneer

In 1838 George Yount, a trapper from North Carolina who is credited as the first nonnative settler in the Napa Valley, took some cuttings from Mission vines that were growing in his friend's vineyard in Sonoma. He planted them outside his log cabin at the southern end of the Napa Valley in the hope that he could produce enough grapes to make wine for his own consumption. Within six years, Yount was making about 900 liters of wine each year, and by the 1850s he was a well-known figure who helped found the town of Sebastopol, about 1.5 miles (3 km) south of his first vineyard. Yount died in 1865 without knowing he was the pioneer of one of the world's most celebrated wine regions. Two years after his death, Sebastopol was renamed Yountville in a lasting tribute to his legacy, and by the end of the 1870s, more than 18,000 acres (7,300 ha) of the Napa Valley were under vine—half the amount grown today.

Mumm Napa

Napa Valley

In 1979 the illustrious French Champagne house Mumm sent winemaker Guy Devaux on a covert mission to the US to find the perfect location for sparkling wine. It was not until 1983 that Devaux identified a site in the Napa Valley with the right climate and soils. By the 1990s, domestic sales of Mumm Napa were outstripping imports from the French Mumm. Ludovic Dervin has continued Devaux's work, and Mumm Napa offers some of the most elegant, reasonably priced sparkling wines in the US. A still Pinot Noir is also now produced. *8445 Silverado Trail, Rutherford • 707 967 7700 • www.mummnapa.com* ☐ *sparkling, red (still)* ★ *Carneros Pinot Noir, Santana DVX, Cuvee M Red*

Opus One

Napa Valley / Oakville

Arguably California's best-known fine wine, Opus One was the 1970s brainchild of California producer Robert Mondavi *(see p. 16)* and Baron Philippe de Rothschild, the owner of Château Mouton Rothschild in Bordeaux. This silky red blend varies in content each year: mainly Cabernet Sauvignon, with degrees of Merlot, Cabernet Franc, Malbec, and Petit Verdot exquisitely balanced together to give a complex layering of spices and berries after some years in the cellar. The first vintage was 1979, which was released in 1983 at $50 a bottle—an unprecedented price for a California Cabernet at the time. For the first 12 years, Opus One was produced at Robert Mondavi's winery across the road *(see right)*, while a dedicated winery was being built here. Completed in 1991, the distinctive limestone building is, like the wine, a mix of the Old and New Worlds in concept, set amid vineyards where Bordeaux-style high-density planting and hand-selection are the norm. *7900 St. Helena Highway, Oakville • 707 944 9442 • www.opusonewinery.com* ☐ *red* ★ *Opus One*

Patz & Hall

Napa Valley, Sonoma & other areas

Patz & Hall was founded in 1988 with one main intention—to produce distinctive Chardonnay on a small-production, single-vineyard basis. As the winery's creative team widened its interests to all things Burgundian, an equivalent emphasis was placed on Pinot Noir. Now using grapes from nine of California's most prestigious vineyards, Patz and Hall has a portfolio of six Chardonnays and four Pinot Noirs, all of which are

Robert Mondavi in the cellar of his Napa Valley winery

distinctly Californian despite being produced using French techniques and even specially imported French equipment. *851 Napa Valley Corporate, Rutherford • 707 265 6700 • www.patzhall.com* red, white ★ *Russian River, Santa Lucia Highlands, Pinot Noir*

Robert Mondavi
Napa Valley / Oakville, Stags Leap & many other areas
Robert Mondavi *(see p. 16)*—the man and the brands—are such a California institution that it is hard to believe the Minnesota-born winemaker only founded his Napa site in 1966, and went through many tough years. Mondavi's secret was simple from the start: indefatigable curiosity and steely determination to excel. He created the Fumé Blanc style of oaked Sauvignon Blanc and pioneered research into oak aging and vineyard density, sharing the results with other wineries. Fanatical about wine education, he was also the major financial backer of Napa's Copia Center *(see p. 34)*, which brings together wine, food, and the arts. Mondavi's extensive vineyards in the Central Coast and Santa Barbara districts of California mostly provide fruit for the less expensive Mondavi blends. The wines from the Napa vineyards are of high quality, in particular those with subdistrict designations from Oakville, Stags Leap, and Carneros. The Reserve wines are significantly superior to the regular bottlings, and the supreme Opus One blend has its own winery in Oakville *(see opposite)*. In 2004 Constellation paid $1.36 billion for the Mondavi Corporation: its subsidiary Centerra Wine Company *(see p. 121)* now owns the Robert Mondavi Private Selection and some related brands, but Mondavi's family is still involved in the business. *Highway 29, Oakville • 1 888 766 6328 • www.robertmondavi.com* *red, white* ★ *Pinot Noir Reserve, Oakville Cabernet Sauvignon*

VINCENT GASNIER'S TOP 10
Great California Cabernet Sauvignons

1. **Peter Michael** Sonoma *p. 54*
2. **Far Niente** Napa Valley *p. 40*
3. **Arrowood** Sonoma *p. 50*
4. **Ravenswood** Sonoma *p. 54*
5. **Shafer** Napa Valley *p. 44*
6. **Araujo** Napa Valley *p. 36*
7. **Spottswoode** Napa Valley *p. 44*
8. **Caymus Vineyards** Napa Valley *p. 37*
9. **Lokoya** Napa Valley *p. 45*
10. **Stag's Leap Wine Cellars** Napa Valley *p. 44*

Robert Mondavi and Baron Philippe de Rothschild first met in Hawaii in 1970, and their families still jointly own Opus One

Shafer
Napa Valley / Stags Leap & Carneros
When publisher John Shafer began searching for vineyards in the late 1960s, he exhibited a fierce obsession with *terroir*. By 1972, he was ready to start growing grapes, and six years later he began to process them. These days, the vineyards stretch over 200 acres (80 ha) and provide the fruit for over 30,000 cases of Cabernet Sauvignon, Merlot, Chardonnay, Sangiovese, and Syrah each year. Under Doug Shafer, the company has espoused sustainable agriculture, making use of solar power, water recycling, and composting techniques. The velvety Hillside Select Cabernet Sauvignon is sourced entirely from a site in Stags Leap. *6154 Silverado Trail, Napa • 707 944 28 77 • www.shafervineyards.com* red ★ *Hillside Select Cabernet Sauvignon, Red Shoulder Ranch Chardonnay*

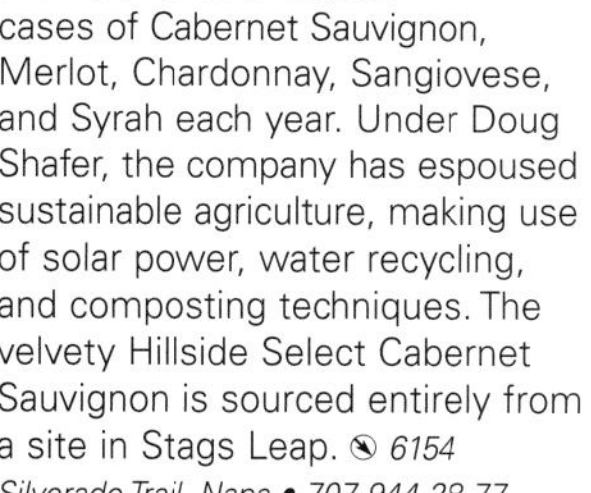

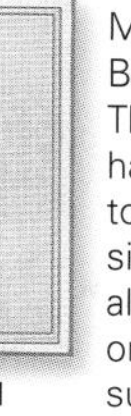
Spottswoode label

The Judgment of Paris
In 1976, British wine merchant Steven Spurrier organized a blind tasting in Paris in which the best California wines were pitted against top growths of Bordeaux and Burgundy. The mostly French team of tasters were amazed to find they had given pride of place to a Stag's Leap Wine Cellars Cabernet *(see right)* and a Chateau Montelena Chardonnay *(p. 37)*, and mortified when the story hit the press. The comparison was unequal, as only recent vintages were tasted and French wines are generally less open and expressive in youth than their California rivals. Nonetheless, the historic tasting showed the wine world that Napa was a serious contender.

Spottswoode
Napa Valley / St. Helena
On an old estate first planted with vines in 1882, Dr. Jack and Mary Novak established this winery in 1972, which Mary and daughter Beth continue to run. This is an estate that has been committed to organic farming since 1985 (olive oil is also produced), using organic fertilizers and sustainable practices where possible to great effect. Despite the wide renown and consistency of its wines, Spottswoode still has a family atmosphere, with no pretensions to grandeur. Consultant winemaker Tony Soter helped established Spottswoode's reputation for immensely stylish Cabernet Sauvignon and lively Sauvignon Blanc, which are the only two wines produced here, always in limited quantities. Current winemaker Rosemary Cakebread has maintained this approach since 1997. *1902 Madrona Ave., St. Helena • 707 963 0134 • www.spottswoode.com* *by appt.* *red, white* ★ *Sauvignon Blanc, Cabernet Sauvignon*

Stag's Leap Wine Cellars
Napa Valley / Stags Leap
Warren Winiarski *(see p. 17)*, one of California's most famous winemakers, acquired his first vineyard site in the Stags Leap district in 1970, and by 1972 had established a winery here. A passionate believer in the suitability of Cabernet Sauvignon to the Napa Valley, Winiarski made his name when his wine outshone first-growth wines from Château Mouton-Rothschild and Château Haut-Brion of Bordeaux at the 1976 Paris Tasting *(see box)*.

The business, still in the skilled hands of Winiarski and his family, continues to make sumptuous Cabernets including a Napa appellation wine from bought-in grapes. The original vineyard, now referred to as S.L.V. on the estate-bottled wines (which helpfully distinguishes it from the district name and other local wineries with Stag's Leap in their names), is planted mainly with Cabernet, as is Fay Vineyard, also in the district. Arcadia Vineyard lies at the foot of Mount George and is planted mainly with Chardonnay. The sublime Cask 23 is a Cabernet reserve wine produced only when conditions have been exceptional. This is one of Winiarski's quintessential reds—rich but elegant, supple, balanced, and age-worthy. Prices are high, but Winiarski also offers a line of sound inexpensive wines under the Hawk Crest label. *5766 Silverado Trail, Napa • 707 944 2020 • www.cask23.com* *red, white* ★ *Arcadia Chardonnay, S.L.V. Cabernet Sauvignon, Cask 23*

ZD Wines

Napa Valley

Although it was in 1968 that Gino Zepponi and Norman deLeuze formed a plan to make Burgundy-style wines using Pinot Noir and Chardonnay, their winery did not appear until 1979. Now certified organic, the ZD production process is renowned for its slow, cool fermentation, and the final product has been the wine of choice at many a White House dinner party. *8383 Silverado Trail, Napa • 800 487 7757 • www.zdwines.com* *red, white* ★ *Reserve Chardonnay, Pinot Noir, Abacus*

Other Producers in the Napa Valley

Abreu Vineyard *2366 Madrona Ave., St. Helena • 707 963 7487*

Acacia Winery *2750 Las Amigas Road, Napa Valley • 707 226 9991 • www.acaciawinery.com*

Philippe-Lorraine Vineyard *1315 Main St., St. Helena • 707 963 0121*

Atalon Vineyard *7600 St. Helena Hwy., St. Helena • 800 224 4090 • www.atalon.com*

Cakebread Cellars *8300 St. Helena Hwy., St. Helena • 800 588 0298 • www.cakebread.com*

Clos du Val *5330 Silverado Trail, Napa • 70 261 5225 • www.closduval.com*

Dunn Vineyard *805 White Cottage Road, N. Angwin • 707 965 3805*

Etude *1250 Cuttings Wharf Road, Napa • 707 257 5300 • www.etudewines.com*

Flora Springs *677 South St. Hwy., St. Helena • 707 963 5711 • www.florasprings.com*

Havens Wine Cellars *2055 Hoffman Lane, Napa • 707 261 2000 • www.havenswine.com*

La Jota Winery *1102 Las Posadas Rd., Angwin, St. Helena • 877 222 0292 • www.lajotavineyardco.com*

Lewis Cellars *4101 Big Ranch Road, Napa • 707 255 3400 • www.lewiscellars.com*

Lokoya Winery *7600 St. Helena Hwy., Oakville • 707 944 2824 • www.lokoya.com*

Neyers Vineyards *2153 Sage Canyon Rd., St. Helena • 707 963 8840 • www.neyersvineyards.com*

Storybook Mountain Vineyards *3835 Hwy. 128, Calistoga • 707 942 5310 • www.storybookwines.com*

Switchback Ridge *4292 Silverado Trail, Calistoga • 707 967 8987 • www.switchbackridge.com*

Turley Wine Cellars *3358 St. Helena Hwy. • 707 963 0940 • www.turleywinecellars.com*

V. Sattui Vineyards *1111 White Lane, St. Helena • 707 963 7744 • www.vsattui.com*

Viader Vineyards and Winery *1120 Deer Park Rd., Deer Park • 707 963 3816 • www.viader.com*

Wine Areas of Sonoma

Sonoma is the most diverse of the North Coast counties, with an enormous range of soil types, mesoclimates, and elevations. Generally, the subregions closer to the Pacific are cooler and better suited to the Burgundian varieties Chardonnay and Pinot Noir. The valley floor and eastern slopes are hotter and ideal for Bordeaux red grapes and Zinfandel.

In total, Sonoma has around 60,000 acres (24,000 ha) in production, and over 260 wineries, ranging in size from tiny operations to vast ranches. Alongside the established Italian families of the region—Seghesio, Foppiano, Martinelli—are relative newcomers equally dedicated to making the most of Sonoma's varied and generous climate. Chardonnay from this region can be exceptional, and Pinot Noir from the Russian River Valley is probably the best expression of this tricky variety in the whole of California. While virtually all the suitable land in the Napa Valley is already planted, new areas in Sonoma are still being developed, and none is more exciting than the cool, lofty ridgetops of the Sonoma Coast. The following are Sonoma's most important AVAs.

gravel, sandy loam, shallow sedimentary, clay, sandstone, gravel, shale *Cabernet Sauvignon, Zinfandel, Merlot, Pinot Noir, Syrah* *Chardonnay, Sauvignon Blanc, Gewürztraminer* *red, white*

Kendall-Jackson label

Alexander Valley & Knights Valley

Alexander Valley AVA can be extremely hot, so many of the 15,000 acres (6,000 ha) of vineyards lie at higher elevations in the foothills of the Mayacamas Mountains. On the valley floor, Zinfandel thrives. The valley is also a source of succulent, rich Cabernet Sauvignon and Merlot grapes.

The adjoining Knights Valley AVA twists through the mountains to Calistoga in Napa. There is only one important winery based here, Peter Michael *(see p. 54)*, although Beringer *(p. 36)* has substantial plantings too. Red vines flourish down on the valley floor, while Chardonnay gives great results at much higher elevations.

Dry Creek Valley

This celebrated region (10,000 acres/4,000 ha of vineyards) runs northwest from Healdsburg, and most of its estates and wineries are strung out along Dry Creek Road. There is a good deal of splendid old-vine (often century-old) Zinfandel planted here; but like other Sonoma regions, Dry Creek Valley is versatile, and some excellent Cabernet Sauvignon and even some white wines can be found. Most of the estates are quite small, but over the past decade the Gallo family *(see p. 52)* has developed vast holdings throughout Sonoma and has its main base in Dry Creek Valley.

Russian River Valley, Green Valley & Chalk Hill

The Russian River Valley AVA has around 10,000 acres (4,000 ha) under vine and is renowned as a cool viticultural region, prone to maritime fog incursions. One sector, where producers Williams Selyem, Rochioli, and Davis Bynum are based, is certainly the

Preceding pages **Vineyard and school house in St. Helena, North Coast California**

source of some of California's best Pinot Noir. The texture of the wine can be silky and sensuous. Nowhere else in California does Pinot develop that seductive damp undergrowth character typical of Burgundy in France. The region is, however, far from uniform, and there are areas where Zinfandel has been established for decades.

Harvesting Chardonnay grapes in Sonoma

Green Valley, while an independent AVA, is really an enclave within the southern Russian River Valley. Here it can be cool, and in some vintages the grapes struggle to ripen. Marimar Torres *(see p. 54)*, sister of the renowned Catalan wine producer Miguel Torres, grows Burgundian varieties here, while Iron Horse *(p. 52)* is the best known of Sonoma's sparkling wine producers. Chalk Hill AVA is another pocket within Russian River Valley, mostly given to the estate of the same name. This is warmer territory just north of the town of Santa Rosa, but it is nonetheless known for its Chardonnay and Sauvignon Blanc.

Sonoma Valley & Sonoma Mountain

Extending from Santa Rosa to Carneros, Sonoma Valley AVA is home to some of the county's best-known producers—Kenwood *(p. 53)*, Chateau St. Jean *(p. 50)*, Landmark, and St. Francis *(p. 55)*. Their wineries are located on the valley floor, though their vineyards are sometimes planted on side valleys. It is a versatile region, producing good Chardonnay, Zinfandel, and red Bordeaux varieties. The loftier Sonoma Mountain AVA lies just to the west. Few wineries are based here; the best known is Laurel Glen *(p. 55)*, which produces tannic and long-lived Cabernets from vineyards at about 820 ft (250 m) elevation.

Sonoma Coast & Northern Sonoma

The vast and almost meaningless Sonoma Coast AVA stretches some distance inland from the long Sonoma County coastline. However, over recent years, vineyards have been planted on high ridges just inland from and sometimes overlooking the Pacific, all with the intention of finding the perfect cool-climate location for Chardonnay and Pinot Noir. Flowers *(p. 55)* is the only important winery located here, but many top producers buy fruit from the area. Sonoma Coast wines often have an intensity and purity reminiscent of fine Burgundy.

Another vast appellation within Sonoma Coast is Northern Sonoma, which exists at the behest of Gallo of Sonoma, as a catch-all AVA for wines the company blends from various districts in Sonoma.

Carneros AVA is shared by Sonoma and Napa Counties **See p. 33**

Vineyard in Knights Valley, Sonoma

Major Producers in Sonoma

Arrowood

Sonoma

Despite being dogged by the legend that he never met a grape that he didn't want to squeeze, Dick Arrowood boasts a wine portfolio that is a model of chastity. He started in the wine business in 1965, and was with Chateau St. Jean *(see right)* for many years until starting up his own company in 1988. Arrowood's ambition for his own winery was to produce reserve-quality Chardonnay and Cabernet Sauvignon. Once that was achieved, he expanded his operation to include limited qualities of Merlot, Riesling, Viognier, Pinot Blanc, Malbec, and Syrah. The Merlot in particular has been silky and rich, and the Late Harvest Riesling is a delicate, floral dessert wine. *14347 Sonoma Hwy., Glen Ellen • 707 935 2600 • www.arrowoodvineyards.com* ◻ *red, white, rosé, dessert* ★ *Hoot Owl Creek, Gewürztraminer, Grand Archer, Late Harvest Riesling*

Chateau St. Jean

Sonoma / Alexander Valley

In the 1970s, this company's first winemaker, Richard Arrowood *(see left)*, produced dazzling dry and sweet white wines from individual vineyards. Today Chateau St. Jean is part of the Beringer Blass empire, and the range is no longer so extensive, though the Chardonnay and Sauvignon Blanc are still impressive. Vineyards are dotted around Sonoma, including two in the Alexander Valley. The chateau itself is located near Kenwood, an attractive listed property dating from the 1920s that is open to visitors. Present winemaker Steve Reeder has introduced some excellent reds: Merlot and the Cabernet Sauvignon-dominated Cinq Cépages. The style is richly fruity, and the emphasis is on wines that are best drunk young. *8555 Hwy 12, Kenwood • 707 833 4134 • www.chateaustjean.com* ◻ *red, white* ★ *Robert Young Vineyard Chardonnay, Cinq Cépages, Sonoma County Reserves*

VINCENT GASNIER'S TOP 10 Zinfandel Producers

1. **Ravenswood** Sonoma *p. 54*
2. **Cline** Contra Costa *right*
3. **Ridge Vineyards** San Francisco Bay *p. 80*
4. **Williams Selyem** Sonoma *p. 55*
5. **Turley Wine Cellars** Napa Valley *p. 45*
6. **Nalle Winery** Sonoma *p. 55*
7. **Gary Farrell** Sonoma *p. 52*
8. **Hartford** Sonoma *p. 55*
9. **Storybook Mountain** Napa Valley *p. 45*
10. **Shafer** Napa Valley *p. 44*

Cline

Sonoma, Contra Costa County

The Cline brothers come from Oakley, in Contra Costa County, where they still own a splendid old vineyard planted with traditional grapes, notably Mourvèdre, Zinfandel,

and Carignane (Carignan). In 1991 they moved the winery to southern Sonoma and planted Rhône varieties in new vineyards while maintaining the old vines in Contra Costa. Anyone weary of Chardonnay and Cabernet should try their sensibly priced Zinfandel, Mourvèdre, Syrah, and Viognier, as well as Carignane and Marsanne. *24737 Hwy 121, Sonoma • 707 963 4310 • www.clinecellars.com* *red, white, sparkling ★ Sonoma Viognier, Ancient Vines Mourvèdre*

Cline label

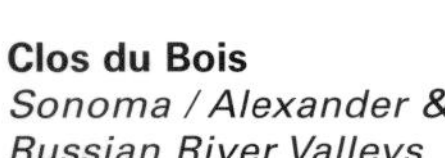

Clos du Bois
Sonoma / Alexander & Russian River Valleys
Clos du Bois bows at the altar of French winemaking when it points out that its 750 acres (300 ha) Alexander Valley vineyards are only 5,577 miles (8,975 km) from France. It also, however, supports the local wine industry, sourcing its French grape varieties from 150 Sonoma growers. This broad range enables Clos du Bois to maintain three brands: the Classic range is an everyday, affordable line; the Appellation Reserves are more upmarket, including fine Pinot Noir from the Russian River Valley. The luxury Proprietary Series benefits from the full attention of winemaker Erik Olsen. *19410 Geyserville Ave., Geyserville • 800 222 3189 • www.closdubois.com* *red, white, rosé ★ Clos du Bois Pinot Grigio, Briarcrest Cabernet Sauvignon, Marlstone, Calcaire Chardonnay*

Ferrari-Carano
Sonoma / Dry Creek Valley
The Caranos are hoteliers from Nevada, and their showmanship is fully in evidence at this lavish Dry Creek estate, which is enjoyed by visitors as much for its gardens and hospitality center as for its wines. Nonetheless, the wines are among Sonoma's best, thanks to the skill of long-term winemaker George Bursick. At first, the winery was known mainly for its elegant, oaky whites—Chardonnay and Sauvignon Blanc—but now the reds win equal acclaim. In addition to standard varietal wines, there is a fine Cabernet Sauvignon-Sangiovese blend called Siena, and Tresor, which is a rich blend of five classic red Bordeaux grape varieties. *8761 Dry Creek Rd., Healdsburg • 707 433 6700 • www.ferrari-carano.com* *red, white ★ Fumé Blanc Reserve, Siena, Tresor*

Zinfandel: California's Heritage Grape

California is fortunate in that its vinous calling card, Zinfandel, is a fascinating grape variety. It seems to be of Croatian origin and identical to the southern Italian Primitivo, but in California it has taken on its own personality. Zinfandel was very widely planted by immigrants, mostly Italian, who settled in the North Coast in the 19th century, delivering robust, full-bodied wines that resembled those from southern Europe. Many of these old vineyards survive; being dry-farmed, they give relatively small crops of intensely flavored grapes. Zinfandel can suffer from uneven ripening: pick too early and it tastes green; pick too late, and it can taste like jelly. The trick is to pick it fully ripe. There is an unfortunate vogue for Zinfandels with very high alcohol levels and for sweet pink "blush" Zinfandel.

Botanist Luther Burbank (1849–1926) described Sonoma as "the chosen spot of all the Earth as far as nature is concerned"

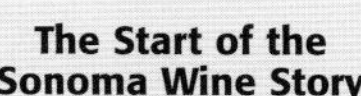

The Start of the Sonoma Wine Story

It is thought that Russian colonists may have planted vines as early as 1812 at Fort Ross on the Sonoma Coast. However, the credit for founding Sonoma's wine industry usually goes to Padre José Altimira. This Spanish Franciscan monk established a mission, San Francisco Solano, in Sonoma Valley in 1823 and a couple of years later planted thousands of so-called Mission vines here, cuttings from which were taken to other parts of California over the next decades. In the 1840s Cyrus Alexander was the first wine pioneer to make a vineyard in the area that was to become known as Alexander Valley. Sonoma's first non-Mission vines were planted by William Hill in 1852, and in 1855 Agoston Harazthy de Mokesa established his prolific Buena Vista winery in Sonoma *(see p. 22)*.

Gallo of Sonoma
Sonoma

To the astonishment and consternation of many small-scale Sonoma growers, the powerful Gallo family *(see p. 83)* reached out from their Central Valley lair in the mid-1980s and bought 3,000 acres (1,200 ha) of land in Sonoma. Since the first releases from the Sonoma arm of Gallo in 1991, wine critics have been surprised by the high quality of the wines. In addition to five single-vineyard labels, which usually represent good value, the Gallos also release very limited quantities of expensive Chardonnay and Cabernet Sauvignon varietals known, confusingly, as the Estate Range. *3387 Dry Creek Rd., Healdsburg • 707 431 5500 • www.gallosonoma.com* *red, white* ★ *Laguna Chardonnay, Frei Ranch Zinfandel, Stefani Vineyard*

Gary Farrell
Sonoma / Russian River Valley

Since 1982, the self-effacing Gary Farrell has been the winemaker fashioning some of the finest Pinot Noirs for Russian River wineries such as Davis Bynum. He has also produced a line of wines under his own label, and in 2000 set up a winery that soon became known for elegant, restrained Chardonnay and Pinot. *10701 Westside Rd., Healdsburg • 707 433 6616 • www.garyfarrell.com* *by appt.* *red, white* ★ *Russian River Valley Pinot Noir, Dry Creek Zinfandel*

Gloria Ferrer
Sonoma / Carneros

Several European sparkling wine houses set up wineries in Carneros in the 1980s: this one was established by the Ferrer family, who own the Freixenet Cava business in Spain. Some of the simpler wines are a touch broad and too overtly fruity to attain real elegance, but the top cuvées are impressive. The crisp Royal Cuvée spends six years on the yeast before disgorgement, and the more toasty Carneros Cuvée is aged for even longer. Sparkling wines remain hard to sell, so like other producers here, Gloria Ferrer has been increasing its output of still wines, including Pinot Noir, Chardonnay, Merlot, and Syrah. *23555 Hwy. 121, Sonoma • 707 996 7256 • www.gloriaferrer.com* *sparkling, red, white* ★ *Royal Cuvée, Carneros Cuvée*

Gloria Ferrer's Royal Cuvée

Iron Horse
Sonoma / Green Valley & Alexander Valley

In the small Green Valley AVA, winemaker Forrest Tancer and owners Barry and Audrey Sterling set up Iron Horse in the 1970s, focusing mainly on Chardonnay

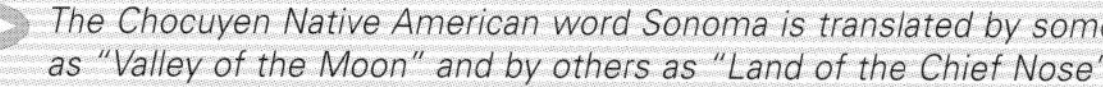

The Chocuyen Native American word Sonoma is translated by some as "Valley of the Moon" and by others as "Land of the Chief Nose"

Kenwood's tasting room in Sonoma

and Pinot Noir. Sparkling wines have been exceptional from this winery, and the still wines, including those sourced from the T-bar-T vineyard in Alexander Valley, should not be overlooked. *9786 Ross Station Rd., Sebastopol • 707 887 1507 • www.ironhorse vineyards.com* *sparkling, red, white, rosé* ★ *Blanc de Blancs LD, Brut Rosé, Russian Cuvée, T-bar-T Benchmark*

Kendall-Jackson
Sonoma & other areas
Jess Jackson started producing wines at his small Lake County vineyards in 1982. The company grew swiftly, acquiring enormous vineyards and making Jackson a billionaire, partly thanks to the success of his off-dry Vintner's Reserve Chardonnay. Today his wines come from all over California, and his empire includes many wineries that operate independently. The Sonoma properties include Hartford *(see p. 55)*, La Crema, Stonestreet, and Matanzas Creek. The winemakers blend in the Australian mode, taking components from various regions to make stylistically consistent wines. *5007 Fulton Rd., Santa Rosa • 707 544 4000 • www.kj.com* *red, white* ★ *Vintner's Reserve Cabernet Sauvignon, Grand Reserve Pinot Noir, Verité Sonoma Merlot*

Kenwood
Sonoma
For over 30 years, Kenwood has maintained its reputation for good-quality wines at all price ranges, from the basic Sonoma Series to the more prestigious Jack London and Reserve ranges. Sauvignon Blanc is not an easy grape in California, but Kenwood has a high reputation for it. The top Cabernet Sauvignon is the outstanding new-oaked Artist Series. Other good reds come from the Jack London Ranch, leased by Kenwood. *9592 Hwy. 12, Kenwood • 707 833 5891 • www.kenwoodvine yards.com* *red, white* ★ *Jack London Zinfandel, Sonoma Sauvignon Blanc*

VINCENT GASNIER'S TOP 10

Good Wines for Everyday Drinking

1. **Fetzer** Mendocino *p. 60*
2. **Alexander Valley Vineyards** Sonoma *p. 55*
3. **Carmenet Vineyard** Sonoma *p. 55*
4. **Geyser Peak: Varietals** Sonoma *p. 55*
5. **Beringer: Alluvium & many varietals** Napa Valley *p. 36*
6. **Laurel Glen: reds** Sonoma *p. 55*
7. **Boeger: varietals** Sierra Foothills *p. 87*
8. **Chateau Ste. Michelle** Columbia Valley *p. 102*
9. **Hawk Crest (Stag's Leap Wine Cellars)** Napa Valley *p. 44*
10. **Robert Mondavi Winery** (basic varietals) Napa Valley *p. 43*

Kistler

Sonoma

Collaborators Mark Bixler and reclusive winemaker Steve Kistler specialize in Pinot Noir and Chardonnay. They own vineyards in the Mayacamas Mountains, but also buy fruit from top vineyards in Sonoma, all bottled separately. From the outset, Kistler wines have enjoyed cult status, and they can be in a league of their own, showing a concentration and mineral complexity rarely found elsewhere in California. Best known for its fruity Chardonnays, Kistler also produces Pinot Noir of remarkable purity and intensity. *4707 Vine Hill Rd., Sebastopol • 707 823 5603 • www.kistlerwine.com* *red, white* ★ *Vine Hill Chardonnay, Chardonnay Cuvée Cathleen, Hirsch Vineyard Pinot Noir*

Sonoma and Simi

Up until as recently as the 1960s Sonoma County was classed as little more than a source of wines to be blended and sold as generic wines. But from 1969 oil magnate Russell Green helped to turn around this view. Already running a successful vineyard in Alexander Valley, Green seized the chance to buy the 1876 Simi Winery, which had long been in decline. His key move was to bring in a number of experts, including the legendary enologist André Tchelitscheff *(see p. 16)*, Robert Stemmler, and Mary Ann Graf, the US's first woman winemaker. The rapid improvement in quality and shower of awards inspired other Sonoma wineries to produce equally powerful wines. Soaring costs forced Green to sell in 1973, but Simi continued to build on its achievements with another pioneering female enologist Zelma Long, and more recently Steve Reeder. *16275 Healdsburg Ave., Healdsburg • 800 746 4880 • www.simiwinery.com*

Marimar Torres

Sonoma / Green Valley

A member of the Spanish Torres wine clan, Marimar Torres bought this Sonoma property in 1982. The cool climate of the Green Valley vineyards is ideal for Chardonnay and Pinot Noir, and production is expanding with the acquisition of additional land along the Sonoma Coast. Torres aims for finesse and balance, and though she does not aim to produce Burgundy clones, her wines do have the elegance and length of flavor often found in fine Burgundy. Since 2003 the estate has been organic. *11400 Graton Rd., Sebastopol • 707 823 4365 • www.marimarestate.com* *by appt.* *red, white* ★ *Chardonnay, Pinot Noir*

Peter Michael

Sonoma

English electronics tycoon Sir Peter Michael bought land in Sonoma in 1981 and harvested his first vintage in 1987. The estate is noted for its range of fine single-vineyard Chardonnays, which can be remarkably intense and complex; the Sauvignon Blanc (L'Après-Midi) and Cabernet Sauvignon (Les Pavots) can also be first-rate. All are expensive. *12400 Ida Clayton Rd., Knights Valley, Calistoga • 707 942 4459 • www.petermichaelwinery.com* *red, white* ★ *Clos du Ciel Chardonnay, Les Pavots*

Ravenswood

Sonoma

Joel Peterson, an immunologist by profession, caught the wine bug in the 1970s. He produced 327 cases in 1976, and by 1991 his outfit, Ravenswood, had become recognized for its superb red wines. Production expanded and Peterson bought a defunct winery in Sonoma. The tasting room was soon packed with visitors, sampling wines and buying

Mary Ann Graf was the first American woman to gain a degree in enology (in 1965) and is one of Sonoma's best-known winemakers

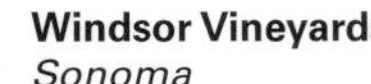

T-shirts with the Ravenswood motto: "No Wimpy Wines." In the 1990s, Ravenswood continued producing single-vineyard wines, but its main focus was a cheap, cheerful line called Vintners Blend, known by happy drinkers as the "People's Premium Wine" and by Peterson as "Chateau Cash Flow." In 2001, the vast Constellation Brands bought Ravenswood, making this boutique winery just a stitch in the corporate tapestry. However, Peterson remained in place, and the folksy tasting room continues to be thronged. Few visitors realize that annual production has soared up to about 400,000 cases. *18701 Gehricke Road, Sonoma • 707 933 2332 • www.ravenswood-wine.com* *red, white* ★ *Vintners Blend, County Series, Vineyard Designates*

Ravenswood

Windsor Vineyards
Sonoma
Windsor has clout. Owned by Australian wine giant Foster's, and with a million customers worldwide, it is America's leading operator in the specialty label corporate and gift market, a niche in which it has been operating since 1959. Although the majority of its business is done via its catalog and website, Windsor does have a tasting center at Healdsburg, where visitors can sample the wide range of varietals and blends, and ponder the design of their personalized labels—cash-flow permitting. *Windsor Vineyards, Center St., Healdsburg • 800 289 9463 • www.windsorvineyards.com* *red, white, dessert, sparkling* ★ *Petite Syrah Private Reserve, Chenin Blanc, Carignane Private Reserve*

Other Producers in Sonoma

Alexander Valley Vineyards *8644 Highway 128, Healdsburg • 800 888 7209 • www.avvwine.com*

Carmenet *1700 Moon Mountain Rd., Sonoma • 707 996 5870 • www.carmenetwinery.com*

Chalk Hill *10300 Chalk Hill Rd., Healdsburg • 707 838 4306 • www.chalkhill.com*

Coturri *6725 Enterprise Rd., Glen Ellen • 707 525 9126 • www.coturriwinery.com*

Davis Bynum *8075 Westside Rd., Healdsburg • 800 826 1073*

Dumol *11 El Sereno, Orinda • 925 254 8922 •www.dumol.com*

Flowers *28500 Seaview Rd., Cazadero • 707 847 3661 • www.flowerswinery.com*

Geyser Peak *22281 Chianti Rd., Geyserville • 707 433 0524 • www.geyserpeakwinery.com*

Hacienda *20580 8th Street East, Sonoma • 707 938 3220*

Hartford Family Winery *8075 Martinelli Rd., Forestville • 707 887 1756 • www.hartfordwines.com*

Kunde Estate *10155 Sonoma Hwy., Kenwood • 707 833 5501 • www.kunde.com*

Landmark *101 Adobe Canyon Rd., Kenwood • 707 833 0053 • www.landmarkwine.com*

Laurel Glen *Glen Ellen • 707 526 3914 • www.laurelglen.com*

Martinelli *3360 River Road, Windsor • 800 346 1672 • www.martinelliwinery.com*

Nalle Winery *2383 Dry Creek Rd., Healdsburg • 707 433 6062 • www.nallewinerycom*

Rochioli Vineyard *6192 Westside Rd., Healdsburg • 707 433 2305*

Seghesio Family Vineyards *14730 Grove Street, Healdsburg • 707 433 3579 • www.seghesio.com*

St. Francis *100 Pythian Rd., Santa Rosa • 800 543 7713 • www.stfranciswine.com*

Williams Selyem *6575 Westside Rd., Healdsburg • 707 433 6425 • www.williamsselyem.com*

Wine Areas of Mendocino & Lake County

Mendocino shares Sonoma's versatility, producing good Chardonnay and Viognier, robust reds, particularly Zinfandel, and fine sparkling wines. Although a relatively small region, with 15,000 acres (6,000 ha) planted and fewer than 40 wineries, it is one of considerable diversity. The chilly Anderson Valley has a very cool, sometimes too cool, ripening season, especially in the lower-lying vineyards. Here it is highly aromatic white wines that come to the fore. Riesling and Gewürztraminer, which ripen well in Germany, are often good in Anderson Valley. The French Champagne house Roederer was also quick to see the potential of Anderson Valley for growing grapes for sparkling wines. Warmer valleys situated farther inland, such as Redwood and McDowell, have the conditions to ripen Cabernet Sauvignon and Chardonnay.

Hidden away in all these regions are very old vineyards that are still in production and increasingly valued by winemakers throughout California. Organic viticulture, pioneered by the Fetzer family *(see p. 60)*, has been pursued avidly and promoted throughout the county *(p. 63)*. Mendocino's most important AVAs are listed opposite. *clay, gravel, volcanic, red clay, loam, alluvial* *Cabernet Sauvignon, Zinfandel, Petite Sirah, Pinot Noir, Syrah, Barbera* *Gewürztraminer, Riesling, Chardonnay, Pinot Gris, Sauvignon Blanc* *red, white, sparkling*

In the Fetzer winery

Anderson Valley, Mendocino Ridges & Yorkville Highlands

The Anderson Valley AVA follows the Navarro River and is the closest region to the Pacific coastline. Some sectors are distinctly cool and foggy because of the maritime influence, and in some years the region is so cool that the grapes do not ripen, or they succumb to rot due to damp weather conditions. Despite this, a host of varieties are grown here, and grapes such as Riesling, Gewürztraminer, and Chardonnay can do particularly well, as does Pinot Noir. Exceptionally good sparkling wine also comes out of the Anderson Valley, notably by the French-owned Roederer Estate *(see p. 63)*, which was set up here in 1982.

A few excellent old vineyards between Anderson Valley and the Pacific have their own AVA called Mendocino Ridges. These are planted mostly with Zinfandel at over 1,150 ft (350 m). Yorkville Highlands AVA is the southern extension of Anderson Valley and is considerably warmer. It only represents about 10 percent of Anderson Valley's 1,000 acres (400 ha) planted to grape vines.

Preceding pages **Undulating vineyard in Knights Valley, Sonoma County**

Redwood Valley & Potter Valley

Some of Mendocino's oldest vineyards are in the county's Redwood Valley AVA, which is showing immense versatility in terms of what can be grown successfully in it. Cooler than neighboring Ukiah, Redwood Valley is nonetheless warm enough to ripen Zinfandel and Italian varieties, as well as a wide range of white grapes. The Potter Valley AVA, to the east of the Redwood Valley, is at a height of around 1,000 ft (300 m), so white grapes (Chardonnay, Sauvignon Blanc) and some Pinot Noir are most commonly planted. Much of the fruit is destined for sparkling wine houses.

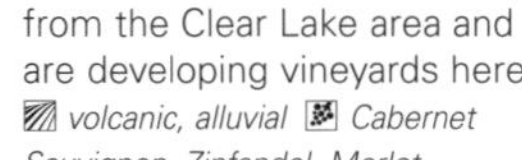

McDowell label

Ukiah Valley

Although not a real AVA, Ukiah Valley is a large region stretching northward from Hopland to Ukiah, producing a substantial proportion of Mendocino's grapes. The best vineyards, red and white, are planted on benchlands flanking the Russian River. Higher up are older vineyards planted with Italian and Rhône varieties.

McDowell Valley

This small AVA in the southern part of Mendocino is more or less the fiefdom of McDowell Valley Vineyards *(see p. 61)*, which specialize almost entirely in Rhône varieties of grapes. The vineyards are planted with some of the oldest Syrah vines in California, which still give first-rate wine. The McDowell Reserve Syrah is smoky and spicy, and sometimes displays a gamey or even slightly jammy character.

LAKE COUNTY

This county has only one major subregion, the Clear Lake AVA, which is situated east of Ukiah Valley and named after the large lake fringed by vineyards. Although a warm region, it has long been known for its Sauvignon Blanc and Cabernet Sauvignon, which are widely planted. Hot days are tempered by nights cooled by cold air descending from the mountains. Many wineries buy fruit from the Clear Lake area and are developing vineyards here.

volcanic, alluvial *Cabernet Sauvignon, Zinfandel, Merlot*
Sauvignon Blanc, Chardonnay
red, white

Mendocino's Italian Connection

Much of the land in Mendocino was originally settled by Italian families. Daniel Gobbi, who was born in Italy in 1823, settled on land near Ukiah in 1856. Between stints of hog-speculating and months on cattle droves he planted 10 acres (4 ha) of Zinfandel to become Mendocino's first grape-grower. Other Italians followed suit, planting mainly Petite Sirah and Zinfandel, but few vineyards and no wineries survived Prohibition. In the 1920s another Italian family, the Parduccis, who had learned winemaking in their native Tuscany, relocated from Sonoma to cheaper lands in Mendocino. They built a new winery at Ukiah, which was up-and-running right after the repeal of Prohibition in 1933. Until 1968 Parducci was Mendocino's only winery and it still exists today as the Mendocino Wine Co. (www.mendocinowinecompany.com).

Mendocino was named by Spanish navigator Juan Cabrillo in 1542 in honor of his patron Antonio de Mendoza, Viceroy of New Spain (Mexico)

Vineyard in the relatively cool Anderson Valley, Mendocino

Major Producers in Mendocino

Fetzer
Mendocino

In 1958 Barney and Kathleen Fetzer bought a run-down ranch in Redwood Valley and started to renovate the property and plant vines. It was another decade before they celebrated their first commercial release. In another decade, the family was turning out about 30,000 cases of reds sourced from local growers each year, and just beginning to branch out into whites. The Valley Oaks property was acquired in 1984, which Fetzer decided to farm organically. Production by the mid-1980s was more than 500,000 cases; this had doubled again to 2.2 million cases a year by 1992, when the company was bought by the Brown Forman Corporation.

Though the Fetzer family is no longer involved with the high-profile winery of its name, the operation has remained true to its principles. Fetzer was a pioneer of organic viticulture in California, and it now offers 10 organic wines under its Bonterra label. Although many of the grapes are from Mendocino, some are sourced elsewhere. Adopting sustainable, energy-efficient practices wherever possible, the company has stated its intention to use 100 percent organic grapes by 2010—an ambitious goal for a large company.

Bonterra by Fetzer

Today, Fetzer sells three million cases of wine each year, a sizeable number of which are exported to the UK. The secret of this success is the outstanding value the wines offer. The basic range is called Bel Arbor; the Barrel Select and Reserve ranges are higher in quality. The white wines are lean and fresh; the reds packed with fruit flavor.

Valley Oaks Visitor Center, Hopland • 707 744 7600 • www.fetzer.com ☐ *red, white* ★ *Bonterra Viognier, Barrel Select Zinfandel*

VINCENT GASNIER'S TOP 10 Best Sparkling Wine Houses of the US

1. **Domaine Carneros** Napa Valley *p. 38*
2. **Scharffenberger** Mendocino *p. 63*
3. **Mumm Napa** Napa Valley *p. 42*
4. **Roederer Estate** Mendocino *p. 62*
5. **Domaine Chandon** Napa Valley *p. 38*
6. **Argyle** Willamette Valley *p. 106*
7. **Dr. Konstantin Frank** Finger Lakes *p. 122*
8. **Wente** San Francisco Bay *p. 81*
9. **Gloria Ferrer** Sonoma *p. 52*
10. **Handley Cellars** Mendocino *opposite*

Greenwood Ridge
Mendocino Ridges

Many of Allan Green's vineyards are high in the hills surrounding Anderson Valley. He inadvertently became a pioneer of the Mendocino Ridges AVA, created to recognize sites at high elevations. Green's Riesling, Pinot Noir, Cabernet, and Merlot

Fetzer is the largest grower of certified organic grapes in the North Coast AVA and one of the largest in the world

come from the ridges. He buys in fruit from other Mendocino vineyards for Chardonnay and Sauvignon Blanc. *5501 Hwy. 128, Philo • 707 895 2002 • www.greenwoodridge.com* *red, white* ★ *Estate Merlot, Estate Chardonnay*

Handley Cellars

Mendocino / Anderson Valley & other areas

Milla Handley founded this winery just near Philo in the Anderson Valley in 1982, devoting herself at first to sparkling wine. Her father's vineyard in Sonoma's Dry Creek Valley provides the fruit for some of the wines, but the main estate vineyard is where Handley has decided to plant her own Pinot Noir, Chardonnay, and Gewürztraminer. This vineyard has been farmed using sustainable methods since 1990, and it achieved full organic certification in 2005. Handley's sparkling wines are no strangers to high praise, but production is strictly limited, which contrasts somewhat markedly with the large scale of Roederer's sparkling wine production a way down the road. However, when the sparklers are all sold out, the red and white varietals are also worthwhile. *3151 Hwy. 128, Philo • 707 895 3876 • www.handleycellars.com* *sparkling, white, red* ★ *Brut Estate, Brightlighter White, Handley Syrah*

McDowell Valley Vineyards

Mendocino

The Syrah vines planted here date from 1948 and 1959, making them among the oldest Syrah in California. These are used for the superb Reserve, but the regular bottling of Syrah is also juicy and beguiling. All the other wines are from Rhône varieties; including an excellent example of the tricky Viognier, as well as an enjoyable Marsanne and dry Grenache rosé. *3811 Hwy. 175, Hopland • 707 744 1053 • www.mcdowellsyrah.com* *red, white* ★ *Viognier, Reserve Syrah*

Mendocino's Sparklers

In the early 1980s, Louis Roederer spent $15 million buying land, planting 500 acres (200 ha) of vines, and building a state-of-the-art winery in Anderson Valley *(see p. 62)*. Wine masters at the famous Champagne house were convinced that the cooler climate here was suited to producing premium sparkling wines. However, Roederer Estate's first wine, a nonvintage 1986-based blend made with the bottle-fermenting method *(méthode champenoise)* was rather disappointing. Fortunately, the situation was reversed with the following year's vintage, and the 1987-based blend was received with enthusiasm by sparkling wine aficionados around the world. The quality of the estate's sparklers has been maintained ever since—they are rich, well-structured, and show a complexity reminiscent of Champagne. Situated just down the road from Roederer, Scharffenberger Cellars *(see p. 63)* produces a very different style of sparkling wine, which is light and elegant with fine fruit flavors. These differences prove how diverse the *terroir* is in Mendocino. Handley Cellars *(above)* is another producer having success with sparklers that in Mendocino are often made from Chardonnay blended with Pinot Noir and a little Pinot Meunier.

Chardonnay grapes

Sparkling wine labels in the US often use the descriptions "Brut" meaning dry, "Sec," or "Demi-Sec," meaning sweet

Monte Volpe
Mendocino

Greg Graziano's ancestors were typical Mendocino immigrant farmers, who grew grapes in the years before Prohibition. The Monte Volpe ("fox mountain") winery honors their traditions by specializing in Italian varietals such as Primo Bianco, Primo Rosso, Sangiovese, Peppolino, and Montepulciano. Graziano cannot replicate the hills of Piemonte or Friuli in the Mendocino highlands, so not every wine is successful. Overall, however, Graziano (who has the passion and pioneering spirit of a missionary) does an excellent job, and has the courage to produce fine versions of wines that cannot always be easy to sell. Other brands include Saint Gregory, which releases wines from the Pinot family, while Enotria focuses on Piemontese varieties such as Nebbiolo and Barbera. *Tasting Room 13251 S. Hwy 101, Ste. 3, Hopland • 707 744 8466 • www.grazianofamilyofwines.com* *red, white* ★ *Monte Volpe Pinot Bianco, Enotria Barbera*

Navarro
Mendocino

In 1973 Ted Bennett and Deborah Cahn bought a sprawling sheep ranch in Anderson Valley, with the intention of raising sheep (about which they knew nothing) until they had mastered the art of growing grapes (about which they also knew nothing). Learning quickly from others and by off-setting the area's unpredictable weather with clone and rootstock diversification, they planted 84 acres (34 ha) with cool-climate varieties and have since built a big reputation for their wines. Navarro Rieslings are among California's finest, always backed with vivid acidity. The Pinot Noir is aged in small French barrels, and can be impressive. *5601 Hwy 128, Philo • 707 895 3686 • www.navarrowine.com* *red, white* ★ *Riesling, Pinot Noir Méthode à l'Ancienne*

The Navarro ranch in Anderson Valley

Sustainably Farmed or Organic Wines

1. **Fetzer: Bonterra** Mendocino *p. 60*
2. **Lemelson Vineyards** Oregon *p. 108*
3. **Spottswoode** Napa Valley *p. 44*
4. **Frog's Leap** Napa Valley *p. 40*
5. **Gallo of Sonoma** Sonoma *p. 52*
6. **Handley Cellars** Mendocino *p. 61*
7. **Viader Vineyards** Napa Valley *p. 45*
8. **Heller** Monterrey Carmel Valley *p. 87*
9. **Coturri** Sonoma *p. 55*
10. **Rubicon Estate: Niebaum-Coppola** Napa Valley *p. 34*

Roederer Estate
Mendocino / Anderson Valley

Most French Champagne houses looking for California vineyards choose Carneros or southern Napa, but Jean-Claude Rouzaud, head of Louis Roederer, chose the Anderson Valley instead *(see p. 61)*. This arm of Roederer was founded

To be called "organic," an American wine must comply with strict critieria, whereas "sustainably farmed" has no legal definition

in 1981. The cool, even uncertain, climate gives the wines the acidic backbone needed for great sparkling wine. Current winemaker, Arnaud Weyrich, gained his enology doctorate at the prestigious French Montpellier School. The Estate Brut is the basic bottling, and it sometimes seems just as good as the more expensive prestige cuvée, the vintage L'Ermitage. The third wine is a sparkling rosé. Many California sparklers have fruit but lack finesse; the Roederer Estate wines have both. *4501 Hwy 128, Philo • 707 895 2288 • www.roedererestate.net* *sparkling* ★ *Estate Brut, Rosé, L'Ermitage*

Scharffenberger Cellars
Mendocino / Anderson Valley
Established in 1981, this sparkling wine house has been through various lives, including the brand name Pacific Echo from 1998 to 2004. It is currently owned by Maisons Marques & Domaines, which is so impressed with the products that it is happy to market this small winery alongside famous French Champagne exports. Despite the upheavals, winemaker Tex Sawyer has been here since 1989, and continues to craft high-quality sparkling blends of Chardonnay and Pinot Noir, using the traditional *méthode champenoise* process of bottle fermentation. Long-term contracts with Anderson Valley growers ensure a reliably high standard of grapes. *8501 Hwy 128, Philo • 707 895 2957 • www.mmdusa.net* *sparkling* ★ *Scharffenberger Brut*

Guenoc Estate
Lake County
This estate—the only winery in the small Guenoc Valley sub-AVA in Lake County—has an interesting history. It was first planted with grapes in 1854, and owned by the famous actress Lillie Langtry from 1888 to 1906, who declared she would make the "greatest claret in the country." Like other wine estates founded in the 19th century, it suffered years of neglect in the first half of the 20th century. However, the Magoon family, who purchased Guenoc in 1963, has positioned it as a producer of top-tier wines and established it as California's leading provider of Petite Sirah. The last couple of years have seen huge investment in state-of-the-art production facilities, and the arrival in 2005 of star winemaker Bob Broman suggests that Guenoc is making a bid for the big time. *21000 Butts Canyon Rd., Middletown • 707 987 2385 • www.guenoc.com* *red, white, fortified* ★ *Langtry Meritage Red Wine, Genevieve Magoon Vineyard Reserve, Guenoc Valley Vintage Port*

Environmentally Friendly Winemaking

Mendocino leads the way with organic viticulture—by 2005 at least 25 percent of the county's grapes were certified organic compared with 5 percent in the rest of California. To be certified organic, US wine estates have to keep within strict limitations on the use of chemicals and certain other practices. While some smaller producers, such as Frog's Leap *(see p. 40)* use 100 percent certified organic grapes, this is much harder for large producers to achieve. However, even big players—like Gallo, Beringer, and especially Fetzer—are increasingly practicing sustainable or natural farming, and only resorting to nonorganic chemicals as a last resort. Sustainable practices include using natural fertilizers and cover crops, solar power, water recycling, and releasing millions of ladybugs as a natural way of controlling aphids and other pests.

CENTRAL & SOUTHERN CALIFORNIA

Introduction
66–67

Wine Map of Central & Southern California
68–69

Wine Areas of Central & Southern California
70–77

Major Producers in Central & Southern California
80–87

CENTRAL & SOUTHERN CALIFORNIA

TO THE SOUTH OF SAN FRANCISCO, *in the Central Coast region, Monterey is home to California's largest commercial vineyards, and sub-AVAs such as Carmel Valley and Chalone are gaining renown. San Luis Obispo, especially Paso Robles, produces supple red wines, and farther south, Santa Barbara County is making huge strides with Chardonnay, Pinot Noir, and Rhône varieties. Inland lies the immense Central Valley, home to America's bulk wine industry.*

Early History

San Diego, near the Mexican border, was the site of California's first vines, grown in the 18th century by Spanish missionaries *(see p. 23)*. Vineyards were planted in the area to the south of San Francisco Bay in the 1830s, and by the late 19th century Santa Clara County had a thriving wine industry. A French-born settler, Etienne Theé, founded Almaden Vineyards near Los Gatos in the 1850s: this was inherited by Theé's son-in-law, Charles Lefranc, who was one of the first winemakers in California to plant European varieties. Lefranc was later joined by Paul Masson *(see box opposite)*.

Key

Central & Southern California AVAs

Meanwhile, the Italian Picchetti brothers were among the first to settle and grow grapes on Montebello Ridge. The Almaden and Picchetti wineries still exist and are among the oldest in California.

By the end of the 19th century, pockets of vineyards were to be found throughout Central and Southern California: the Santa Ynez Valley, in Santa Barbara County, had a flourishing wine industry before Prohibition, but most vineyards were lost during this era. Only a handful, such as Paul Masson's, survived the 1920s and 30s by selling grapes wholesale and being awarded special status to produce "medicinal" wines.

VINCENT GASNIER'S TOP 10 Wines for Celebrations

1. **Opus One** (red) Napa Valley *p. 42*
2. **Dominus: Cabernet Sauvignon** (red) Napa Valley *p. 39*
3. **Ridge Vineyards: Monte Bello** (red) San Francisco Bay *p. 80*
4. **Kistler: Pinot Noir** (red) Sonoma *p. 54*
5. **Williams Selyem: Pinot Noir** (red) Sonoma *p. 55*
6. **Colgin: Abreu** (red) Napa Valley *p. 37*
7. **Colgin** (other reds) Napa Valley *p. 37*
8. **Caymus: Cabernet Sauvignon** (red) Napa Valley *p. 37*
9. **Harlan Estate** (reds) Napa Valley *p. 40*
10. **Domaine Drouhin: Chardonnay or Pinot Noir** (red or white) Willamette Valley *p. 107*

Post-Prohibition Industry

In 1933, two impoverished brothers, Ernest and Julio Gallo, launched a small winery in Modesto in the Central Valley. Their output grew at a phenomenal rate, bolstered by mass marketing after 1945. Through the Gallos, the Central Valley was to become the setting for the world's biggest

Preceding pages **Late summer vineyards beneath the Santa Lucia Mountains of San Luis Obispo County**

Vineyards in the dramatic Arroyo Grande Valley, San Luis Obispo

wine empire *(see p. 83)*. However, neither the Central Valley nor San Francisco Bay have the ideal conditions for viticulture.

In the 1950s, researchers at the University of California identified the cooler climate farther south in Monterey as better for winemaking. Two large companies, Paul Masson and Mirassou, were the first to make the move in 1957, buying 1,300 acres (530 ha) in the Salinas Valley. Following them, Bonny Doon, Chalone, and Mount Eden confirmed Monterey's suitability for high-quality wines.

Recent Developments

South of Monterey, the area stretching from Paso Robles to the Santa Ynez Valley began to be replanted with vines in the 1970s, and is rapidly gaining recognition. Santa Barbara has become one of the most favored places for Pinot Noir specialists. The Pinot Noir vines were originally planted with a view to supplying the sparkling wine industry farther north, but the mesoclimate at Monterey—16 miles (26 km) inland—is ideal for making wines that vie with the best of Burgundy. Cabernet Sauvignon and Chardonnay are also giving some world-quality wines in parts of the Central Coast region.

The Champagne King of California

Paul Masson is one of the most famous names in California wine history. Born in Burgundy in 1859, Masson came to California in 1878, where his association with winemaker Charles Lefranc led to his interest in wine. Operating from bases at Almaden Vineyards in Los Gatos and the Santa Cruz Mountains, his sparkling wines and lavish socializing brought him fame as "California's champagne king." Although he died in 1940, Masson's name endures through the brand name. Orson Welles helped to market this in the 1970s, declaring "we will sell no wine before its time." It is now owned by Constellation *(see Centerra p. 121 & North Lake p. 121)*.

Wine Map of Central & Southern California

The Central Coast AVA is very large, stretching for about 250 miles (400 km) from San Francisco in the north to Santa Barbara in the south, and encompassing about 360 wineries and 90,000 acres (37,000 ha) of vineyards. It is subdivided into further AVAs and sub-AVAs, the broadest of which are San Francisco Bay, Monterey, San Luis Obispo, and Santa Barbara. Inland, the huge Central Valley AVA is where the majority of American table wines originate. The Southern California AVA lies farther south, a loose grouping of sub-AVAs stretching from Los Angeles to the Mexican border.

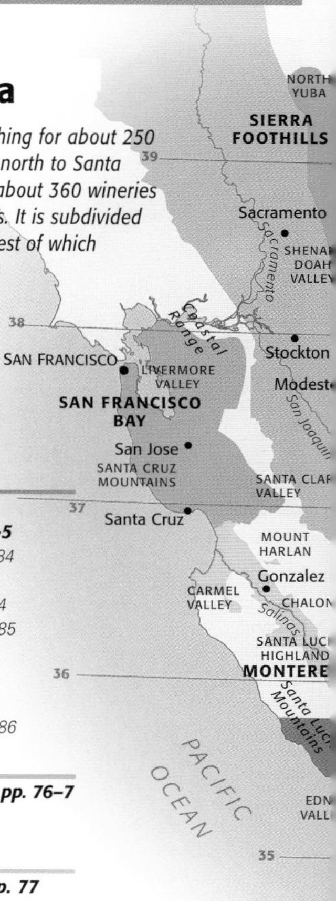

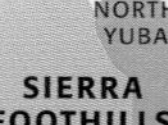

MAIN AVAs & MAJOR PRODUCERS

San Francisco Bay *p. 70*
J. C. Cellars *p. 80*
Ridge Vineyards *p. 80*
Testarossa *p. 80*
Wente Vineyards *p. 81*

Monterey & San Benito *pp. 70–72*
Calera Wine Company *p. 82*
Chalone Vineyard *p. 81*
Paraiso Springs *p. 81*

San Luis Obispo *pp. 72–3*
Alban Vineyards *p. 82*
Bonny Doon *p. 81*
Justin Vineyards *p. 82*
Meridian *p. 82*
Tablas Creek *p. 82*
Wild Horse *p. 84*

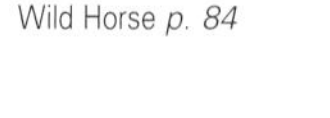

Santa Barbara County *pp. 74–5*
Andrew Murray *p. 84*
Arcadian *p. 84*
Au Bon Climat *p. 84*
Blackjack Ranch *p. 85*
Byron *p. 85*
Firestone *p. 85*
Ojai Vineyard *p. 86*
Rancho Sisquoc *p. 86*
Sanford *p. 86*

Sierra Foothills *pp. 76–7*
Domaine de la Terre Rouge *p. 86*

Central Valley *p. 77*
Gallo *p. 83*
Quady Winery *p. 87*

Southern California *p. 77*
Moraga Vineyards *p. 87*

Vineyards beneath the Santa Lucia Mountains

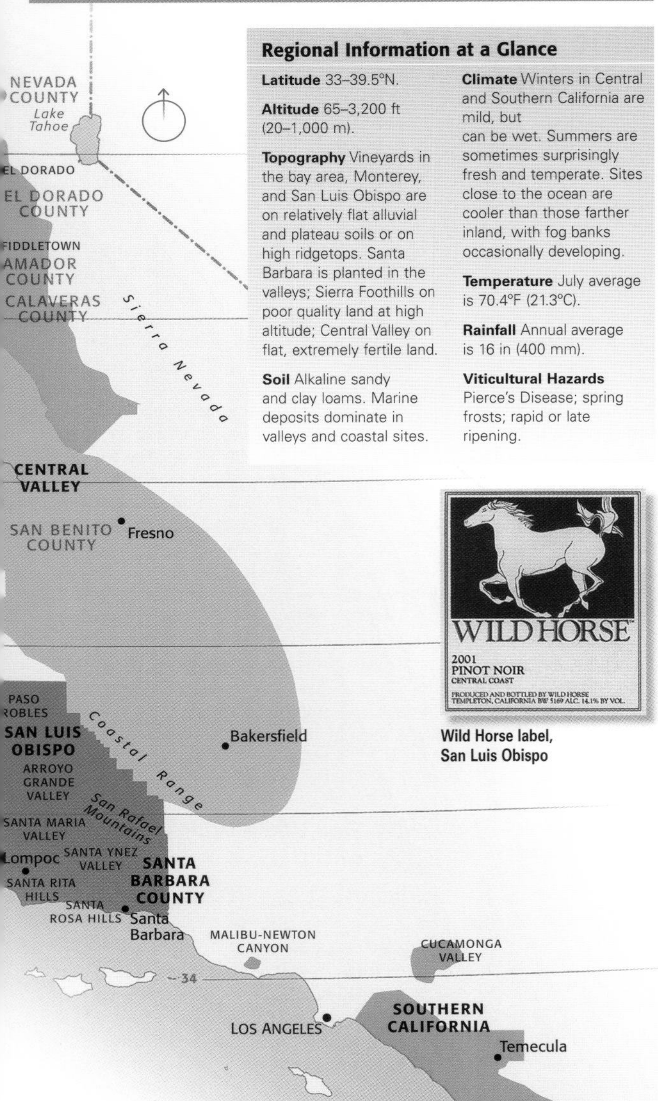

Regional Information at a Glance

Latitude 33–39.5°N.

Altitude 65–3,200 ft (20–1,000 m).

Topography Vineyards in the bay area, Monterey, and San Luis Obispo are on relatively flat alluvial and plateau soils or on high ridgetops. Santa Barbara is planted in the valleys; Sierra Foothills on poor quality land at high altitude; Central Valley on flat, extremely fertile land.

Soil Alkaline sandy and clay loams. Marine deposits dominate in valleys and coastal sites.

Climate Winters in Central and Southern California are mild, but can be wet. Summers are sometimes surprisingly fresh and temperate. Sites close to the ocean are cooler than those farther inland, with fog banks occasionally developing.

Temperature July average is 70.4°F (21.3°C).

Rainfall Annual average is 16 in (400 mm).

Viticultural Hazards Pierce's Disease; spring frosts; rapid or late ripening.

Wild Horse label, San Luis Obispo

Good recent vintages in Central & Southern California include 1994, 1995, 1998, 1999, 2000, 2003, and 2005

Wine Areas of Central & Southern California

San Francisco Bay

This was an important wine region in the late 19th century, but many vineyards were destroyed by the phylloxera bug. The expansion of the San Francisco suburbs also limited the potential vineyard area.

The most important sub-AVA today is the **Livermore Valley**, to the east of San Francisco Bay. This is planted mainly with white grapes—including Sauvignon Blanc descended from cuttings taken from Château d'Yquem in France in the 1880s—and dominated by the Wente group of wineries. To the south of the bay is the **Santa Cruz Mountains** AVA, which produces great Cabernet Sauvignon and other grapes at high elevations. Most of the vineyards in this area are remote and dispersed. Other sub-AVAs are so small and marginal that their names are rarely encountered on labels. Between San Jose and Gilroy lies the **Santa Clara Valley**, whose once-thriving wine industry is now close to extinction due to urban sprawl.

Many wineries to the south of the bay, including Bonny Doon and Ridge *(see pp. 80–81)*, buy supplementary grapes from other regions. *gravel, loam, shale* *Cabernet Sauvignon, Pinot Noir, Zinfandel* *Chardonnay, Sauvignon Blanc, Semillon* *red, white, sparkling*

Wente Vineyards in Livermore Valley

Monterey County

The Monterey region begins at Watsonville and continues in a southeasterly direction down the Salinas Valley. It was in the 1950s–60s that viticultural experts recommended the valley as a good site for Cabernet Sauvignon. They calculated there were sufficient hours of sunshine to ripen Cabernet, but overlooked the strong cool winds that roar down the valley and inhibit ripening. Many early wines from Monterey had an unpleasant vegetal character. However, the problems of the past have long since been corrected, and Monterey is now best known for its white varietals: Chardonnay, Riesling, and others. There are a few subregions where Bordeaux red grape varieties can ripen, but in terms of red wine Monterey as a whole is better suited to Pinot Noir and Syrah.

Fine White Wines of the US

1. **Kistler: Chardonnay** Sonoma *p. 54*
2. **ZD: Chardonnay** Napa Valley *p. 45*
3. **Blackjack Ranch: Chardonnay** Santa Barbara County *p. 85*
4. **Rancho Sisquoc** Santa Barbara County *p. 86*
5. **Arrowood: Saralee's Vineyard Viognier** Sonoma *p. 50*
6. **Martinelli: Three Sisters** Sonoma *p. 55*
7. **Dumol: Chloe Chardonnay** Sonoma *p. 55*
8. **Cuvaison: Carneros Estate** Napa Valley *p. 38*
9. **Peter Michael: Sauvignon Blanc L'Apres-Midi** Sonoma *p. 54*
10. **Walter Hansel: Chardonnay** Santa Barbara County *p. 87*

Chalone Vineyard below the Pinnacles National Monument, Gavilan Mountains

The county-wide **Monterey** AVA applies mostly to Salinas Valley, which is known for its big vegetable farms. The northern end is very cool, but the valley becomes progressively warmer toward the southeast, as the maritime influence diminishes. Large-scale investment has been important here, with hundreds of acres planted by individual companies. Kendall-Jackson of Sonoma *(see p. 53)* alone owns 2,500 acres (1,000 ha) here, and the San Bernabe Vineyard is the largest in California, with 8,650 acres (3,500 ha) under vine. But relatively few producers are based in Monterey, and much of the fruit is sold to very large wineries elsewhere. Chardonnay is the most important variety, and the wines often display a tropical fruit character.

The vineyards of the **Carmel Valley** AVA lie in a verdant valley between the Salinas Valley and the ocean to the west. The mesoclimate in the valley is warmer than that in the Salinas, and is largely free from fog. Even though the vineyards are planted at elevations of up to 2,000 ft (600 m), red Bordeaux varieties do well here and account for 70 percent of plantings. The wines are rich, fleshy, and modestly structured. Some Chardonnay is also grown. Large-scale wineries of note in this district include Joullian, Heller, and Georis *(see p. 87)*.

Near Gonzalez on the western side of Salinas Valley is a series of terraces, slightly elevated over the side of the valley, known as the **Santa Lucia Highlands** AVA. Somewhat sheltered from the cold Pacific blasts that roar down Salinas Valley, and hovering just above the fog line, these highlands are home to some of Monterey's top vineyards. Few wineries are based here, but the extensive and highly regarded vineyards sell their fruit to many producers. Some North Coast wineries have even bought land here. Pinot Noir and Syrah can be excellent, as can Riesling, but low market prices for the latter mean that many vineyards are being grafted over to more fashionable and lucrative grape varieties.

Chalone is a one-winery AVA high in the Gavilan Mountains, at an altitude of 1,800-2,000 ft (550–600 m), on the eastern side of Salinas Valley. It took courage to plant vines here back in 1919, when there was no electricity or adequate water supply. The vineyards were obscure until wine entrepreneur Dick Graff purchased them in 1965. Today, some 500 acres (200 ha) are in production, and after a rough patch and a change of winemakers, the Chalone Vineyard estate is once again on top *(see p. 81)*. The 1919 vines are the oldest Chardonnay and Chenin Blanc in Monterey.

The harvest in Monterey is typically two weeks later than in other Californian wine regions

Calera vineyard in the Gavilan Mountains, Mount Harlan

San Benito County

On the eastern side of the Gavilan Mountains, within San Benito County, are six tiny AVAs; **Mount Harlan** is the only one of any significance. Only just across the county border from Monterey, it deserves consideration because of its unusual *terroir*. The site was selected in the mid-1970s by Burgundy enthusiast Josh Jensen for its limestone soil, which he believes to be one of the secrets of great Burgundy. The only winery here is Jensen's Calera Wine Company *(see p. 82)*, justly renowned for its Chardonnay and Pinot Noir, both of which are planted at 2,300 ft (700 m), high above the fog line. Mount Harlan's Chardonnays are sturdily reliable, and the Pinots have on occasion been exceptional. The other AVAs of San Benito County are, in the main, used by much larger producers that are based elsewhere, including Beaulieu and Williams Selyem; the products are usually labeled under the Central Coast AVA.

silt, loam, well-drained sandy loam, clay, alluvial loam, decomposed granite, clay, limestone *Pinot Noir, Syrah, Merlot, Cabernet Sauvignon* *Chardonnay, Riesling, Pinot Blanc, Sauvignon Blanc, Viognier* *red, white*

San Luis Obispo

The county of San Luis Obispo encompasses 25,000 acres (10,000 ha) of vineyards, four excellent sub-AVAs, and 110 wineries. The mesoclimatic conditions vary greatly; many vineyards are planted on flat land, while others are high in the Santa Lucia Mountains. Unlike Monterey, which ships most of its grapes to wineries beyond its borders, San Luis Obispo has a host of small, thriving wineries, which attract many visitors. There is a growing interest in Rhône varieties in the area. The red wines (notably Cabernet Sauvignon, Syrah, and Zinfandel) tend to be supple and seductive; the Burgundian grape varieties do well in cooler areas.

Best Rosé (Blush) Producers

1. **Bonny Doon** San Francisco Bay *p. 81*
2. **Joseph Phelps** Napa Valley *p. 41*
3. **Verdad** Santa Barbara *p. 87*
4. **Eberle** San Luis Obispo *p. 87*
5. **Heitz Cellar** Napa Valley *p. 40*
6. **Robert Mondavi** Napa Valley *p. 43*
7. **Thornton** Southern California *p. 87*
8. **V. Sattui** Napa Valley *p. 45*
9. **Kongsgaard** Napa Valley *p. 41*
10. **Beringer** Napa Valley *p. 36*

The largest and warmest sub-AVA of the county, and the one that is currently enjoying the greatest accolades is **Paso Robles**.

Vineyards lie both east and west of the laid-back little town of Paso Robles, and there are around 85 wineries within this AVA. To the east there stretches a large plateau, where the majority of vineyards are planted. To the west the terrain is quite different: more mountainous, with vineyards on isolated slopes among the forests of the Santa Lucia Mountains. The mesoclimates are also different, since the so-called Westside vineyards receive much more rainfall than those on the plateau. The plateau can be very hot during the day, but its elevation of 1,300 ft (400 m) means that nights are relatively cool, so the grapes never become baked. The main soil types have been formed from the weathering of granite, serpentine, shale, and sandstone.

Tablas Creek Vineyard label, Paso Robles

Broadly speaking, Paso Robles plateau wines have supple tannins, are medium-bodied, and show a great deal of youthful charm. Zinfandel, Cabernet Sauvignon, and Syrah are best drunk within five years, but they can often be kept longer. Westside wines reflect the more rugged terrain, have fiercer tannins, and often need up to five years in bottle to reveal their complexity and profundity. There is a plethora of small wineries here, ranging from decidedly rustic in quality to sophisticated boutique operations. Some of them benefit from ownership of very old Zinfandel vineyards, and newer plantings of Bordeaux and Rhône varieties show great promise.

Adjoining Paso Robles Westside is the very small **York Mountain** AVA, which has a rather cooler mesoclimate than Paso Robles and is best known for red varieties such as Syrah and Pinot Noir, although ripening can be problematic. There is a handful of vineyards and one winery here.

Just south of the town of San Luis Obispo is the **Edna Valley** AVA, which has little in common with Paso Robles. Open to the Pacific to the south and west, it has a strongly maritime climate and a very long growing season. Fog can provoke botrytis mold and other maladies. Chardonnay tends to dominate, and the wines are usually rich and plump. There are about 1,350 acres (550 ha) in production, with little room for further expansion. The region is dominated by a single winery, the eponymous Edna Valley.

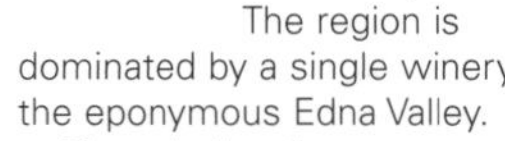

The winding **Arroyo Grande Valley** is, in effect, the southeastern extension of Edna Valley. Much of this AVA has a mesoclimate similar to that of its neighboring AVA, though slightly warmer and less breezy, and both Chardonnay and Pinot Noir are grown here with great success. Farther inland, where the temperatures are higher, there are small pockets of Zinfandel. Alban Vineyards on the western edge of the subregion is an outpost of Rhône varieties of exceptional quality. Coastal fog and breezes affect conditions at the mouth of the valley *sandy loam, silty clay, marine deposits, marine sediment, degraded granite and tufa, clay, light clay* *Cabernet Sauvignon, Zinfandel, Merlot, Syrah, Pinot Noir* *Chardonnay, Sauvignon Blanc, Viognier* *red, white*

Paso Robles is home to several dynamic winemakers who belong to a group known as the Rhône Rangers **See p. 75**

Byron Vineyards and winery at the foot of the San Rafael mountains, Santa Barbara County

Santa Barbara County

In 1969, the total vineyard surface in Santa Barbara County was less than 13 acres (5 ha); today there are 20,000 acres (8,000 ha) under vine. This used to be ranching country, with undulating grassy hills, and it was easy to convert some of those gentle slopes and valley floors to vineyards.

Santa Barbara has a unique topography in its east-west valleys—they are the only valleys in the coastline between Alaska and Cape Horn to be orientated as such. The viticultural benefit of this orientation is that it lets in maritime breezes that are good for the Burgundian varieties Chardonnay and Pinot Noir, while the more inland sites are warm enough for Merlot. Also capable of ripening here are Syrah, Sauvignon Blanc, Riesling, Cabernet Franc, and even Cabernet Sauvignon, but only in specific sites.

Given the cool climate, sun exposure is of primary importance, and vineyards planted in poorly exposed spots risk grapes not ripening. Growers like to point out that Santa Barbara was producing exciting wines from the outset, even when vines were planted more or less at random, without any great knowledge of clonal selection and other viticultural practices. Now that these issues are far better understood, quality is likely to improve even further.

Maritime influences ensure that the vineyards planted in the county's **Santa Maria Valley** AVA are among the coolest in California. Most of them lie on terraces or shelves above the valley floor, but not on the exposed ridgetops of the San Rafael Mountains just to the north. Many of these vineyards are very large and owned by producers based on the North Coast such as Robert Mondavi, Kendall-Jackson, and Beringer. There are also large commercial vineyards, such as Bien Nacido, selling fruit to wineries throughout the state. Chardonnay is by far the dominant variety; the fruit can have a firm acidic structure, which is unusual in California, and this acidity consolidates the grapes' intensity of flavor. The wine often has an exotic or fruit-salady flavor, which can be an acquired taste. Pinot Noir is also grown successfully in Santa Maria.

Santa Ynez Valley is located south of Santa Maria Valley, and curves inland from the town of Lompoc. With every 2 miles (3 km) from the ocean, average temperatures increase by about 1°F (0.5°C), so there is a marked

difference between westerly sites such as the Sanford Winery and Benedict vineyards and easterly locations like those of the Firestone and Zaca Mesa vineyards. A wide range of grape varieties can be grown here, with Burgundian varieties and Riesling doing well toward the cooler west, and Bordeaux and Rhône grapes flourishing in the warmer east. Merlot and Cabernet Franc are more reliable than Cabernet Sauvignon, which can display vegetal tones. Rainfall is almost nonexistent in summer, and spring frosts are very rare.

Sanford, Santa Rita Hills

Santa Rita Hills AVA was created in 2001, at the urging of leading growers such as Richard Sanford and Bryan Babcock. An enclave within the Santa Ynez Valley AVA, it has 12,300 acres (500 ha) under cultivation and tends to be rather cooler than the rest of Santa Ynez, often experiencing dense maritime fogs. The grape variety with the greatest potential here is Pinot Noir, which is dark-colored and potent, yet fragrant. *marine sediment, sandy loam, clay loam, silty loam, shale, calcium* *Pinot Noir, Merlot, Syrah* *Chardonnay, Riesling, Pinot Blanc, Sauvignon Blanc, Viognier* *red, white, sparkling*

California's Rhône Rangers

Since the 1970s, a few wine producers have argued, persuasively, that California's hot climes are better suited to Mediterranean grapes than the usual Burgundy and Bordeaux varieties. These "Rhône Rangers" have cropped up across California. Founding member Randall Grahm *(see p. 81)* of Bonny Doon Vineyard pays homage in his wines and labels to celebrated Mediterranean wines, while the Perrin family, owner of Châteauneuf's best-known estate, Château de Beaucastel, in France, has planted the best clones of Rhône varieties in the hills of San Luis Obispo's Westside. Syrah, the archetypal Rhône grape, is enjoying a boom here and in Santa Barbara, where the climate is warm but not excessively hot. There are also some stunning Syrahs emerging from the rustic Sierra Foothills. Grenache is often used to make richly fruity rosés, while Viognier has proved more difficult—perhaps because of the California propensity to throw everything into new oak and overcharge for the result. Even so, exciting Viogniers are emerging from places as diverse as Mendocino, Napa, and Santa Barbara. Less familiar whites like Marsanne and Roussanne are also being cultivated, and some North Coast growers are showing interest in old-vine Carignane just when many southern French growers are grubbing the variety up from their vineyards. Producers include Fetzer, McDowell Valley Vineyards, Joseph Phelps, Tablas Creek Vineyard, Alban Vineyards, and Andrew Murray Vineyards.

San Luis Obispo's Westside

Fortified Wines and Marvelous Muscats

A few decades ago, California's wine industry was dominated by fortified wines, which gave drinkers more alcohol for their money. Quality was usually dismal, as producers took shortcuts to simulate sherry and port styles. Today, such wines may be out of fashion, but there are some superlative examples worth trying. Port-style wines are sometimes made from Zinfandel, Petite Sirah, or even Cabernet Sauvignon, and a handful of wineries, including the vast Mondavi Woodbridge operation in Lodi AVA, produce good fortifieds from Portuguese grapes such as Touriga Nacional. The Sierra Foothills region, which never abandoned the tradition of fortified wine production, is also a good source of these wines, and of rich Muscats. In the Central Valley, where quality rarely rises above mediocre, Ficklin has always specialized in port-style wines that are regularly among California's best. The standard bearer for elegant Muscats is Quady *(see p. 87)* in the Central Valley, which has mastered the art of producing highly perfumed Muscats and—thanks in part to brilliant packaging—has made them an international success.

Quady Winery Muscat label

Sierra Foothills

The planting of the Sierra Foothills area was a by-product of the gold rush of the 1850s, when farmers and entrepreneurs made wines for thirsty prospectors. By the late 1860s, there were 10,000 acres (4,000 ha) under vine. Although only half that area is in production today, some vineyards date from the late 19th century, and the area is arguably the most fascinating of California's wine regions. What makes the Foothills so intriguing is the combination of lofty terrain, long winemaking history (evident in some very old vineyards), and remaining links with the gold rush, for example, at Ironstone (www.ironstonevineyards.com), where an enormous gold nugget is on proud display.

The vineyards are at a high elevation, between 1,300 and 3,000 ft (400 and 900 m), which moderates the heat of this inland region, east of Sacramento. There are four AVAs. **El Dorado** is the largest, with no vineyards below 1,300 ft (400 m). It is planted with a range of grapes, including Zinfandel, Barbera, Cabernet Sauvignon, Merlot, Chardonnay, and Viognier. South of El Dorado, in Amador County, are **Shenandoah Valley** and **Fiddletown**, both renowned for their old-vine Zinfandel. The southernmost area is Calaveras County, which has no AVA, but is home to some important wineries.

The growers of the Foothills are generally open-minded, and there are substantial plantings of Rhône and Italian varieties. Fortified wines can be outstanding, with port-style wines from Zinfandel and Barbera, and rich Muscats. Winemaking standards vary, with state-of-the-art facilities alongside rustic and mediocre wineries.

A few vineyards lie on the fringes of the Foothills, such as the handful of wineries within Nevada County. The impressive terraced vineyards of the

Syrah, the classic red grape of the Rhône in France, is a relative newcomer to California, taking off here in the 1970s

Renaissance Winery, which enjoy their own AVA, **North Yuba**, successfully produce everything from Riesling to Cabernet. *granite, volcanic deposits* *Syrah, Zinfandel, Cabernet Sauvignon, Barbera* *Chardonnay, Sauvignon Blanc* *red, white, rosé, fortified*

Central Valley

Stretching for 400 miles (650 km) across the center of California, the vast, flat Central Valley supplies a quarter of the food and beverages consumed in the US. With about 190,000 acres (77,000 ha) under vine, the Central Valley is also by far the largest of California's wine regions, producing around 60 percent of all the state's grapes. The soils are rich, and the climate is blisteringly hot and dry; this is one of the world's sunniest regions, so irrigation is essential. The heat makes high-quality grapes virtually impossible to cultivate; instead, the valley is a source of fruity, easy-drinking wines at an affordable price.

A handful of producers make excellent port-style and Muscat wines, but they are a drop in the ocean of Chardonnay, Chenin Blanc, French Colombard, Merlot, and Zinfandel. A few northerly regions around Sacramento can make some claim to quality: Zinfandel from Lodi and Chenin Blanc from Clarksburg are certainly worth a try. *alluvial loam* *Merlot, Cabernet Sauvignon, Zinfandel* *Chardonnay, Chenin Blanc, Colombard, Sauvignon Blanc* *red, white, rosé, sparkling, dessert, fortified*

Quady Winery, Central Valley

Southern California

In the 19th century, vineyards were flourishing in Los Angeles itself, but they were wiped out by Pierce's Disease, a bacterial malady spread by insects, for which there is no cure. In recent years, this disease has destroyed vineyards elsewhere in southern California, notably in Temecula, which was once a Chardonnay stronghold. However, metropolitan Los Angeles has a tiny AVA called **Malibu-Newton Canyon**. Around San Bernardino is the **Cucamonga Valley** AVA, dominated by Zinfandel; and there is another AVA in the far south, consisting of 75 acres (30 ha) around San Diego, called **San Pasqual Valley**. With a few exceptions, none of these regions is strongly focused on quality, and the wineries survive by catering to the enormous local population. Zinfandel, Chardonnay, and Sauvignon Blanc are the dominant grape varieties. *varied* *Zinfandel* *Chardonnay, Sauvignon Blanc* *red, white*

VINCENT GASNIER'S TOP 10

Exceptional California Syrah Wines

1. **Araujo: Eisele Vineyard** Napa Valley *p. 36*
2. **Arrowood: Saralee's Vineyard** Sonoma *p. 50*
3. **J. C. Cellars** San Francisco Bay *p. 80*
4. **Martinelli** Sonoma *p. 55*
5. **Ojai Vineyard: Thompson** Santa Barbara *p. 86*
6. **Pax: Alder Springs The Terraces** Mendocino *www.paxwines.com*
7. **Blackjack Ranch: Maximus** Santa Barbara *p. 84*
8. **Alban Vineyards: Lorraine** San Luis Obispo *p. 82*
9. **Havens** Napa Valley *p. 45*
10. **Qupé** San Luis Obispo *p. 87*

Syrah is not directly related to Petite Sirah (sometimes spelled Syrah), which has been grown in California since the 19th century

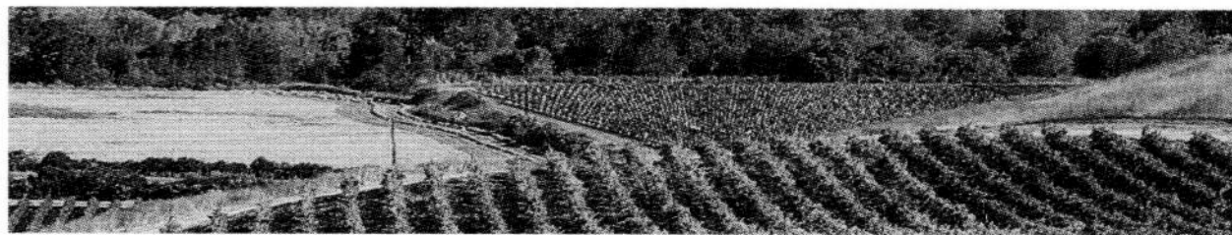

Fall vineyard in Santa Ynez Valley, Santa Barbara County

Major Producers in Central & Southern California

J. C. Cellars
San Francisco Bay
Specializing in hand-crafted, single-vineyard Syrah, Petite Sirah, Viognier, and Zinfandel, J. C. Cellars was set up as a small-production winery by Jeff Cohn in 1997, while he was still winemaker at Rosenblum Cellars down the road. Cohn has now left Rosenblum to concentrate on J. C., which has benefited from massive investment in new equipment. In 2004 and 2005, Cohn's products were the winners of the "Syrah Shootout," a tasting conducted by 38 rival winemakers. Watch out for Late Harvest Viognier, made only in years when the weather conditions have encouraged botrytis. *3000 Washington St., Alameda • 510 749 9463 • www.jccellars.com* *red, dessert*
★ *Rockpile Vineyard Syrah Haley's Reserve, Pourquoi Pas Syrah*

Ridge Vineyards
San Francisco Bay & other areas
This famous winery was founded on the site of an 1880s vineyard by Stanford University professors in 1959. Paul Draper became winemaker in 1969, and he is still at the helm. His finest wine is the estate Cabernet Sauvignon from grapes grown in the 2,000 ft (600 m) high Monte Bello vineyard. From one of California's premier vineyards, it is aged, unusually, in American oak. Ridge also produces some stunning Zinfandels from old vineyards in Sonoma and Paso Robles. *17100 Monte Bello Rd., Cupertino • 408 867 3233 • www.ridgewine.com* *red, white*
★ *Santa Cruz Mountains Chardonnay, Monte Bello Cabernet Sauvignon, Geyserville Zinfandel*

Ridge Vineyards

Testarossa
San Francisco Bay & other areas
This winery near San Jose was founded by Rob and Diana Jensen in 1993. They own no vineyards so buy in grapes from nine top sites in Monterey and Santa Barbara

VINCENT GASNIER'S TOP 10 Fabulous Dessert Wines

1. **Dolce** Napa Valley *p. 38*
2. **Arrowood: Late Harvest** Sonoma *p. 50*
3. **Chateau St. Jean: Dessert** Sonoma *p. 50*
4. **Beringer: Nightingale** Napa Valley *p. 36*
5. **Bonny Doon: Dessert** San Luis Obispo *opposite*
6. **Martinelli: Muscat** Sonoma *p. 55*
7. **Ojai: Dessert** Santa Barbara County *p. 86*
8. **J. C. Cellars: Late Harvest** San Francisco Bay *above*
9. **Washington Hills: Sweet Whites** Columbia Valley *p. 104*
10. **Quady: Essensia** Central Valley *p. 87*

Preceding pages **Cabernet Sauvignon vineyards in the fall sunshine, San Luis Obispo County**

County. The Chardonnays tend to be rich and toasty, with good acidic bite. The Pinot Noirs are spicy and well structured, with a distinctively California style. The Syrah is excellent, too. *300-A College Ave., Los Gatos • 408 354 6150 • www.testarossa.com* *red, white* ★ *Michaud Vineyard Chardonnay, Sleepy Hollow Vineyard Pinot Noir, Gary's Vineyard Syrah*

Wente Vineyards
San Francisco Bay / Livermore Valley

This family-owned estate, founded in 1883 by Carl Wente, dominates Livermore Valley and also has substantial holdings in Monterey, planted with Pinot Noir and other grape varieties. The wines are commercial in the best sense—made in large quantities to a consistent level of quality. The standard varietals are labeled Family Selections, and the estate-grown wines are bottled as Vineyard Selections. Wente also makes a fine sparkling wine aged for five years before disgorgement. *5565 Tesla Rd., Livermore • 408 456 2300 • www.wentevineyards.com* *red, white, sparkling* ★ *Estate Chardonnay, Late Harvest Riesling, Brut Reserve*

Chalone Vineyard
Monterey / Chalone

The vineyards at this remote mountainside property date from 1919, but wines were not bottled here until 1960. Chardonnay and Pinot Noir dominate; Syrah and Viognier were planted in the late 1990s. Bacterial problems in the winery damaged Chalone's reputation in the 1990s, but today the winery is back on track. Chenin Blanc may be out of fashion, but the old-vine version here shows how stunning it can be. *(See also p. 70.)* *Stonewall Canyon Rd. & Hwy. 146 W., Soledad • 831 678 1717 • www.chalonevineyard.com* *by appt* *red, white* ★ *Chenin Blanc, Viognier, Pinot Noir*

Randall Grahm & Bonny Doon

A highly intellectual and witty character, Randall Grahm *(see p. 17)* wandered into the California wine industry in the 1970s and became its most admirable gadfly. His Bonny Doon Vineyard in Santa Cruz is his way of demonstrating that California's climate is better suited to Mediterranean and Rhône grape varieties than to Cabernet and Chardonnay. His wines pay homage to Bandol and Châteauneuf-du-Pape, and display idiosyncratic acts of courage, such as the attempt to produce a "Pacific Rim" Riesling from West Coast regions. These are not California's best wines, but Grahm's rejection of conventional wisdom about varieties, styles, and markets has stimulated other California winemakers to redefine the future of the industry. *2 Pine Flat Rd., Bonny Doon • 831 425 3625 or 2485 W. Hwy. 46, Paso Robles • 805 239 5614 • www.bonnydoonvineyard.com* *red, white, dessert* ★ *Ca'del Solo, EuroDoon, Rhonefandel, Riesling Asylum, Viognier Doux*

Paraiso Springs Vineyards
Monterey / Santa Lucia Highlands

Rich Smith is primarily a grape farmer, but he sets aside certain blocks of land from his 3,000 acres (1,200 ha) to make his own wines of great purity and direct fruit flavors. Riesling and Pinot Blanc have been good in the past, and the Pinot Noir and Syrah show the intense fruitiness of which Monterey is capable. *Paraiso Springs Rd., Soledad • 831 678 0300 • www.paraisovineyard.com* *red, white* ★ *Pinot Noir, Syrah*

Calera Wine Company
Mount Harlan
An admired estate with a style of its own, Calera was planted to test a theory. Josh Jensen often visited Burgundy in the 1970s and was convinced that the secret of great Pinot Noir was the limestone soil. Back in California, he found limestone 2,200 ft (670 m) up in the Gavilan Mountains, and planted four different sites with the grape. Results were mixed: some vintages were magnificent, others, earthy and stewed. The limestone soils do offer excellent drainage, but bacterial problems have undermined fruit quality in certain vintages. However, the Viognier, made since 1987, is splendid. *(See also p. 72)* *11300 Cienega Rd., Hollister • 831 637 9170 • www.calerawine.com* *by appt.* *red, white* ★ *Viognier, Mount Harlan Chardonnay, Selleck Pinot Noir*

Alban Vineyards
San Luis Obispo
John Alban was converted to Rhône wines when he visited Condrieu, and from 1990 onward he has dedicated his vineyard to the varieties of the Rhône. Low yields give his wines immense concentration, and whether he is turning his hand to Roussanne or Viognier, Syrah, or Grenache, Alban seems incapable of making a bad wine. It is no wonder that other producers line up to buy his grapes. *8575 Orcutt Rd., Arroyo Grande • 805 546 0305* *red, white* ★ *Viognier, Reva Syrah, Grenache*

Justin Vineyards & Winery
San Luis Obispo / Paso Robles
Former banker Justin Baldwin bought this Westside Paso Robles property in 1982 and now has 72 acres (29 ha) in production. Over the years he has experimented to see which varieties work best in these virgin sites. The Cabernet Sauvignon and Syrah varietals have proved successful, as have his Bordeaux blends called Isosceles and Justification. High quality and skillful marketing have brought swift recognition. *11680 Chimney Rock Rd., Paso Robles • 805 238 6932 • www.justinwine.com* *red, white, fortified* ★ *Sauvignon Blanc, Syrah*

Meridian Vineyards
San Luis Obispo / Paso Robles
Founded by veteran winemaker Chuck Ortman, Meridian has been through many changes in ownership, but Ortman remains at the helm. Under Beringer Blass, production at this already large winery is set to expand further. With thousands of acres at his disposal, Ortman makes a wide range offering exceptional value for money. *7000 Hwy. 46 E, Paso Robles • 805 237 6000 • www.meridianvineyards.com* *red, white* ★ *Pinot Noir Reserve, Paso Robles Syrah, Paso Robles Zinfandel*

Tablas Creek Vineyard
San Luis Obispo / Paso Robles
For many years the French Perrin family and American wine importer Robert Haas searched California for the perfect place to grow Rhône varieties. Eventually they chose Westside Paso Robles, as its soils and rugged terrain resembled those of the family's estate, Château de Beaucastel, in Châteauneuf-du-Pape. Importing vines from France and growing them organically, they have produced complex, flavorful blends called Esprit de Beaucastel. The red combines Mourvèdre, Syrah, and Grenache; the white blends Marsanne, Viognier, and Roussanne. *9339 Adelaida Rd., Paso Robles • 805 237 1231 • www.tablascreek.com* *by appt.* *red, white* ★ *Espirt de Beaucastel*

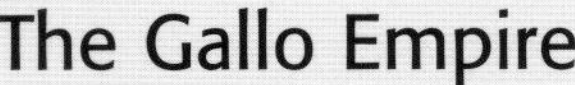

The Gallo Empire

Gallo's lavish advertising features a family company that is content to tend its vineyards and invite the public to enjoy the results. In reality, this is an industry phenomenon: a single producer making about as much wine as the whole of Australia. Founded by brothers Ernest and Julio Gallo, the business took off just as Prohibition ended in the mid-1930s. Thanks to a well-developed distribution network, market awareness, and ruthless promotion, Gallo grew fast and by 1967 had a third of the US market. It is still based deep in California's Central Valley, where it produces tens of millions of cases of table wine each year, sold under about 50 labels. It was the domaine in Sonoma (see p. 52)*, set up by the founders' grandchildren, that saved Gallo from a reputation for mediocrity in the 1980s, and keeps up the image today, offering indisputably high quality at a fair price. The multibillion-dollar business is still firmly in the hands of the Gallos, with about 20 family members working in various capacities in 2006, and the elderly Ernest still a figurehead.*

Special Relationship

From the early years, Julio oversaw the vineyards, while Ernest dealt with bankers, suppliers, bottlers, and buyers. Business strategies were usually a joint decision right up until Julio's death in 1993.

Contact Information

www.gallo.com • Tasting room in Sonoma (see p. 52)
red, white, sparkling, fortified ★ Gallo of Sonoma, Turning Leaf, Indigo Hills

A Hard Beginning

Ernest Gallo was born in California in 1909; Julio a year later. The family were immigrants from Piemonte in Italy, and had a small vineyard in Modesto. Life was hard, and the brothers' father shot their mother and then himself dead in 1933, in the Depression. However, in that same year, the brothers' first winery, E. & J. Gallo, was launched. An intricate understanding of the wine business, coupled with ferocious tenacity in the face of poverty (the brothers even slept by their fermentation tank), saw the business make a $30,000 profit on 177,847 gallons of red table wine in its first year. The Gallos never looked back.

Gallo vineyard in Central California

Gallo was the world's largest vintner until 2004, when a fast succession of mergers put Constellation Brands ahead

Wild Horse

San Luis Obispo & other areas

Starting in the early 1980s, the irrepressible Ken Volk has brought forth an astonishing range of wines from his own land and various Central Coast vineyards. He is renowned for his Pinot Noir and the Rhône range called Equus, and he delights in producing highly individual wines from Malvasia, Trousseau Gris, and Négrette. Quality fluctuates, which is not surprising given the huge range of often quirky wines produced here. But the wines are serious, and the Pinot Noir and Syrah can be first rate. In 2003 Wild Horse was bought by Peak Wines, with Volk remaining as winemaker. *1437 Wild Horse Winery Ct., Templeton • 805 434 2541 • www.wildhorsewinery.com* ☐ *red, white* ★ *Malvasia Bianca, Equus Roussanne, Cheval Sauvage Pinot Noir*

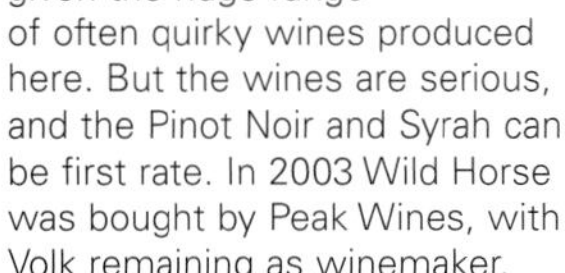

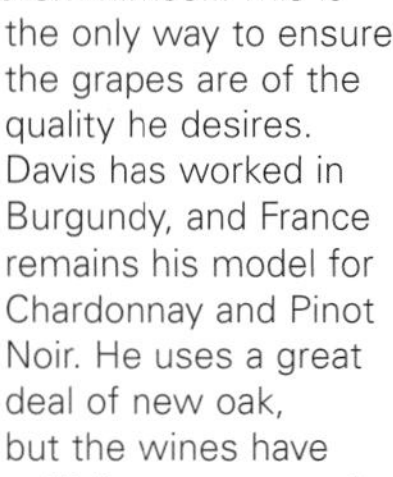

Wild Horse: Cheval Sauvage label

Andrew Murray Vineyards

Santa Barbara County / Santa Ynez Valley

Restaurateur James Murray took his son (now winemaker) Andrew on gastronomic trips to France, where they became acquainted with Rhône wines. They planted 50 acres (20 ha) of Rhône varieties in Santa Ynez Valley in 1990. Fruit is also bought in from Central Coast vineyards, but the top wines are from the estate: a ripe, floral Viognier and a range of spicy, clove-scented Syrahs, which year after year show the suitability of the valley to these two varieties. *Los Olivos • 805 686 9604 • www.andrewmurrayvineyards.com* ☐ *by appt.* *red, white* ★ *Estate Viognier, Roasted Slope Syrah*

Arcadian Winery

Santa Barbara County, Monterey & other areas

Joseph Davis does not own any vineyards. Instead, he leases plots of land from growers in Santa Barbara County and Monterey, and farms them himself. This is the only way to ensure the grapes are of the quality he desires. Davis has worked in Burgundy, and France remains his model for Chardonnay and Pinot Noir. He uses a great deal of new oak, but the wines have sufficient concentration for the wood not to be dominant. These are Burgundy-style wines of purity and intensity. *Santa Ynez • 805 688 1876 • www.arcadianwinery.com* ■ *red, white* ★ *Bien Nacido Chardonnay, Pisoni Vineyard Pinot Noir, Gary's Vineyard Syrah*

Au Bon Climat Winery

Santa Barbara County / Santa Maria Valley

Jim Clendenen is one of the great pioneers of Santa Maria Valley and he has been named Winemaker of the Year several times. His Au Bon Climat Winery, founded in 1982, means "a well exposed vineyard," and he has produced some very fine Chardonnay and Pinot Noir, both from his own vineyards and from those of the region's leading growers. Clendenen favors restraint over power, yet the wines remain very Californian in their generosity and richness. There is also a range of Italian varietals bottled under the Podere dell'Olivos label. *Rte. 1, Santa Maria Mesa Rd., Santa Maria • 805 937 9801 • www.aubonclimat.com* ☐ *by appt.* *red, white* ★ *Talley Vineyard Chardonnay, Isabelle Pinot Noir*

A vine planted in 1842 on a farm in Santa Barbara grew into a giant: its trunk was 10 ft (3 m) round, and it yielded 10 tons of grapes a year

Blackjack Ranch

Santa Barbara County

Roger Wisted first became interested in winemaking at the age of 14, and he was collecting and making the stuff long before the legal age for drinking it. Another teenage interest was casino games: in 1990 Wisted invented the card game California Blackjack, which he licensed to clubs across California. The commercial success of California Blackjack gave Roger Wisted the means to start a winery and a name for it, too. Shunning mass production and looking to French techniques for inspiration, Wisted uses Cabernet Sauvignon and Merlot to produce highly complex and elegant wines. *220 Alamo Pintado Rd., Solvang • 805 686 9922 • www.blackjackranch.com* *red, white* ★ *Chardonnay Blackjack Ranch Vineyard Reserve, Wilkening Vineyard Reserve*

Byron

Byron

Santa Barbara County / Santa Maria Valley

Ken Brown founded this winery in the 1980s. It was sold to Robert Mondavi in 1990, although Brown remains in charge. The principal wines are Pinot Noir, Chardonnay, Pinot Blanc, and Pinot Gris. Byron has over 600 acres (250 ha) of vineyards, but also buys fruit in from other top sites in Santa Barbara. The wines are perfect examples of the elegantly poised Santa Maria style; some of the simpler wines are more satisfying than the oaky bottlings. *5230 Tepusquet Rd., Santa Maria • 805 934 4770 • www.byronwines.com* *red, white* ★ *Pinot Gris, Santa Maria Chardonnay, Byron Vineyard Pinot Noir*

Firestone Vineyard

Santa Barbara County / Santa Ynez Valley

Set up by Brooks Firestone in the 1970s, this Santa Ynez Valley estate is now owned by the Japanese Suntory group, although the Firestone family is still involved. The winery has a reputation for outstanding value. Production has expanded considerably, and many grapes are now bought in, but Riesling has always been reliable, as are the Merlot and much improved Cabernet Sauvignon. Wines can lack concentration and length, but they are well crafted. *5000 Zaca Station Rd., Los Olivos • 805 688 3940 • www.firestonewine.com* *red, white* ★ *Gewürztraminer, Late Harvest Riesling, Merlot Reserve*

VINCENT GASNIER'S TOP 10 Great Riesling Makers

1. **Chateau Montelena** Napa Valley *p. 37*
2. **Rancho Sisquoc: Flood Family Winery** Santa Barbara County *p. 86*
3. **Sanford Winery** Santa Barbara County *p. 86*
4. **Windsor Vineyards** Sonoma *p. 55*
5. **Kendall-Jackson: Vintner's Reserve** Sonoma *p. 53*
6. **Claiborne & Churchill** San Luis Obispo *p. 87*
7. **Navarro** Mendocino *p. 62*
8. **Robert Mondavi Private Selection** Napa Valley *p. 43*
9. **Gainey Vineyard** Santa Barbara County *p. 87*
10. **Argyle Winery** Willamette Valley *p. 106*

Assistant winemaker in the lab at Quady

Ojai Vineyard
Santa Barbara County
Ojai's (pronounced "oh-high") founders, Helen and Adam Tolmach, have always been uncompromising. They are more than usually demanding of their grape providers, and they refuse to change their production philosophy, which is to keep things as low-intervention as possible. The Tolmachs might baulk at being called entrepreneurs, as they purportedly make wines purely to keep themselves amused; yet they have gained a reputation for crafting some of Santa Barbara's finest Syrah, Pinot Noir, Grenache, and sweet wines.
805 649 1674 • www.ojaivineyard.com ● *red, white, dessert* ★ *Roll Ranch, Bien Nacido, Talley Reserve*

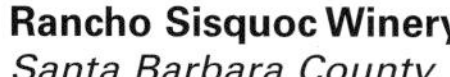

Rancho Sisquoc Winery
Santa Barbara County
In 1972 Harold Pfeiffer decided, as an experiment, to devote 12 (5 ha) of his 37,000 acres (15,000 ha) ranch to planting Johannesburg Riesling and Cabernet Sauvignon grapes. Today, the Rancho Sisquoc Winery has expanded to occupy 320 acres (130 ha) of Santa Barbara County's eastern-most vineyards. Its owners today, the Flood family, have convinced winemaker Alec Franks that small is beautiful, therefore, the winery produces no more than 10,000 cases of varietals a year, which sell out as soon as they appear.
6600 Foxen Cyn. Rd., Santa Maria • 805 934 4332 • www.ranchosisquoc.com ○ *red, white* ★ *Sisquoc River Red, Sisquoc Sauvignon Blanc, Johannesburg Riesling*

Sanford Winery
Santa Barbara County
Richard Sanford was one of the first Pinot Noir growers in the county, establishing his vineyard in 1971. Ten years later he founded his winery and expanded his holdings to 350 acres (140 ha). The white wines have a broad, oaky, slightly confected style, but the Pinot Noir is exceptional. Winemaker Doug Fletcher's fruit focus is unblinking, and his team uses a unique gravity racking system, whereby hydraulic elevators raise and lower vats to reduce handling. This reverence for the grape has made Sanford a major Santa Barbara player.
7250 Santa Rosa Rd, Buellton • 805 688 3300 ○ *red, white* ★ *Barrel Select Chardonnay, La Rinconada Pinot Noir*

Domaine de la Terre Rouge
Sierra Foothills
Founded in 1987 by William Easton, Terre Rouge produces the Sierra Foothills' best wines from Rhône varieties. The finest Syrah comes from a parcel of land called Pyramid Block, and the best grapes are usually reserved for the

very oaky Ascent bottling. Whites include a Rhône-style blend called Enigma and a rich Viognier. Under the Easton label, there are some powerful yet elegant Zinfandels and juicy Barberas. *10801 Dickson Rd., Fiddletown • 209 245 3117 • www.terrerougewines.com* red, white, fortified ★ *Enigma, Pyramid Block Syrah, Estate Zinfandel*

Quady Winery
Central Valley

Andrew Quady dabbled with port-style wines in the mid-1970s while working for other wineries. He also experimented with fortified Muscats, and in 1981 released Essensia, an enchanting, beautifully packaged, orange-scented Orange Muscat, which was a smash hit. He then created other wines: Elysium, a rose-scented Black Muscat; sweet and dry vermouths; and fortified wines from Zinfandel and Portuguese varieties. This area is too hot for fine wines, but Quady has proved Madera is an ideal location for world-class sweet wines. *1318 Rd 24, Madera • 559 673 8068 • www.quadywinery.com* *dessert, fortified* ★ *Essensia, Elysium*

Moraga Vineyards
Southern California

Tom Jones's small Moraga Canyon plot in Los Angeles' exclusive Bel Air suburb must be the most unlikely spot in the US for a quality-orientated vineyard. The canyon's mesoclimate has the advantage of higher rainfall and cooler nights than downtown LA. There is only one red and one white wine: the Cabernet Sauvignon-dominated Bordeaux-style blend made in an opulent and oaky style is as expensive, and as impressive, as a fine Napa Cabernet. *650 Sepulveda Blvd, Los Angeles • 310 476 3051 • www.moragavineyards.com* *red, white* ★ *Moraga Cabernet*

Other Producers in Central & Southern California

Boeger Winery *(Sierra Foothills) 1709 Carson Rd., Placerville • 530 622 8094 • www.boegerwinery.com*

Cedar Mountains *(San Francisco Bay) 7000 Tesla Rd., Livermore • 925 373 6636*

Claiborne & Churchill *(San Luis Obispo) 2649 Carpenter Canyon Rd. • 805 544 4066 • www.clairbornechurchill.com*

Eberle Winery *(San Luis Obispo) Hwy. 46 East, Paso Robles • www.eberlewinery.com*

Gainey Vineyard *(Santa Barbara County) 3950 East Highway 246, Santa Ynez • 805 668 0558 • www.gaineyvineyard.com*

Georis Winery *(Monterey) 4 Pilot Rd., Carmel Valley • 831 659 1050 • www.georiswine.com*

Heller Estate *(Monterey) W. Carmel Valley Road, Carmel Valley • 831 659 6220 • www.hellerestate.com*

Joseph Filippi *(Southern California) 12467 Base Line Rd., Rancho Cucamonga • 909 899 5755 • www.josephfilippiwinery.com*

Joullian *(Monterey) 2 Vilalge Drive Suite A, Carmel Valley • 831 659 8100 • www.joullian.com*

Laetitia Estate *(San Luis Obispo) 453 Laetitia Vineyard Drive, Arroyo Grande • 805 481 1772 • www.laetitiawine.com*

Morgan Winery *(Monterey) 590 C. Brunken Ave., Salinas • 831 751 7777 • www.morganwinery.com*

Qupé *(San Luis Obispo) Los Olivos • 805 937 9801 • www.qupe.com*

Thornton Winery *(Southern California) 32575 Rancho California Rd., Temecula • 951 699 0099*

Verdad *(San Luis Obispo) Los Olivos • 805 784 0747 • www.verdadwines.com*

Walter Hansel *(Santa Barbara) 2800 Corby Ave, Santa Rosa • 707 525 3614*

PACIFIC NORTHWEST

Introduction
90–91

Wine Map of the Pacific Northwest
92–93

Wine Areas of Washington
94–96

Wine Areas of Oregon
97–98

Major Producers in the Pacific Northwest
102–109

PACIFIC NORTHWEST

ALTHOUGH OREGON AND WASHINGTON *are as diametrically opposed to one another as Bordeaux is to Burgundy, they are both more closely allied to France than to other US winemaking states. Lying, like their French counterparts, between 43° and 47° latitude, they are separated from each other by the great Columbia River and divided in two by the Cascade Mountains. The interplay between sun, weather, and these geological features defines regional wine styles. Farther inland, Idaho has an embryonic wine industry.*

The North Pacific's warm current brings onshore rain to the US's northwestern states, instead of the fog that is a dominant feature of North Coast California to the south. The warm current also keeps the average temperatures higher in the Pacific Northwest than the area's northerly latitude might suggest. As a consequence, whereas the climate of California lends itself to big, fruity, higher alcohol wines, the climate of the Pacific Northwest is more suited to light wines that often resemble those of northern Europe.

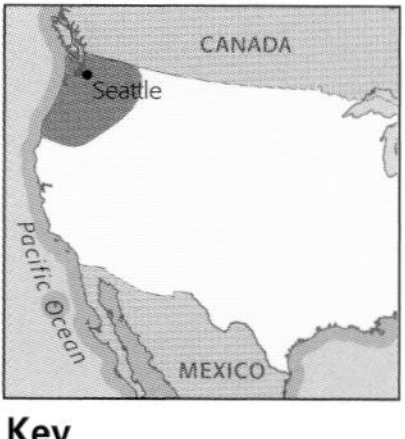

Key

Pacific Northwest

Grandpa Grape

Dr. Walter Clore (1911–2003) was a key figure in Washington's wine history. A visionary horticulturalist based at the Prosser research station from 1937–76, he studied the growth patterns of 250 grape varieties, including American, European, and hybrid vines. Over the years, he convinced local winemakers, especially those at Columbia Crest and Chateau Ste. Michelle, that superior *vinifera* varieties could flourish in the state. He also helped to develop the Lemberger red variety and predicted the massive expansion of the US wine industry. Fondly referred to as "Grandpa Grape" in his lifetime, Clore was honored by Columbia Crest in 1999 with an artisan-style Bordeaux blend called the Walter Clore Private Reserve.

Oregon

It was in Oregon in the 1960s that the cool-climate viticulture of the New World was born. Two enthusiasts, Richard Sommer and David Lett, were convinced that Pinot Noir had to have a long ripening period if they were to re-create the same delicately spiced perfume, velvety texture, and fine structure that the grape finds in Burgundy. After undertaking an almost kamikaze-like pursuit to that end, Oregon's winemakers eventually achieved their goal *(see p. 99)*.

With 14,000 acres (5,600 ha) of vineyards and more than 300 wineries by 2006 (up from 250 in 2003), Oregon now produces around 1.1 million cases of wine each year. Despite the recent fast growth in Oregon's industry, most wineries are often relatively small, family affairs run by dedicated winemakers. The majority are clustered within the coastally influenced, cool, wet Willamette Valley, to the west of the Cascade Mountains. The focus here is primarily on cool-climate grapes: Pinot Noir, Pinot Gris, Sauvignon

Preceding pages **Vineyard with Mount Hood in the background, Willamette Valley, Oregon**

Canoe Ridge Vineyard in Walla Walla, Washington

Blanc, Gewürztraminer, Riesling, and Pinot Blanc. The ratio of red to white wines is 60:40.

Washington

Washington State's wine industry is grander in scale than Oregon's, and, like Oregon, in a period of dramatic growth. In the 1980s, the state had about 5,000 acres (2,000 ha) of vineyards and some 20 wineries. By 2006, the vines were reaching over 30,000 acres (12,000 ha), and the number of wineries was more than 360, with a new one opening every couple of weeks. The state's wine output is traditionally ranked second in the US after California (although some surveys using different criteria now rank New York State in second place). Wines from Washington State are exported to over 40 countries.

Washington's wine regions mainly follow river valleys to the east of the Cascade Mountains. This environment is semidesert, and vines could not survive without irrigation. The state has an average of 17.4 hours of sunlight per day, which is about two hours more than California's North Coast wine regions. The sunlight allows a range of vines to ripen consistently. In the 1990s most of the production was white (Chardonnay and Riesling); this has changed in the past ten years, with reds such as Cabernet Sauvignon, Merlot, and Syrah now accounting for about 60 percent of production.

Pinot Gris grapes

Idaho

The vineyards of Idaho are planted mainly in volcanic ash soils above the Snake River. The high altitude—peaking at around 3,300 ft (1,000 m)—results in the region being sunny during the day but very cold at night. This extreme temperature difference produces wines with a very high acidity and alcohol balance. Ste. Chapelle, established in 1978, is the largest winery (now owned by Constellation Brands), and it has consistently proved that Idaho can produce excellent Chardonnay, Riesling, and Chenin Blanc. Ste. Chapelle's success has encouraged others, and Idaho now has about 20 wineries.

Wine Map of the Pacific Northwest

To the east of the Cascade Mountains lie Washington's four main AVAs: the all-encompassing Columbia Valley; Yakima Valley within Columbia Valley; Red Mountain within Yakima Valley; and Walla Walla. Puget Sound is the only AVA in west Washington and is of little significance. Oregon's AVAs lie to the west, set between the Coastal Range and the Cascades. They run 200 miles (320 km) from the damp north to the drier south: Willamette Valley, Umpqua Valley, Rogue Valley, and its sub-regions, Applegate and Illinois river valleys.

MAIN AVAs & MAJOR PRODUCERS

Columbia Valley *p. 95*
Chateau Ste. Michelle *p. 102*
Columbia Winery *p. 102*
McCrea Cellars *p. 103*
Ste. Michelle Wine Estates *p. 103*

Yakima Valley & Red Mountain *p. 96*
DeLille Cellars *p. 103*
Hedges Cellars *p. 104*
Washington Hills Cellars *p. 104*

Walla Walla *p. 96*
Canoe Ridge Vineyard *p. 104*
Cayuse Vineyards *p. 104*
L'Ecole No. 41 *p. 105*
Long Shadows Vintners *p. 105*
Woodward Canyon Winery *p. 105*

Willamette Valley *p. 98*
Amity Vineyards *p. 106*
Archery Summit Winery *p. 106*
Argyle Winery *p. 106*
Beaux Freres *p. 106*
Bergstrôm *p. 106*
Domaine Drouhin *p. 107*
Elk Cove Vineyards *p. 107*
Ken Wright Cellars *p. 107*
Lemelson Vineyards *p. 108*
Owen Roe Winery *p. 108*
Panther Creek Cellars *p. 108*
Ponzi Vineyards *p. 109*
WillaKenzie Estate *p. 109*
Willamette Valley Vineyards *p. 109*

Umpqua Valley *p. 98*
Abacela Vineyards & Winery *p. 109*

Rogue, Applegate & Illinois River Valleys *p. 97*

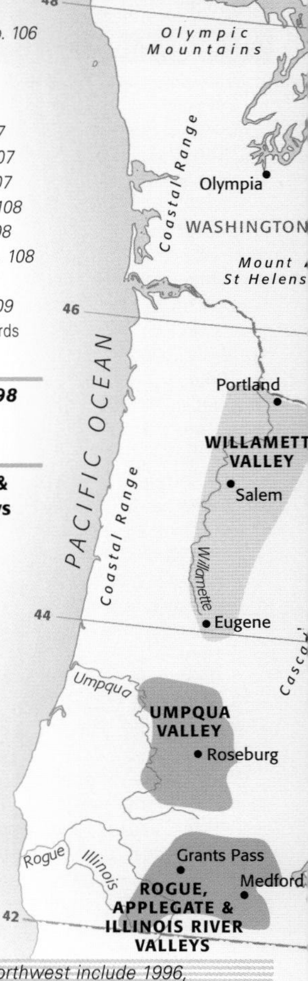

Woodward Canyon Winery label, Washington

Good recent vintages in the Pacific Northwest include 1996, 1997, 1999, 2001, 2002, and 2004

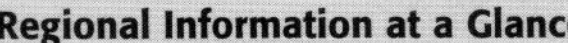

Regional Information at a Glance

Latitude 45–48.5°N. (Washington); 42–45.5°N (Oregon).

Altitude 0–900 ft (270 m) in Washington; 300–2,600 ft (90–800 m) in Oregon.

Topography The Cascade Mountains are a barrier to the moist, moderate marine climate of the Pacific. Oregon's wine regions are sandwiched between the Coastal Range and the Cascades.

Soil Basaltic sand, loess, and river gravel in Washington; volcanic, granite, and clay in Oregon.

Climate Little rain finds its way past the Cascade Mountains to fall on Washington's bone-dry wine area. Summers are hot, but dramatic diurnal temperature shifts preserve acidity and ensure slow ripening. The Pacific influence on Oregon results in cool summers and damp falls.

Temperature July average 70°F (21°C) in Washington; 66°F (19°C) in Oregon.

Rainfall Annual average is 8 in (200 mm) in Washington; 43 in (1,100 mm) in Oregon.

Viticultural Hazards Some freezes in Washington; fungal diseases, underripeness in Oregon.

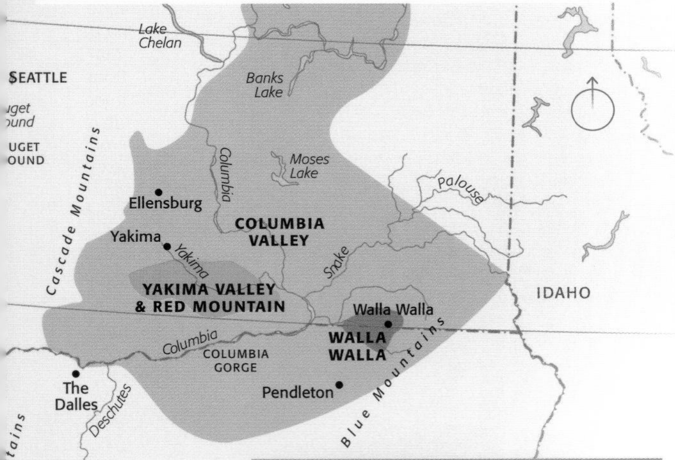

Domaine Drouhin's gravity-fed winery, Willamette Valley, Oregon

Wine Areas of Washington

The first recorded planting of vines in Washington was around 1825 at Fort Vancouver on the Columbia River, by Hudson's Bay Company traders. The first winery was established in the 1860s at Walla Walla, and the first *vinifera* varieties were planted at Yakima in 1871. However, it wasn't until the 1930s, when government funding became available, that vine-growing and winemaking on a truly commercial scale took off. The funds were used to develop an irrigation system in the state and transform what was an arid desert into agricultural land.

After this, Washington's wine industry grew rapidly. The varieties were mainly native *labrusca* up until the early 1960s when larger plantings of *vinifera* took place. Large wineries grew up in populated areas around Seattle and were supplied by grapes shipped over the mountains from sun-blessed, dry eastern areas. This allowed efficient production and cross-regional blending between a range of mesoclimates. Starting with large volumes of well-priced, consistent, everyday wines, producers then added reasonably priced midrange, reserve, and super premium labels. Washington red varietals are earning a strong reputation for their character-filled flavors, smooth textures, and finely honed structure, particularly with Merlot and Cabernet Sauvignon. There is also increasing interest in Nebbiolo and Syrah.

Although Washington State has a notoriously wet climate, eastern Washington, where most of the vineyards are situated, enjoys a drier, hotter mesoclimate. Many of the vines are ungrafted; the oldest vines are allowed to become dormant before the coldest winter temperatures set in by cutting off the water supply. Interestingly, Washington is one of the few parts of the wine world where the phylloxera bug has never been a problem for *vinifera* varieties of vine *(see box opposite)*.

Vineyard planted on a riverbed in Walla Walla, Washington State

Columbia Valley

The Columbia Valley AVA represents about 98 percent of Washington's production and has three sub-AVAs within it: Yakima Valley, Red Mountain, and Walla Walla *(see p. 96 for all)*. The Columbia Valley AVA was established in 1984 as a catch-all to facilitate cross-regional blending. Its own designated vineyards encompass the state's widest range of mesoclimates, from the hottest vineyards along the Wahluke Slope—Mattawa, Saddle Mountains, Frenchman Hills, and Indian Wells—to the cooler south, where temperate, frost-free vineyards dot the upper slopes of the subregion Columbia Gorge: Alder Ridge, Cold Creek, Zepher Ridge, and Canoe Ridge.

Soils range from highly infertile ancient gravels to sand, clay, and basalt. Out of necessity, vineyards are planted on slopes between 65 and 1,000 ft (20 and 310 m) above sea level, close to the Columbia River to keep frost at bay in winter and vines cool in summer.

This all-encompassing AVA was first recognized for its high-quality, delicately perfumed, racy Rieslings in the early 1970s. Chardonnay and Merlot have predominated since then, but the dry, medium- and late-harvested Rieslings are still among the best in the US. Matured-on-the-vine ice wines are made when conditions are suitable. Sadly, Washington's early success with vibrantly fruited, razor-sharp, highly unfashionable Semillon and Chenin Blanc is underappreciated. The refreshingly crisp Sauvignon Blancs are among the country's better versions, and are often ridiculously cheap.

Merlot has been Washington's star red since 1976. It is generally richer, riper, and more alcoholic than in Bordeaux, and more finely structured and juicier than in California wines. Cabernet Sauvignon also ripens consistently, producing concentrated, powerful wine, but it is overshadowed by Merlot. The two grapes marry well, often forming a blend with Cabernet Franc or Malbec—or both, in full Meritage glory. All can appear remarkably Bordeaux-like.

The 1990s saw phenomenal growth in plantings of Syrah. Its style is very much that of France's northern Rhône Valley. In this spirit, Washington's own Rhône Ranger movement, mirroring that of California *(see p. 75)*, has been known to add a dash of Viognier for aromatic lift and structure.

Less well known but trendy varieties such as Marsanne, Roussanne, Malbec, Mourvèdre, Nebbiolo, Sangiovese, Barbera, Zinfandel, Grenache, and Cinsaut are starting to produce exciting wine. Lemberger, developed by Dr. Walter Clore *(see p. 90)* is making a strong comeback too. Big, brash, and fruity, it may turn out to be Washington's answer to California's Zinfandel. *gravels, sand, clay, basalt* *Merlot, Cabernet Sauvignon* *Chardonnay* *red, white*

A Cool Advantage

Washington's growing conditions are occasionally marred by vine-killing freezes, but the cold has its upside. The phylloxera louse *(see p. 11)* cannot cope with the extreme cold or sandy soils common to the Columbia basin, so Washington State remains phylloxera-free, allowing *vinifera* vines to be grown ungrafted on their own roots. Many winemakers believe that this results in healthier vines and grapes, which in turn produces purer characteristics akin to those found in 19th-century French wines before phylloxera devastated the vines there.

Washington's high level of sunlight hours is ideal for ripening thick-skinned grape varieties such as Cabernet Sauvignon

Semillon vineyard in Yakima Valley

Yakima Valley & Red Mountain

Hemmed in by the Rattlesnake and Horse Heaven hills, the relatively cool Yakima Valley was the first AVA to be designated in Washington State—in 1983. Silt loam soils dominate in the famous Otis, Red Willow, Sagemoor, Wycoff, Boushey, and Elerding vineyards. These focus on Chardonnay, Riesling, Merlot, Cabernet Sauvignon, and Cabernet Franc, but newcomers Pinot Gris, Sangiovese, Barbera, Syrah, Malbec, and Viognier are also on the increase. The hottest location within the Yakima Valley is the relatively new sub-AVA of Red Mountain (established in 2001). Its vineyards straddle a sharp bend in the Yakima River, made famous for producing ultra-ripe Bordeaux and Rhône varieties on its "roasted slopes". The free-draining vineyards are suited to Cabernet Sauvignon, Cabernet Franc, Merlot, Malbec, Viognier, and Syrah; Ciel du Cheval is its best vineyard. *gravels, clay, sand, basalt* *Merlot, Cabernet Sauvignon* *Chardonnay* *red, white*

Walla Walla

Established in 1984, Washington's Walla Walla AVA (the Native American name means "land of many waters") has a great concentration of boutique wineries. Ripe with potential, some of them are planted on ancient, infertile river beds peppered with cobbles. With Walla Walla's wide range of hot and cool mesoclimates, the harvest of a single variety can take up to three weeks from one side of the valley to the other. Pepper Bridge and Seven Hills Vineyards, among others, produce bold Cabernet Sauvignon and Merlot alongside frilly, racy Viognier and rich, smooth Syrah. *gravels, loess-based soils* *Cabernet Sauvignon* *Chardonnay* *red, white*

VINCENT GASNIER'S TOP 10 Best Wineries in the Pacific Northwest

1. **Argyle Winery** Willamette Valley *p106*
2. **Domaine Drouhin** Willamette Valley *p107*
3. **Cayuse Vineyards** Walla Walla *p104*
4. **Columbia Winery** Columbia Valley *p102*
5. **DeLille Cellars** Yakima Valley *p103*
6. **Ken Wright Cellars** Willamette Valley *p107*
7. **Woodward Canyon Winery** Walla Walla *p105*
8. **Ponzi Vineyards** Willamette Valley *p109*
9. **Chateau Ste. Michelle** Columbia Valley *p102*
10. **Elk Cove Vineyards** Willamette Valley *p107*

Wine Areas of Oregon

Oregon's first *vinifera* varieties were planted in the Rogue River Valley in 1854. As in Washington, Oregon's early wine industry was almost entirely focused on the *labrusca* variety Concord until the birth of cool-climate viticulture in the 1970s *(see p. 99)*. Since then, Pinot Noir has predominated.

From the outset, Oregon wineries have been mainly family operations with grapes grown on small plots of 4–20 acres (1.5–8 ha), and hand-picked. Viticulture follows traditional Burgundian practices; some vineyards are planted at a density of 1,200–1,800 vines per acre (3,000–4,500 per ha). And, as in Burgundy, the wine producers of Oregon have adapted to extreme vintage variations. Improved clonal selection of grapes, lower yields, and the influence of 20- to 35-year-old vines have now evened out annual variations and are delivering high levels of concentration and complexity.

Pinot Noir label, Eyrie Vineyards

Since 1979, when an Oregon wine came second in a famous blind tasting of Pinot Noirs from Burgundy and elsewhere *(see p. 99)*, the winemakers of Oregon have held firm. Unique in a world favouring homogeneous, hot-climate wine styles, they refuse to sell out and insist that one day their Pinot Noir wines will be as famous as Burgundy throughout the wine-drinking world.

The best Oregon wines are Pinots from the Willamette Valley, but Chardonnay is also showing great potential. Other interesting whites include early-picked Muscat and Pinot Gris.

Rogue, Applegate & Illinois River Valleys

Dwarfed by the Pinot Noir-dominated north, Rogue Valley AVA and subregions are now coming of age. With rainfall of 7–20 in (180–510 mm), Rogue Valley is markedly drier than Willamette Valley. Its huge range of elevated (1,000–2,500 ft / 310–780 m) vineyards and soil types presents unlimited possibilities. An early focus on Pinot Gris, Chardonnay, Sauvignon Blanc, and Pinot Noir is shifting into Sangiovese, Viognier, Syrah, Tempranillo, and Bordeaux varieties. Especially good are the ripe, finely structured, claret-like blends of Cabernet Sauvignon, Cabernet Franc, Merlot, and Malbec. The climate of Rogue Valley encourages these relatively hot-climate varieties to ripen slowly in the way that Pinot Noir does further north. The resulting intense varietal characters and finer structures are more typical of Washington than of Oregon.

Given the delicately aromatic, fine bodied, refreshingly tangy Viognier and richly ripe, tightly structured Syrah already evident here, the Rogue Valley could be Oregon's response to California's Rhône Rangers *(see p. 75)*.

Near the Californian border and closer to the ocean, gathering 35 in (890 mm) of rain annually, the Illinois River Valley, a subregion of Rogue Valley, favors northern Willamette varieties Riesling, Pinot Gris, Gewürztraminer, and Pinot Noir. *granite, mixed loams, clay* *Merlot, Cabernet Sauvignon* *Pinot Gris, Chardonnay* *red, white*

Umpqua Valley
Sandwiched between the north's warmer, wetter Pinot country and the higher, drier, Syrah vineyards to the south, this AVA has a transitional climate and is still finding its feet. Successful experimentation with Tempranillo, Syrah, Merlot, Dolcetto, Malbec, Cabernet Franc, Viognier, and Albariño suggests a way forward. *metamorphic, sedimentary, volcanic, alluvial* *Pinot Noir* *Chardonnay* *red, white*

Willamette Valley
Set between the Cascade and Coast ranges, the cool, wet Willamette Valley follows the course of the Willamette River for about 90 miles (150 km) from Eugene in the south to the Columbia River near Portland in the north. The valley contains about 70 per cent of Oregon's population, and the majority of the state's wineries. The mesoclimate is maritime-influenced, although the Coast range protects the valley from Pacific storms. The growing season is long and gentle; the winters wet and mild. Mature, multi-clone vineyards are planted in relatively infertile soil, mostly on gentle slopes, 295–700 ft (90–215 m) above sea level.

The wine industry of the Willamette Valley has been focused on Pinot Noir since the 1970s *(see opposite)*, and it is one of the world's finest sources for the variety. Forty years into the adventure, distinct *terroir* can now be readily tasted through single-vineyard bottlings from different parts of the valley and the foothills of the Coastal Range. AVA status has already been granted to **McMinnville**, **Dundee Hills**, and **Yamhill Carlton**, and it is pending for **Ribbon Edge**, **Chehalem Mountains**, and **Eola Hills**.

Tending Pinot Noir vines

With their focused fruit, delineated structure, and intense aromatics, the best Pinot Noirs of Oregon's Willamette Valley lean more toward the wines of Burgundy than those of the New World. Often needing four to seven years to open up, many are best left for two decades to develop fully.

Of other grape varieties planted in the valley, Gamay, Dolcetto, and St-Laurent are the most promising reds. The signature white and second most-planted grape is dry, freshly fruited, and richly textured Pinot Gris, although Pinot Blanc could eventually trump Pinot Gris with its racier acidity and its luscious peachy fruit. Commercially unfashionable, aromatic Rieslings and Gewürztraminers can show intensely focused, Alsace-like varietal characters. Growers have also adopted Dijon clones of Chardonnay after early plantings of "hot climate" Californian clones delivered tart, fruitless wine. Current models wear subtle Côte de Beaune-like fruits undercut by minerally, delicately floral, earthy aromatics, and tightly knit, steely acidity. *volcanic, granite, clay, marine sediment* *Pinot Noir & others* *Pinot Gris & Blanc, Chardonnay* *red, white*

The Birth of Cool-climate Viticulture

The thoroughly modern New World concept of cool-climate viticulture found its first footing in Oregon. Vitis vinifera *was introduced here by Henderson Luiellen in 1847 and Peter Britt in 1852, but few of the earliest wineries survived beyond Prohibition in the 1920s. It was not until the 1960s that serious viticulture in Oregon really took off, under the guidance of Richard Sommer and David Lett.*

Believing California's hotter climates were unsuited to grape varieties from Burgundy, Alsace, and Germany, these two visionary winemakers bucked conventional beliefs that Oregon was far too cool and damp to grow grapes, and headed north in search of slower, gentler ripening conditions, more akin to those found in Northern Europe.

Richard Sommer explored the Umpqua Valley first, successfully establishing the Hillcrest vineyard and the Riesling variety there in 1961. Taking a giant leap of faith into the considerably cooler, wetter, northern Willamette Valley, David Lett planted Pinot Noir, Pinot Meunier, Pinot Gris, Riesling, and Muscat at the Eyrie Vineyards (www.eyrievineyards.com) in 1965. Others soon followed.

David Lett's hunch ultimately paid off. In 1979, his 1975 Eyrie Vineyards Pinot Noir won second place at the Gault-Millau Wine Olympics in Paris, competing against a top flight of Burgundies, including Joseph Drouhin. Oregon was cast into the limelight as the first place outside Burgundy to produce Burgundy-style Pinot Noir.

Having bought heavily into a "Burgundian" climate, the Oregonians soon felt its downside: frost, rot, harvest rains, under-ripe and high-acid grapes, and extreme annual variations. Turning to Europe for practical help, rather than other New World areas, the Oregonians effectively opened up the first beach-head outside Europe for low-tech, Old-World winemaking practices. The Swiss taught them how to micro-manage vines, exposing the fruit to light and wind through leaf plucking. From the French they learned the importance of site selection and microclimates, close planting on slopes, good drainage, gentle handling, "cold soak" pre-fermentation maceration, and non-filtered, gravity-fed production. Eventually jettisoning their original "hot climate" Pinot Noir vines, Oregonian growers imported better suited "cool-climate" Dijon clones from Burgundy.

Oregon's experiments with Pinot Noir brought about the codification of cool-climate practices now commonly used throughout the New World. Burgundy producer Joseph Drouhin, having been caught out in the 1979 Wine Olympics, itself set up in Oregon in the 1980s *(see p. 107)*.

Young Pinot Noir vines in the cool Willamette Valley

Cool-climate viticulture requires a long, gradual ripening season in moderate temperatures to protect the delicacy of the fruit

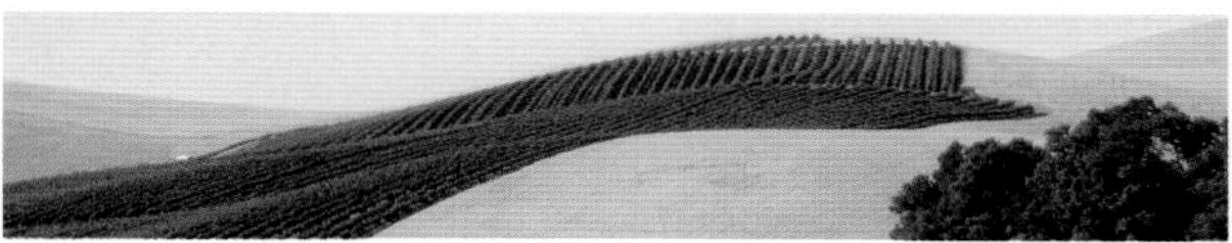

Vineyard in Yakima Valley, Washington

Major Producers in the Pacific Northwest

Chateau Ste. Michelle
Columbia Valley & other areas

This is Washington State's most famous and oldest winery (founded in 1933), and continues to take production very seriously. Château Ste. Michelle won a reputation in the early 1970s for low-priced, consistent varietals. Now its comprehensive portfolio of single-vineyard Chardonnays, Merlots, and Cabernets ranks among the USA's finest. White wines are produced under the direction of Erik Olsen, while reds are the responsibility of Ron Bunnell at the River Ridge plant. Both winemakers are given great freedom by the owner, Ste. Michelle Wine Estates *(see opposite)*, on condition that they excel, which they continually do. The magazine *Wine Spectator* gave its Single Berry Select the highest rating ever awarded to a wine from Washington, and more accolades are showered upon the winery every year. *14111 NE 145th Woodinville, WA • 425 488 1133 • www.ste-michelle.com* *red, white, ice wine ★ Single Berry Select, Eroica Riesling*

Geology of the Pacific Northwest

The viticultural regions of the Pacific Northwest have been shaped by huge flood erosion as well as ongoing volcanic activity (Mount St. Helen last erupted in 1982). Geological evidence shows that as glaciers retreated 16,000 years ago, Lake Missoula, one of the greatest ancient inland lakes, burst its ice dam, releasing a tsunami 200 ft (60 m) high and 12 miles (20km wide). This wave scoured out the massive Columbia Gorge, blasting westward through the Cascades' ancient basalt, and eventually depositing boulders and silt onto the Willamette Valley floor. In its wake it left a 245 ft- (75m-) deep gravel bed covering Columbia Valley, and shallow, stone-studded, free-draining, infertile, phylloxera-free, sandy topsoil—perfect for grape-growing.

Columbia Winery
Columbia Valley

Originally known as Associated Vintners, this historic winery was created by a group of visionary amateur winemakers in 1962, who were convinced—correctly, as events have proven—that European *vinifera* grape varieties could thrive in the state. Called Columbia Winery since 1983, it is now owned by the mighty Constellation Brands. However, under the winemaking guidance of Master of Wine David Lake since 1979, the company retains a human touch, making characterful, varietally correct, and flavor-filled wines. Lake always pushes the boundaries: after introducing Cabernet Franc, Syrah, and Pinot Gris to Washington, he helped to establish exotic varieties such as

Preceding pages **Cabernet Franc vineyard at Woodward Canyon Winery in Walla Walla, Washington**

Sangiovese and Barbera, and led the way with *terroir*-distinct, single-vineyard wines. *14030 NE 145th St, Woodinville, WA • 425 488 2776 • www.columbiawinery.com red, white ★ Cabernet Franc, Viognier, Syrah*

McCrea Cellars
Columbia Valley
Former saxophonist Doug McCrea riffs his way through Syrah, Grenache, Viognier, Mourvèdre, Roussanne, and Counoise at his winery; sometimes blending, other times focusing on getting the most out of the varietal. With fruit grown primarily in Red Mountain, his range includes an elegantly styled French-oaked Syrah: Amerique, an American-oaked Syrah, Cuvée Orleans Syrah (with Viognier); Boushey Grande Côte Syrah; and spicy, stone fruit-driven Viognier. *13443 SE 118th Ave, Rainier, WA • 800 378 6212 • www.mccreacellars.com by appt red, white ★ Syrah, Syrah-Grenache, Syrah-Viognier*

Ste. Michelle Wine Estates
Columbia Valley & other areas
Known as Stimson Lane Estates until 2004, this smartly branded company owns Chateau Ste. Michelle *(see opposite)*, the name of which has inspired the rebranding. The company also owns Columbia Crest, Domaine Ste. Michelle, Snoqualmie, Stimson Estate Cellars, and other Washington wineries that together produce over half of the wine ouput of the state. Columbia Crest, set up as a volume label in 1984, is now a high-quality producer in its own right. Still in a period of growth, Ste. Michelle owns several Californian wineries and has ties with Antinori of Italy (the Col Solare label) and Dr. Loosen of Germany *(see box p. 104)*. *14111 NE 145th St, Woodinville, WA • 425 488 1133 • www.ste-michelle-wine-estates.com red, white ★ Merlot, Riesling, Chardonnay*

Columbia Crest, Ste. Michelle Wine Estates

DeLille Cellars
Yakima Valley
DeLille Cellars produced Washington's first ever Meritage, and continues to churn out densely packed, unfiltered, long-lived Bordeaux-style blends from impeccably grown, site-specific fruit. Low yields, merciless grape sorting, and declassification of any substandard lots ensure excellence. Chaleur and Harrison Hill, both intense, savoury Cabernet blends, complement D2, a smooth, gamey Merlot-led wine. The Graves-influenced Sauvignon-Sémillon blend and the peppery, dusty tannined Doyenne (mainly Syrah) are equally compelling. *14208 NE Redmond Rd, Woodinville, WA • 425 489 0544 • www.delillecellars.com by appt red ★ Chaleur, D2, Doyenne*

Outstanding Pinot Noir Wines

1. **Acacia** Napa Valley *p. 45*
2. **Kistler** Sonoma *p. 54*
3. **Williams Selyem** Sonoma *p. 55*
4. **Goldeneye (Duckhorn)** Napa Valley *p. 39*
5. **Patz & Hall** Napa Valley *p. 42*
6. **Bergström** Willamette Valley *p. 106*
7. **Ponzi** Willamette Valley *p. 109*
8. **Calera** Mount Harlan *p. 82*
9. **Laetitia Estate** San Luis Obispo *p. 87*
10. **Sanford** Santa Barbara County *p. 86*

A bottle of Columbia Crest 2002 Walter Clore Private Reserve sold for an unprecedented $100,000 in a Houston Wine Auction in March 2006

Hedges Cellars

Red Mountain

The wines made by Hedges Cellars are built to last: they are densely packed with savory aromas, condensed flavors, juicy textures, and firm tannins. Top wines include a sweetly ripe, early-drinking Columbia Valley blend (Merlot-Cabernet Sauvignon-Cabernet Franc-Syrah), and the meaty, tightly wound Three Vineyards and complex, floral Red Mountain Reserve (both blends of Cabernet Sauvignon-Merlot). Intense, pure Cabernet Sauvignon and earthy, tightly knit Merlot are also noteworthy, as is the port-style wine made with genuine Portuguese varieties such as Touriga Nacional and Sousão. *195 NE Gilman Blvd., Issaquah, WA • 425 391 6056 • www.hedgescellars.com* red, fortified ★ *Cabernet Sauvignon, Merlot & blends*

Washington's Eroica

Before Allen Shoup established Long Shadows *(see opposite)*, while he was still at Stimson Lane *(see Ste. Michelle p. 103)*, he had formed partnerships in the 1990s with several prominent Old-World winemakers. One of these, Dr. Ernst Loosen of the famous 200-year-old Riesling estate in the Mosel Valley of Germany, was invited to help create a top-notch Washington Riesling that could educate American palates about the potential of a grape that is often disappointing in the US. The result of the collaboration was Eroica, first released in 1999, and named after Beethoven's Third Symphony. The success of Eroica—now overseen by Bob Bertheau at Chateau Ste. Michelle, and the Loosen Estate in Germany—has encouraged Washington growers to expand their plantings of Riesling as quickly as possible.

Washington Hills Cellars

Yakima Valley & Red Mountain

Washington Hills' branding offers a full range of excellent value wines. Basic Washington Hills delivers crisp, quaffable styles, strong on Riesling, Chenin Blanc, and Gewürztraminer. Midrange Bridgman consistently overdelivers, with sassy Cabernet Franc; tart, peachy Viognier; cherrylike Sangiovese; and mango-infused Sauvignon Blanc. The Apex Reserve Syrah has layers of pepper, liquorice, and savory black fruit, while Apex Gewürztraminer icewine is pure, expensive, and worth every cent. *111 E Lincoln Ave., Sunnyside, WA • 1 800 814 7004 • www.washingtonhills.com* *red, white, dessert, icewine* ★ *Syrah, Gewürztraminer, Cabernet Franc*

Canoe Ridge Vineyard

Walla Walla

This important vineyard in the upper Columbia Gorge takes its name from a crest of land named by 19th-century explorers Lewis and Clark for its resemblance to an overturned canoe. California's Chalone Wine Group, which established the vineyard in 1990, makes deeply perfumed, velvety, Pinot Noir-like Merlots and crisp, delicate Chablis-style Chardonnays. *1102 W Cherry, WA • 509 527 0885 • www.canoeridgevineyard.com* *red, white* ★ *Merlot, Chardonnay, Cabernet Sauvignon*

Cayuse Vineyards

Walla Walla

Dubbed the "Bionic Frog" in Australia's Barossa Valley, and now proudly sporting WWSYRAH license plates on his Ford pickup, international *terroir*-ist vigneron Christophe Baron infuses Walla Walla with Gallic flair and charm. Farmed biodynamically and fermented with indigenous yeasts,

his unfiltered, unfined, single-vineyard wines reek of originality, personality, and authenticity. Abhorring "Mike Tyson-style wines that knock you out," Baron likes to create food-friendly styles that "excite the taste buds and stimulate the intellect." *17 E Main, WA • 509 526 0686 • www.cayusevineyards.com* *by appt.* *red, white* ★ *Syrah, Syrah-Viognier*

L'Ecole No. 41
Walla Walla

Inhabiting the town of Lowden's original schoolhouse (hence the name), long-established L'Ecole makes excellent age-worthy tank- and barrel-fermented Semillons. The top reds are a finely structured Merlot and an expansive, creamy, unfiltered Apogee Merlot-Cabernet blend. The meaty, smooth, viscous Walla Walla Cabernet Sauvignon and inky Syrah, packed with dried black fruits and well-managed tannins, are also of note. *41 Lowden School Rd., WA • 509 525 0940 • www.lecole.com* *red, white* ★ *Semillon, Syrah, Apogee*

Long Shadows Vintners
Walla Walla

For 20 years, Allen Shoup was chief winemaker at Stimson Lane (now called Ste. Michelle; *see p. 103)*, where he collaborated with international wine stars *(see box opposite)* and helped to shape the Washington wine industry. Shoup retired from Stimson Lane in 2000, then set up Long Shadows, which is a consortium of leading winemakers (ones who have cast "long shadows" in the wine world), including Michel Rolland, based in Pomerol, France; Armin Diel of Germany; and John Duval of Penfolds, Australia. These highly regarded consultants were invited by Shoup to choose sites in the Columbia Valley where they could focus on supreme single varietals or blends. Of the six boutique wineries established by 2006, the Pedestal Merlot, made under Rolland's guidance, Duval's Sequel Syrah, and Diel's Poet's Leap Riesling had all received high praise. Quantities are small—no more than a few hundred cases from each winery in each vintage—and offered by mailing list first, before general release to selected outlets. *P. O. Box 33670, Seattle, WA • 206 396 9628 • www.longshadows.com* *red, white* ★ *Feather, Pirouette, Pedestal, Poet's Leap, Chester-Kidder, Sequel*

Artist Series #8
woodward canyon
1999
Washington Cabernet Sauvignon
Alcohol by Volume 13.9%
Contains Sulfites

Woodward Canyon Winery Artist Series label

Woodward Canyon Winery
Walla Walla

The high-density, low-yield vines of this pioneering boutique winery, established by Rick Small in 1981, produce complex, silky, seamless wines. Winemaking here is noninterventionist: wines are unfiltered, unfined, never acidified, and never overdone. Famous for elegantly styled, earthy Celilo Chardonnay, floral, velvety Merlot, and powerful, tannic, Old-Vines Cabernet Sauvignon, Woodward Canyon is now exploring Walla Walla's potential for Barbera, Dolcetto, and Pinot Noir. *11920 W Hwy. 12, Lowden, WA • 509 525 4129 • www.woodwardcanyon.com* *red, white* ★ *Celilo Chardonnay, Cabernet Sauvignon, Merlot, Columbia Valley "Old Vines"*

Amity Vineyards

Willamette Valley

This quirky, veteran 1970s-era producer consistently makes complex, age-worthy, old-vine Pinot Noir, richly fruited Gamay, and exemplary, varietally correct aromatics: dry Riesling, Gewürztraminer, and Pinot Blanc. It is also noteworthy for one of the world's few sulfur-free wines, the organic Pinot Noir—labeled Eco-Wine—and the winery's early period Oregon-funk architecture. *18150 Amity Vineyards Rd., Amity, OR • 888 264 8966 • www.amityvineyards.com* ☐ *red, white* ★ *Pinot Noir, Gewürztraminer, Pinot Blanc*

Archery Summit Winery

Willamette Valley

This massive French château-inspired, gravity-fed winery, underground cellar, and high-density vineyard provide a counterpoint to neighboring Domaine Drouhin on the Dundee Hills skyline. With a dollop of California gloss, it produces a range of intensely fruity, spicily oaked, single-vineyard Pinot Noirs. *NE Archery Summit Rd., Dayton, OR • 503 864 4300 • www.archerysummit.com* ☐ *red* ★ *Pinot Noir*

The Marriage of Burgundy and Oregon

Domaine Drouhin and many other Oregon wineries on these pages have successfully married some of the techniques of Burgundy with Oregon. Vines are planted at a much higher density than is the norm in the New World (almost four times as much), and sometimes with Burgundy-style trellising, which results in small vines with intensely flavored fruit. Grapes are handpicked and hand-sorted, and often fermented in oak barrels shipped over from France. The results are impressive.

Argyle Winery

Willamette Valley

Australia's first wine foray into the US focused the attention of winemaker Brian Croser of Petaluma on making top-quality Oregon sparkling wine using the traditional method of bottle fermentation. Current winemaker Rollin Sales gathers accolades for richly fruited Chardonnays and Pinot Noirs. The portfolio includes balanced sparkling Blanc de Blancs, rosé, and vintage wines, all with clear cool-climate character and rich autolytic notes. *691 S Pacific Hwy., Dundee, OR • 888 417 4953 • www.argylewinery.com* ☐ *red, white, sparkling* ★ *Blanc de Blancs, Chardonnay, Pinot Noir*

Beaux Freres

Willamette Valley

Michael Etzel cultivates the same varietal on the same small stretch of land year after year. Beaux Freres, which Etzel co-owns with superstar wine critic Robert Parker, adheres to Burgundian wine growing and production methods. These, combined with Etzel's devotion to *terroir*-specificity, have made Beaux Freres the producer of one of the US's finest Pinot Noirs. *15155 NE North Valley Rd, Newberg • 503 537 1137 • www.beauxfreres.com* ☐ *red* ★ *Beaux Freres Pinot Noir, Belles Soeurs Pinot Noir.*

Bergström Winery

Willamette Valley

Although this winery was founded in 1997 by John and Karen Bergström, it is their son and winemaker Josh who provides its energy and direction. Bergström's vineyards are not unique among Willamette producers in being laid out to Burgundian specifications; but very few are tended by someone like Josh, who inspects

his land at least once every 14 days in order to reposition leaves so that they are facing the optimal direction. *18405 NE Calkins Lane, Newberg • 503 544 0468 • www.bergstromwines.com* ☐ red
★ *Bergström Whole Cluster, Arcus Vineyard, Cumberland Reserve*

Domaine Drouhin
Willamette Valley

French *négociant* (wine merchant) Joseph Drouhin was amazed by the quality of Oregon wine at the 1979 Paris Wine Olympics *(see p. 99)*, and marked the first Burgundian foray into the New World in 1987, with the establishment of Domaine Drouhin in Oregon's Willamette Valley. Drouhin planted a plot of Chardonnay and Pinot Noir with double the usual US vine density and filled his tastefully designed, gravity-fed winery with state-of-the-art French technology. Marrying French soul to Oregon soil, this US arm of Drouhin produces elegant, underplayed, generously fruited, multilayered benchmark Pinot Noirs, and highly underrated, understated, earthy Dijon-clone Chardonnays. Expensive but worth it, the reserve Pinot, Laurène, is made only in the best years. *6750 Breyman Orchards Rd., Dundee, OR • 503 864 2700 • www.domainedrouhin.com* ☐ *by appt.* *red, white* ★ *Pinot Noir, Chardonnay*

Elk Cove Vineyards label

Elk Cove Vineyards
Willamette Valley

Founded in 1974 by Pat and Joe Campbell, Elk Cove is still proudly owned and operated by the Campbell family, with son Adam in charge of the winemaking. Typical of Oregon's early quality producers, Elk Cove's production evolved from estate-bottled Pinot Noir into a variety of subregionally distinct single-vineyard wines, La Bohème and Dundee Hills being the more famous. The Pinot styles consistently err on the side of subtlety, balance, and elegance, often with an impressive silky texture. The best will age for about two decades. Dry, late-harvested Riesling, Gewürztraminer, and Pinot Gris can be outstanding value, and the Syrah and Viognier from Rogue Valley's Del Rio Vineyard also show promise. *27751 NW Olson Rd., Gaston, OR • 877 355 2683 • www.elkcove.com* ☐ *red, white* ★ *Pinot Noir, Gewürztraminer, Pinot Gris*

Ken Wright Cellars
Willamette Valley

Reversing traditional pricing arrangements, which were based on tonnage, it was Ken Wright who negotiated the US's first price-per-acre contracts in the 1980s, allowing winemakers to determine concentration, quality, and ripeness. Oregon's leading *terroir*-ist, Wright produces 8–12 very low-yield single-vineyard Pinot Noirs, each clearly delineating a wide range of soil types and microclimates. His Tyrus Evan Rogue Valley label offers a massively fruited, tightly structured Cabernet Franc, a fine-grained Malbec, a savory, claretlike Bordeaux blend, and a creamy, superripe Pinot-style Syrah. All suggest that Rogue Valley could rival Willamette's reputation for Pinot Noir. *236 N Kutch St., Carlton, OR • 503 852 7070 • www.kenwrightcellars.com* ☐ *by appt.* *red, white* ★ *Pinot Noir, Pinot Blanc*

The barrel store at Panther Creek Cellars

Lemelson Vineyards
Willamette Valley

Eric Lemelson designed his winery in 1997 with the ambition of constructing the perfect Pinot Noir production facility. It was, he believed, what the fruit of his six vineyards deserved, with their carefully chosen differences of soil and elevation. The resulting facility turned out to be one of Oregon's most sophisticated gravity wineries. The jewel in its crown is the world's only mobile sorting platform—a 13-ft (4-m) high metal structure that allows the operator to glide above the stainless-steel fermentation tanks for precise sorting of grape clusters and other processes. The single-vineyard and reserve Pinots vary in quality from year to year, but usually receive great acclaim. Some whites are also produced.
12020 NE Stag Hollow Rd., Carlton • 503 852 6619 • www.lemelsonvineyards.com ☐ *red, white* ★ *Jerome Reserve Pinot Noir, Resonance Pinot Noir, Lemelson Chardonnay*

Owen Roe Winery
Willamette Valley & other areas

Co-owned by Jerry Owen and winemaker Jerry O'Reilly, Owen Roe sources its grapes from vineyards in Oregon's Willamette Valley and Washington's Columbia Valley, including Walla Walla, to add variety to their range (O'Reilly's, Owen Roe Woodcut, and Photograph labels). O'Reilly claims that he entered the wine business to discover truth and reality in nature; the demand for the 45,000 cases that the winery produces each year suggests that he at least discovered the truth and reality of making popular wines. *31590 NE Schaad Rd., Newberg • 503 678 6514 • www.owenroe.com* ☐ *red* ★ *Abbot's Table, Sharecropper's Pinot Noir*

Panther Creek Cellars
Willamette Valley

Ken Wright built Panther Creek's reputation through a series of unfiltered, high-quality, low-yield single-vineyard Pinot Noirs. Since Wright's departure in the mid-1990s to set up his own winery *(see p. 107)*, Panther Creek has continued to produce generously fruity, well-balanced, smartly structured, ageworthy wines under the direction of winemaker Michael Stevenson and consultant Mark Vlossak. *455 North Irvine St., McMinnville OR • 503 472 8080 • www.panthercreekcellars.com* ☐ *red, white* ★ *Pinot Noir, Melon, Pinot Gris*

Ponzi Vineyards
Willamette Valley
One of Oregon's Pinot Noir pioneers of the early 1970s, Ponzi continues to improve the quality and breadth of its range. Its Pinot Noir consistently ranks as one of Oregon's most reliable and complex wines: silky smooth and dressed in smoky bacon and mushroom savouriness. Pinot Gris, Chardonnay, Arneis, and late-harvest Riesling all show rich texture and clean, well-outlined ripe fruit. *14665 SW Winery Lane, Beaverton OR • 503 628 1227 • www.ponziwines.com* *red, white* ★ *Pinot Noir, Pinot Gris, Arneis*

WillaKenzie Estate
Willamette Valley
In 1992 Burgundian Bernie Lacroute traded his career developing computer companies for one growing vines with organic techniques. His handsome gravity-fed winery produces richly fruited, fine-grained Pinots Noir, Pinot Gris, and Meunier; a powerful Gamay; and the country's first screw-capped Pinot Noir. The wines consistently deliver more than might be expected at such good prices. *19143 NE Laughlin Rd., Yamhill, OR • 503 662 3280 • www.willakenzie.com* *red, white* ★ *Pinot Noir, Gamay, Pinot Meunier*

Willamette Valley Vineyards
Willamette Valley & other areas
Now NASDAQ-listed with 4,500 shareholders, this winery offers a range of single-vineyard Pinot Noir styles from organically managed, mature vines in the Willamette Valley. The purchase of Tualatin Vineyards ensures a supply of old-vine fruit, while the Rogue Valley-focused Griffin Creek label offers a delicate Viognier and well-rounded Syrah with plenty of ripe fruit. Visionary management and smart winemaking deliver well-priced, well-made wine. *8800 Enchanted Way SE, Turner, OR • 503 588 9463 • www.wvv.com* *red, white* ★ *Pinot Noir, Pinot Gris, Viognier*

Willamette Valley Vineyards label

Abacela Vineyards
Umpqua Valley
After a long search throughout the US for a suitable climate for Tempranillo, Abacela settled on the Umpqua Valley's south-facing, rocky hillsides. It is hard to find anything drab in the range: alongside the Tempranillo are Syrah, Merlot, Dolcetto, Grenache, Sangiovese, and Malbec, and also great whites like Albariño and Viognier. *12500 Lookingglass Rd., Roseburg, OR • 541 679 6642 • www.abacela.com* *red, white* ★ *Syrah, Tempranillo, Malbec*

VINCENT GASNIER'S TOP 10 Fabulous Fortified Wines

1. **Dolce** Napa Valley *p. 38*
2. **Hedges Cellars** Red Mountain *p. 104*
3. **Justin Vineyards** Paso Robles *p. 82*
4. **Quady Winery** Central Valley *p. 87*
5. **Merryvale** Napa Valley *p. 41*
6. **Cedar Mountains** Livermore Valley *p.87*
7. **Windsor Vineyards** Sonoma *p. 55*
8. **Joseph Filippi** Southern California *p. 87*
9. **Guenoc Estate** Lake County *p. 63*
10. **Terre Rouge** Sierra Foothills *p. 86*

ATLANTIC NORTHEAST & OTHER REGIONS

Introduction
112–113

Wine Map of
New York State
114–115

Wine Areas of
New York State
116–118

Major Producers
in New York State
120–123

Other Wine Regions
of the US
124–125

ATLANTIC NORTHEAST

THE ATLANTIC NORTHEAST *is the oldest viticultural region in the US, but harsh winters have prevented its wine industry from developing to the degree of that in California. It was not even until the late 1950s that European vines were planted instead of native varieties. Today, New York State contains the region's most important vineyards, while Virginia possibly has the greatest potential.*

The eastern seaboard of North America has a greater variety of microclimates and soils than the West Coast, which would allow it to rival California as quality wine country were it not for the harsh winters here. The seasonal frosts render grafted vines vulnerable to damage, and so consequently it is the native *labrusca*—a hardy vine—that has historically been grown in these parts. The *labrusca* varieties include Concord, Catawba, Ives, Delaware, and Niagara, and they tend to produce overly sweet, highly aromatic wines. These have never really found favor with the majority of wine lovers.

Key

New York State

Such vines were, however, grown for several centuries, the first vineyard having been planted on Long Island by the Dutch in the 17th century—although records state that it failed to survive the winter. By the 1800s hybrids flourished across New York State, thanks to horticulturalists who crossed thousands of European *vinifera* varieties with the sturdier native vines. The temperance movement caused a temporary halt to the development of wine production, emerging in the early 20th century to lay the blame for society's ills at the door of alcohol. In 1919 Prohibition *(see p. 119)* effectively crushed the wine industry; until the law reverted in 1933 and alcohol was redeemed, growers survived by making juice and sacramental wines and selling grapes to illicit winemakers.

New York State

The 1950s were a turning point for winemaking in New York State. Konstantin Frank, a professor of plant science at the New York State Viticultural Research Station, started to expound his beliefs that Old-World *vinifera* such as Riesling, Pinot Noir, and Chardonnay could thrive in the cold Finger Lakes area of New York State. His opinions were based on research he had conducted in Odessa in his native Ukraine. Charles Fournier, the president of Gold Seal, New York's top winery at the time, took a gamble and hired the visionary émigré as his director of research. Dr. Frank successfully grafted *vinifera* vines onto hardy American rootstock. In the great freeze of February 1957—when the state's *labrusca* vines failed to produce grapes—Frank's Riesling and Chardonnay vines were hardly damaged

Dr. Konstantin Frank label

Preceding pages **Vineyard and traditional building at Keuka Lake in the Finger Lakes area**

Vineyard above Canandaigua in the Finger Lakes region

and went on to produce a bumper crop. Frank dubbed his achievement "the second discovery of America."

Dr. Frank's success in introducing European grape varieties to New York state was surprisingly not followed by large-scale plantings of *vinifera* varieties by the major wine companies. Instead, the production of decent wine stayed largely in the hands of small producers. In 1976, new legislation permitted such wineries to sell directly to customers, making their businesses more economically viable. As a result, the industry exploded: by 2003 there were 177 wineries in New York State, compared with 19 in 1976. New York State's output is now fourth in the US after California, Washington, and Oregon, and its reputation for sweet, cheap, and kosher wines for immigrant Jews is consigned to history. Boutique winemakers growing individual *vinifera* varieties work for passion and prestige here. Handcrafted European-style Riesling, Cabernet Franc, Chardonnay, and Merlot rule the roost and are gradually building an international reputation.

The Great Lakes

Inland, the northern states of Michigan, Ohio, and Pennsylvania border the Great Lakes, which create microclimates tempering the extremes of winter and providing conditions in which European grapes can flourish. The state of Michigan, for example, now has more than 90 wineries near the shore of Lake Michigan (which very rarely freezes), some producing creditable Chardonnay, Riesling, Gamay, and Merlot wines.

Virginia

Farther south, Virginia's hot and humid weather during the growing season and at harvest time hampers grape-growing. However, with the use of improved canopy management, several wineries out of the 100 or so established in Virginia are producing excellent wines, the majority sited in the Monticello AVA. Virginia now follows New York State with the fifth largest wine output in the US. As viticultural techniques and technology advance, Virginia is likely to be an exciting area in the future. It has even been tipped as the next Napa Valley.

Global beverage giant Constellation Brands owns major administrative operations but relatively few vineyards in New York State

Wine Map of New York State

Between the shores of Lake Erie and the eastern tip of Long Island are four major American Viticultural Areas (AVAs). Lake Erie is the biggest, but most of its output is grape juice. Some 300 miles (500 km) west of New York City, near Ithaca, is the scenic, noteworthy Finger Lakes area; north of Manhattan is the Hudson River Valley; and to the east is "New York's Bordeaux"–Long Island's North Fork–and the South Fork, known as The Hamptons. Central New York State is developing as a wine region, but has not yet been designated an AVA.

MAIN AVAS & MAJOR PRODUCERS

Long Island *pp. 116–117*

Bedell Cellars *p. 120*
Palmer Vineyards *p. 120*
Paumanok Vineyards *p. 120*
The Lenz Winery *p. 120*
Wölffer Estate *p. 121*

Hudson River Valley *p. 117*

Finger Lakes *pp. 117–118*

Centerra Wine Company *p. 121*
Château LaFayette Reneau *p. 122*
Dr. Konstantin Frank *p. 122*
North Lake Wines *p. 122*
Standing Stone Vineyards *p. 123*

Lake Erie *p. 118*

Johnson Estate *p. 123*

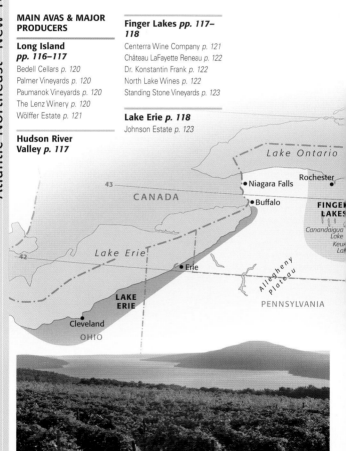

Vines growing by the shore of one of the Finger Lakes in New York State

Good recent vintages in the Atlantic Northeast include 1995, 1998, 1999 (white), 2000, 2001, 2004, and 2005

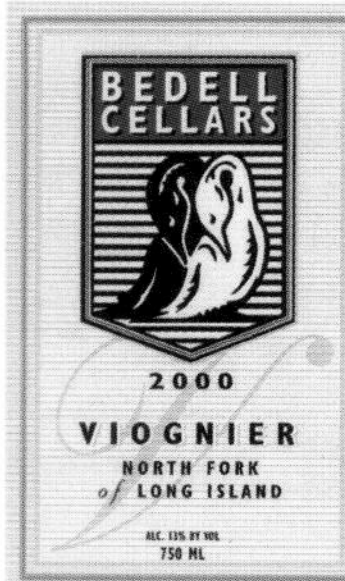

Bedell Cellars label

Regional Information at a Glance

Latitude 40.5–43°N.

Altitude 0–800 ft (245 m).

Topography Diverse terrain. Ice-age glaciers left behind a landscape of sloping hillsides, deep valleys, and bodies of water ranging from the carved-out Finger Lakes to the wide, majestic Hudson River.

Soil Deep, well-drained, glacial soils, silt, and loam composition.

Climate Cool nights and warm, but not hot, days characterize these wine districts, all of which benefit from a lake, river, or ocean effect.

Temperature July average is 75°F (24°C).

Rainfall Annual average is 36–44 in (915–1,120 mm).

Wind Lake and ocean breezes keep wine regions cooler in summer. In winter, warm southwesterly winds from the Atlantic moderate temperatures.

Viticultural Hazards Black rot; insects; bird damage; hurricanes.

Long Island vineyard

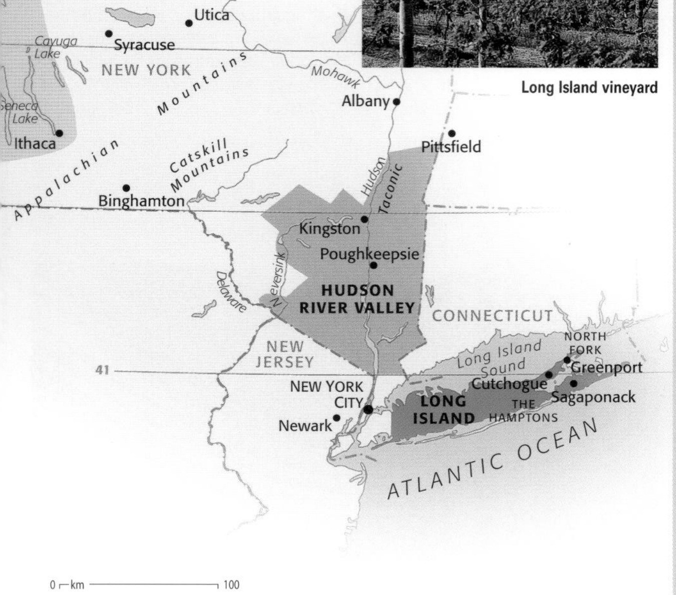

Wine Areas of New York State

LONG ISLAND

Today, burgeoning Long Island lays claim to 52 vineyards on two peninsulas, exclusively growing the classic European grape varieties, such as Cabernet Sauvignon, Merlot, Chardonnay, and Riesling. The North Fork area of the island, a slim strip bounded by Long Island Sound, Peconic Bay, and the Atlantic, holds the majority of these interesting viticultural zones. So far, no problem with the *phylloxera* aphid has emerged anywhere on Long Island. It is ironic that while troubled California is forced to replant its old louse-weakened vines, the relatively young Long Island vines will soon come to surpass them in maturity.

fertile sand, loam, silt *Merlot, Cabernet Sauvignon, Cabernet Franc*
Chardonnay, Gewürztraminer, Riesling
red, white, rosé, sparkling, dessert

Bedell Cellars label, North Fork

North Fork

Rave reviews continue to pour in for North Fork wines. Many of Manhattan's best restaurants have been quick to include these local wines on their lists.

Vineyards were attempted in this region in the 17th century, but it was not until 1973 that Alex and Louisa Hargrave successfully planted the first *vinifera* vines on their potato farm in Cutchogue. Over the years they were forced to battle a range of droughts, diseases, and hurricanes. In 2003, Long Island grandly celebrated the 30th anniversary of the Hargraves' success (even though the couple sold the winery in 1999).

The pioneering spirit of these agriculturalists has inspired other winemakers who now produce world-class Cabernet Sauvignon, Merlot, Bordeaux-style blends, and Chardonnay. The top producers of

Vineyard on the west side of Lake Keuka

North Fork—Bedell Cellars and The Lenz Winery *(see p. 120)* among them—exhibit elegant European-style leanings over bold California-style wines. With a long growing season of 215–235 days (up to three weeks longer than the island's South Fork), the North Fork enjoys a lengthy period of freeze-free temperatures. Salt-spraying hurricanes and sporadic droughts pose an ongoing threat to the harvest, but it is the flocks of ravenous starlings and robins that have been more destructive. Netting the vines seems to be the best solution to the problem, albeit an expensive one.

Barrels outside the Lenz Winery, North Fork, Long Island

The Hamptons

Famous for its swanky mansions and glamorous summer parties, The Hamptons is also a surprisingly productive agricultural area, settled by European immigrant farmers in the 17th century. The deep, well-drained soil is loam-rich, and consequently needs less irrigation than the vineyards of the North Fork. Of the three wineries on the South Fork—Wölffer Estate *(see p. 121)*, Channing Daughters, and Duck Walk—Wölffer is the most ambitious and accomplished; its Chardonnay and Merlot show satisfying depth and balance.

Perhaps the reason for The Hamptons' dearth of wineries is the prohibitive cost of property here. What was once a charming collection of sleepy maritime villages, favored by New York artists wishing to chill out, is now an area swimming with boutiques, restaurants, and nightclubs. It is a particularly heady place on summer weekends, even without wine.

HUDSON RIVER VALLEY

Grapes have been grown in the lush, bountiful Hudson River Valley for 300 years, and the region is home to Brotherhood, America's oldest continuously operating winery. Brotherhood is one of the few wineries that lasted through Prohibition, which it did by making sacramental and "medicinal" wines. Native American grape varieties such as Delaware, Concord, Catawba, and Niagara dominate here, as well as French-American hybrid Seyval Blanc.

The vast valley, which is scattered with lovely river-straddling cities, is on a latitude parallel with northern Spain, though it has a shorter growing season. Nearly 30 wineries are in operation, focusing on light-bodied, fruity wines. Millbrook Vineyards and Winery is the region's flagship producer, making a sprightly Tocai Friulano and textbook Cabernet Franc, among other varietals. *glacial deposits of shale, slate, limestone* *Pinot Noir, Cabernet Franc* *Chardonnay, Tocai Friulano, Seyval Blanc* *red, white*

FINGER LAKES

Ice-age glaciers gouged out the 11 Finger Lakes in west central New York. The four largest resemble the tapered fingers of the Great Spirit described by Iroquois legend—hence the lakes' native names.

French-American hybrid grape varieties grown in New York State include Seyval Blanc, Vidal Blanc, Chelois, Baco Noir, and Aurore

Vineyards above Canandaigua Lake in the Finger Lakes

More than 80 wineries have tamed this former wilderness, taking advantage of the ideal growing conditions for a staggering variety of grapes. Lakes with sloping hillsides buffer extremes in temperature during winter and summer, and the 190-day-plus growing season contributes to outstanding ripening conditions for Riesling, Gewürztraminer, and Pinot Noir. Sparkling wines are another forte, and Glenora Wine Cellars in Dundee is one of the largest producers in the east US.

Along the southeastern shore of Seneca Lake is the so-called "banana belt," a viticultural phenomenon that boasts the highest daytime temperatures and longest growing season of all the Finger Lakes. The heaviest concentration of wineries is in this pocket, including Wagner Vineyards, Château LaFayette Reneau, Standing Stone Vineyards, Silver Thread Vineyard, and Red Newt Cellars. The mesoclimate seems to coax Gewürztraminer and Riesling to their most vibrant, honeyed heights, while also adding intensity to reds such as Merlot and Cabernet Sauvignon.

Central New York State, a region of pastoral farmland just to the east of the Finger Lakes region, is now undergoing strong development as a viticultural area, but it has yet to win AVA status. With well over a dozen wineries currently in operation—some of which buy in grapes from other regions—the area is starting to show promise. *shallow topsoil on sloping shale beds* *Cabernet Franc, Pinot Noir, Merlot, Cabernet Sauvignon* *Chardonnay, Riesling, Gewürztraminer* *red, white, sparkling, dessert*

LAKE ERIE

Lake Erie is a multistate AVA, covering 40,000 acres (16,188 ha) in New York, Pennsylvania, and Ohio. Since the 19th century, native *labrusca* grape producers have cornered the market here, making this the US's grape juice capital. Local wine production reflects that tradition, putting out wines that are juicy and sweet.

Increasingly, however, French-American varieties, such as Seyval Blanc and Vidal Blanc, and noble grapes such as Riesling and Chardonnay, are being widely planted. Of the dozen or so wineries here, Johnson Estate and Merritt Estate are the biggest, oldest, and most respected. The lake offers a unique macroclimate—extended summer sunlight, few thunderstorms, constantly flowing air that minimizes botrytis and other fungal problems—but severe winter weather menaces vines about every three years. *gravel-and-shale soils of glacial origin* *Chancellor, Merlot, Cabernet Sauvignon* *Chardonnay, Riesling, Vidal Blanc* *red, white, sparkling, dessert*

Prohibition

The Prohibition era lasted from January 1920 to December 1933, during which time the manufacture and sale of intoxicating liquors were outlawed. It was a disaster for the domestic wine industry, and even beyond those 14 "dry" years, Prohibition dramatically influenced the nation's relationship with alcohol.

Survival

Although the 18th Amendment to the US Constitution ushered in national Prohibition, there were legal loopholes that permitted a few wineries to continue limited operation. Some produced dried "grape bricks" for home wine production, which was permitted, while a few producers were designated to make wine for sacramental and medicinal purposes.

Illegal drinking

Despite the efforts of police, Prohibition was widely flouted. The production and sale of wine, beer, and liquor were widespread, though the supply of bootleg liquor was largely in the hands of criminals.

Aftermath

The 21st Amendment to the Constitution ended Prohibition. Each state is now responsible for its own system of alcohol distribution and sales. All states operate a tiered system, whereby producers must sell to wholesalers, who sell to retailers, who then sell to consumers. In some areas, known as control states, it is the state itself that is the wholesaler and retailer.

The Temperance Movement

America's rapid, "Wild West" expansion had made the 19th century a chaotic time, and World War I increased the sense of social strife. The temperance movement was born out of a grassroots reaction to this disorder, and concern about alcohol abuse became a key issue. However, after it became clear that Prohibition also had many negative effects, leaders of the temperance movement called for reform, and the laws were changed again.

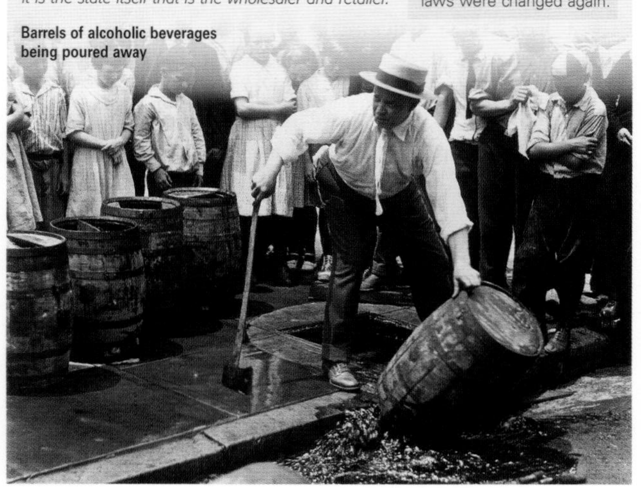

Barrels of alcoholic beverages being poured away

Left **Fox Run bottles** Right **Wölffer Estate**

Major Producers in New York State

Bedell Cellars

Long Island/North Fork

From small beginnings making wine in his basement, Kip Bedell founded this acclaimed winery in 1980. He realized that the North Fork's cool climate and well-drained soils were ideal for Merlot, and his Merlot wines are consistently delicious: mouth-filling and silky with hints of raspberry and black cherry. Michael Lynne, wine aficionado and Co-CEO of New Line Cinema, acquired Bedell Cellars in 2000, with Bedell remaining as winemaker alongside John Irving Levenberg, who has worked in Bordeaux, New Zealand, and the Napa Valley. Lynne also bought the Corey Creek and Wells Road vineyards, signaling a new era of big business. Bedell Cellars now makes plummy Bordeaux-style wine, complex Cabernet Sauvignon, and lightly oaked Chardonnay. The limited edition Artist Series wines feature labels designed by artists such as Barbara Kruger and Eric Fischl.

36225 Main Rd., Cutchogue • 631 734 7537 • www.bedellcellars.com red, white, rosé, dessert ★ Merlot, Corey Creek Chardonnay, C-Block South Merlot, Main Road Red, Main Road White

Bedell Cellars

Palmer Vineyards

Long Island/North Fork

Palmer makes some of Long Island's best-known wines. Owner Robert Palmer's experience as an ad man helps, but the round-but-not-opulent Chardonnay and silky, smoky, black cherry Cabernet Franc live up to the hype. The tasting house, an 18th-century period farmhouse, is worth a visit. *108 Sound Ave., Aquebogue • 631 722 9463 • www.palmervineyards.com red, white, rosé, sparkling ★ Cabernet Franc Reserve, Chardonnay Reserve*

Paumanok Vineyards

Long Island/North Fork

Taking its name from the Native American word for Long Island, Paumanok, founded by Ursula and Charles Massoud in 1983, is a real family affair. Ursula was born into a line of German winemakers, and the couple's three sons are also passionately involved in the winery. Charles's smooth Merlot and rich Cabernet Sauvignon are consistently good, as is his juicy, melony Chardonnay; the Cabernet Franc is supple with savory hints of tobacco. Charles is also one of the few in New York State to make Chenin Blanc, with crisp citrus and peach flavors.

1074 Main Rd., Rte. 25, Aquebogue • 631 722 8800 • www.paumanok.com red, white ★ Merlot, Chenin Blanc

The Lenz Winery

Long Island/North Fork

Founded in 1978, Lenz has some of the most mature vineyards on Long Island. The amazing Old Vines Merlot, from some of the oldest Merlot vines known to have been planted in North America, is spicy and voluptuous with hints of charcoal. In 1996, owners Peter

and Deborah Carroll were so confident that Lenz's wines could compete with the world's best, they instigated public blind tastings to prove it. Indeed, the Merlots and Chardonnays made news by standing up to higher-priced French and California rivals. Long Island wines had landed, and the Carrolls have never looked back. *Main Rd., Rte. 25, Peconic • 631 734 6010 • www.lenzwine.com* *red, white, sparkling* ★ *Old Vines Merlot, Gewürztraminer, White Label Chardonnay*

Wölffer Estate
Long Island/The Hamptons
International business magnate Christian Wölffer lavished millions on this Tuscan-style winery in the heart of The Hamptons. The estate's world-class equestrian center and venue for lavish social events ensure its popularity with the wealthy locals. As for the wines, German-born winemaker Roman Roth's European-style, food-friendly tipples are classically elegant. They range from a well-structured Premier Cru Merlot (retailing at $100), with its lush berry flavors that promise to age well, to a more modest rosé evoking roses and citrus, which is perfect for a picnic. *139 Sagg Rd., Sagaponack • 631 537 5106 • www.wolffer.com* *red, white, rosé, sparkling* ★ *Estate Selection Merlot, Reserve Chardonnay, Cabernet Franc*

Centerra Wine Company
Finger Lakes
Owning about 50 brands, including Paul Masson fortified wines and Inglenook, Centerra is one of the biggest US wine companies and itself owned by global beverage giant Constellation Brands. Many of the wines are made in California, while the Finger Lakes operation is mainly administrative, but there are two local wineries: Canandaigua and Widmer's. *116 Buffalo St., Canandaigua • 888 659 7900 • www.cwine.com* *Widmer's* *red, white, dessert, sparkling, fortified* ★ *Robert Mondavi Private Selection, Woodbridge by Robert Mondavi, Turner Road, Talus Collection*

Touring the Wine Districts of New York State

New York State's picturesque wine districts are well worth exploring by car. Wineries that are open to the public are clearly signposted by road signs bearing clusters of grapes. Scores of wineries hug the shores of Lake Seneca and other Finger Lakes. The **Hermann J. Wiemer Vineyard**, run by a celebrated master of Riesling, offers self-guided vineyard walks. **Wagner Vineyards** has a restaurant and tasting room where you should try its smoky, plummy Meritage, a Bordeaux blend, and its tangy, spicy Riesling Icewine. Also in the Finger Lakes is **Glenora Wine Cellars**, which features a fine restaurant and inn with breathtaking views. This is a leader in the region for its impressive sparkling wines, especially Riesling and Gewürztraminer. **Millbrook Vineyards & Winery**, in the Hudson River Valley, hosts concerts, outdoor films, and giant harvest parties. On the upmarket Long Island tasting circuit, the **Pindar** and **Pellegrini** vineyards are key players, with live music, food festivals, and deluxe wine-and-food pairing dinners.

Millbrook Vineyards & Winery

For addresses and websites of the wineries above, **See p. 123**

Chateau LaFayette Reneau
Finger Lakes

The *terroir* of South Seneca Lake enriches LaFayette Reneau's structured, German-style Riesling, and full-bodied Merlot with mocha and black cherry undertones. The Pinot Noir has lively hints of raspberry and cherry, and the Cabernet Sauvignon is layered with plum, leather, and chocolate. Winemaker Tim Miller often wins medals for his wines, and owners Dick and Betty Reno run a small inn with panoramic lake views. *Rte. 414, Hector • 607 546 2062 • www.clrwine.com* *red, white, rosé, sparkling, dessert* ★ *Cabernet Sauvignon, Merlot, Johannisberg Riesling*

Up-and-coming Producers in New York State

Some of New York State's finest producers are relative newcomers to the scene, or have such a limited output that they are virtually unknown outside the local area. **Schneider Vineyards** is a North Fork Cabernet Franc specialist of note. In the Finger Lakes, **Shalestone Vineyards** and **Silver Thread Vineyard** sell 90 percent of the wine they make on site: Shalestone produces five stirring, well-structured reds from European *vinifera* varieties, while so far Silver Thread is the only local winery to take a wholly organic approach to winemaking, and makes delicious Riesling and Pinot Noir. Finger Lakes winemaker David Whiting is another star: having done stints at Château LaFayette Reneau and Standing Stone Vineyards *(right)*, he opened **Red Newt Cellars** in 1999 and makes compelling, diverse varietals. **Fox Run Vineyards**, also in the Finger Lakes, excels at floral, fruity Riesling, and has been expanding its output with Gamay, Merlot, Cabernet Franc, and Gewürztraminer grape varieties.

Fox Run bottle

Dr. Konstantin Frank
Finger Lakes

The professor of plant science, Dr. Frank, who founded this seminal winery in 1962 *(see p. 112)*, knew how to farm with minimal use of chemicals. So does his grandson Fred: he spreads hay across fields to restore soil nutrients and builds birdhouses to encourage birds which control insects. The wines include full, earthy reds, crisp, ripe Rieslings, Rkatsiteli, a vibrant, appley grape of Georgian origin, and toasty sparkling wines that often outscore pricier French examples. *9749 Middle Rd., Hammondsport • 607 868 4888 • www.drfrankwines.com* *red, white, sparkling* ★ *Château Frank Brut, Rkatsiteli, Cabernet Sauvignon*

North Lake Wines
Finger Lakes

Owned by Constellation Brands, North Lake is a sibling of the Centerra Wine Company *(see p. 121)*. Under its umbrella are 35 wine brands, including Paul Masson table wines, Taylor California Cellars, Taylor New York, and the new California label Smashed Grapes, as well as a number of imported wines. *235 North Bloomfield, Canandaigua • 866 334 9463 • www.nlwines.com* *red, white, sparkling, dessert* ★ *Dunnewood Vineyards, Belaire Creek, Foolish Oak*

Standing Stone Vineyards
Finger Lakes

Standing Stone's spicy, golden, pungent Gewürztraminer is arguably the best in the US. Tom and Marti Macinski's wines are

beautifully complex. The garnet-hued, red currant-flavored Pinnacle (a Bordeaux-style blend), and cherry-chocolatey Cabernet Franc are of note. The couple bought the pioneering Gold Seal winery land in 1991, inheriting New York State's first plantings of European *vinifera* varieties of grapes. The site is small—just 40 acres (16 ha)—but bursting with potential. *9934 Rte. 414, Hector • 800 803 7135 • www.standingstonewines.com red, white, dessert ★ Gewürztraminer, Pinnacle, Cabernet Franc*

Johnson Estate
Lake Erie
Aurore, Chambourcin, Ives Noir – the tradition of weird-sounding but well-made Native American and French-American hybrid grape varieties is proudly upheld at Johnson, the oldest family-owned estate winery in New York State (1961). Semisweet, fruity wines such as the fun and lively Seyval Blanc are the specialty. The Freelings Creek Merlot evokes cherry pie, and the French-American hybrid Chancellor is a more austere red with good acidity. Johnson Estate is also one of the wineries on the US side of the Great Lakes making icewine *(see p. 132)* from grapes that have frozen on the vine. The luscious Vidal Blanc Icewine is made from a French-American hybrid descended from Ugni Blanc vines grown in southern France. *8419 West Main Rd., Westfield • 716 326 2191 • www.johnsonwinery.com red, white, rosé, sparkling, dessert, icewine ★ Vidal Blanc Icewine, Chancellor, Seyval Blanc*

Other Producers in the Atlantic Northeast

Am Rhein Wine Cellars *(Virginia) 243 Patterson Drive, Bent Mountain • 540 929 4632 • www.roanokewine.com*

Breaux Vineyards *(Virginia) Breaux Vineyards Lane, Purcellville • 540 668 6299 • www.breauxvineyards.com*

Chateau Grand Traverse Winery *(Michigan) Center Rd., Traverse City • 231 223 7355 • www.cgtwines.com*

Cooper Vineyards *(Virginia) Shannon Hill Rd., Louisa • 540 894 5253 • www.coopervineyards.com*

Fox Run Vineyards *(Finger Lakes, NY) 670 Rte. 14, Penn Yan • 800 636 9786 • www.foxrunvineyards.com*

Glenora Wine Cellars *(Finger Lakes, NY) 5435 Rte. 14, Dundee • 800 243 5513 • www.glenora.com*

Hermann J. Wiemer Vineyard *(Finger Lakes, NY) Rte. 14, Dundee • 800 371 7971 • www.wiemer.com*

Keswick Vineyards *(Virginia) Keswick • 434 244 3341 • www.keswickvineyards.com*

Millbrook Vineyards & Winery *(Finger Lakes, NY) 26 Wing Rd., Millbrook • 800 662 9463 • www.millbrookwine.com*

Pellegrini Vineyards *(Long Island, NY) 23005 Main Rd., Cutchogue • 631 734 4111 • www.pellegrinivineyards.com*

Pindar Vineyards *(Long Island, NY) Main Rd., Peconic • 631 734 6200 • www.pindar.net*

Red Newt Cellars *(Finger Lakes, NY) 3675 Tichenor Rd., Hector • 607 546 4100 • www.rednewt.com*

Schneider Vineyards *(North Fork, NY) 2248 Roanoke Ave., Riverhead • 631 727 3334 • www.schneidervineyards.com*

Shady Lane Cellars *(Michigan) Shady Lane, Suttons Bay • 231 947 8865 • www.shadylanecellars.com*

Shalestone Vineyards *(Finger Lakes, NY) 9681 Rte. 414, Lodi • 607 582 6600 • www.shalestonevineyards.com*

Silver Thread Vineyard *(Finger Lakes, NY) 1401 Caywood Rd., Lodi • 607 582 6116 • www.silverthreadwine.com*

St. Julian Wine Company *(Michigan) 716 South Kalamazoo St., Paw Paw • 269 657 5568 • www.stjulian.com*

Wagner Vineyards *(Finger Lakes, NY) 9322 Route 414, Lodi • 607 582 6450 • www.wagnervineyards.com*

OTHER WINE REGIONS OF THE US

THE WINE LAWS IN THE US ALLOW ANY STATE *to be recognized as its own viticultural area. Consequently, almost every state in the US has some kind of winemaking industry. These wines can be made either from grape-vines–such as* vinifera *or* labrusca*–or from other types of soft fruit, such as citrus fruit. The most prominent of these regions are covered here.*

Texas

Arguably the most successful fledgling winemaking state is Texas, growing from being the smallest wine area in 1983 to the fifth largest today. The history of wine in Texas is actually older than that of California. Sacramental wines were made here by Franciscan monks in the 1650s—no fewer than 130 years before they were made in California. In the mid-19th century German settlers discovered the indigenous Mustang grape, which is still used to produce wine today. The first commercial winery in Texas was Val Verde, founded in 1883.

Key

• Other wine regions

Before Prohibition the Texas wine industry was blossoming; there were 19 wineries by 1919, and a Texas wine secured a gold medal at the Paris Exposition. The state's post-Prohibition revival began in the mid-1950s when a professor of viticulture, Robert Reed, planted some vine cuttings in his garden. He then went on to experiment with several different grape varieties until, in 1987, the potential of Texas as a promising viticultural area was recognized by the French. In that year, famous Bordeaux *négociant* (merchant house) Cordier bought 1,000 acres (405 ha) of land at Fort Stockton for a vineyard, called Ste. Geneviève. By 2006 there were about 100 wineries in the state.

The soil in Texas tends to be sandy loam topsoil with clay subsoils in the valley areas. Cabernet Sauvignon, Semillon, Chardonnay, and Riesling all grow successfully.

Florida

French Huguenots made wine at Fort Caroline in 1564, which in theory makes Florida the oldest winemaking state in the US. However, little else happened in the way of viticulture until the end of the 19th century, when new settlers from other parts of the country brought *labrusca* and Muscadine traditions with them. Today, Florida has a successful fruit wine industry. "Orange wine" is especially popular, alongside wines made from Key lime, mango, or passion fruit. Many growers have tried and failed to succeed in growing *vinifera* grapes, which succumb easily to disease in Florida's warm, moist climate. However, proving that the pioneer spirit is not dead, the number of wineries in the state is growing.

Other States

In **Minnesota** growers bury their vines under several feet of soil to help them survive the winter months. Consequently, native varieties and hybrids prevail, although one notable exception is

Winery building at Becker Vineyards, in the emerging wine state of Texas

Northern Vineyards where wines are made from own-grown *vinifera* varieties such as Chardonnay, Gewürztraminer, Pinot Gris, and Pinot Noir.

These same grape varieties are successfully grown in **Montana**, even though the growing season is too short for grapes. Mission Mountain Winery has won some acclaim for its wines made in Montana, although it often has to supplement them with grapes grown outside the state.

The desert state of **Nevada** is another environment where the growing season is too short and grapes really should not grow. However, the first experiments in vine-growing began here in 1992, giving rise to several new vineyards over the next decade.

New Mexico is another state with a very old winemaking tradition—16th-century Spanish settlers made sacramental wines in the Rio Grande Valley, and their European vines are still the source of many of the wines produced by approximately 20 wineries today.

In the 19th century **Wisconsin** was the place where the famous Agoston Haraszthy *(see p. 22)* planted his first vineyard before moving on to the easier climate of California. Modern-day growers in Wisconsin have to be prepared to see their vines suffer winter damage. It is mainly fruit wines that dominate here, but Wisconsin has also seen some success with the early-ripening varieties of Riesling and Vidal Blanc.

Producers in Other Regions

Becker Vineyards *(Texas) Stonewall, Gillespie County • 830 644 2681 • www.beckervineyards.com*

Chautauqua Vineyards *(Florida) 364 Hugh Adams Rd., DeFuniak Springs • 850 892 5887 • www.chautauquawinery.com*

Flat Creek Estate *(Texas) Singleton Bend East, Marble Falls, Burnet County • 512 267 6310 • www.flatcreekestate.com*

Florida Orange Groves *(Florida) 1500 Pasadena Avenue S., St. Petersburg • 800 338 7923 • www.floridawine.com*

Llano Estacado Winery *(Texas) FM 1585, Lubbock • www.llanowine.com*

Mission Mountain Winery *(Montana) Flathead Lake, Dayton • 406 849 5524 • www.missionmountainwinery.com*

Northern Vineyards Winery *(Minnesota) 223 N. Main St., Stillwater • 651 430 1032 • www.northernvineyards.com*

San Sebastian Winery *(Florida) 157 King Street, St. Augustine • 888 352 9463 • www.sansebastianwinery.com*

Sea Breeze Winery *(Florida) 13201 Hutchison Blvd., Panama City Beach • 850 230 3330 • www.seabreezewinery.com*

Ste. Genevieve Winery/Cordier Estates *(Texas) Fort Stockton • 800 336 2166*

WINES OF CANADA

Introduction
128–129

Wine Areas of Canada
130–131

Major Canadian Producers
132–133

CANADA

WITH ITS HOT, HUMID SUMMERS and icy cold winters, Canada may not appear to have the ideal conditions in which to make fine wine. But in the last 30 years there has been a wine revolution in the country. A number of forward-thinking winemakers planted cool-climate grape varieties in the 1970s and 80s, and these 20- to 30-year-old vines are now producing wines on a par with the rest of the winemaking world.

History

Canada's first *vitis vinifera* grape vines were planted by European settlers in the early 1800s. But while native species of grape vines were flourishing in the wild, the imported vines succumbed to disease too easily. Table wines made from the native, mainly *labrusca*, grape varieties turned out to have a rather strange taste, but when fortified into sherry or port styles they became much more palatable. With a steady export market to England, the Canadian wine industry was born.

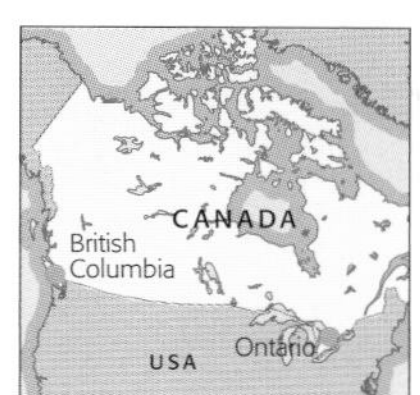

Key

Canadian wine regions

From 1900 to 1950 the Canadian wine producers faced the same problems as their US neighbors—namely Prohibition and two world wars—which limited further developments in the industry. By the 1960s, however, the world wine market shifted toward drier table wines with a lower alcohol content. At the same time, technological advances in the vineyard introduced disease-resistant clones so that by the 1970s European grape varieties were thriving in Canada.

Best Canadian Reds

1. **Mission Hill: Merlot** Okanagan
2. **Cedar Creek: Pinot Noir** Okanagan
3. **Blue Mountain: Pinot Noir** Okanagan
4. **Jackson-Triggs: Shiraz** Okanagan
5. **Nichol: Merlot** Okanagan
6. **Quails' Gate: Cabernet Sauvignon** Okanagan
7. **Sumac Ridge: Cabernet Sauvignon** Okanagan
8. **Inniskillin: Cabernet Franc** Niagara
9. **Thirty Bench: Cabernet Franc** Niagara
10. **Chateau des Charmes: Cabernet Franc** Niagara

See pp. 132–3 for all

The Wine Industry Today

In 1988 Canada signed a free trade agreement with the US. In order to compete in the new market conditions, the better Canadian wine producers realized that they needed to increase their efforts to produce premium wines. To that end, growers in Ontario and British Columbia pulled out their native grape varieties and replaced them with *vinifera* grapes such as Chardonnay and Pinot Noir. Also in 1998, the Vintners Quality Alliance was launched in Ontario. This group of dedicated winemakers agreed to comply with a set of quality standards in order to improve the quality of Canadian wines overall and to assure consumers of that quality.

Preceding pages **Okanagan Valley vineyard, British Columbia**

Mission Hill vineyard, Oliver, British Columbia

Since 1988 Canadian winemakers have increasingly produced wines of complexity and structure. The number of commercial wineries now exceeds 100, and the VQA standard is recognized by consumers worldwide. Sales of VQA wines were over 10 million liters by the year 2000.

Grape Varieties & Wine Styles

Riesling is currently the most successful white grape variety, particularly in Ontario where it produces long-lived, crisp, dry wines with hints of lime and grapefruit, as well as honeyed late harvest dessert wines, and the unique icewine *(see p. 132)*. Chardonnay is producing wines ranging from gently oaked versions, using either American or French oak, to crisp, unoaked versions, creamy Sur Lies (wine that is left on lees, then bottled without racking), and sparkling wines. In British Columbia, Pinot Blanc and Pinot Gris are appearing with depth and complexity. Rich, lychee-laden Gewürztraminers and aromatic Sauvignon Blancs are also coming to the fore.

As for the red varieties, Pinot Noir is showing such promise that Burgundy producer Boisset has teamed up with Vincor, Canada's largest producer, to build a winery in Niagara for it. Cabernet Franc is being used as a varietal wine in its own right, producing light, raspberry and spice versions as well as richer wines with chocolate and cassis overtones. Merlot is the top red varietal grown in British Columbia, producing velvety varietal wines with rich plum fruit.

The VQA Standard

The Vintners Quality Standard (VQA) is Canada's symbol of quality wine and is similar to other regulatory systems such as the AOC system in France. The symbol is used on wine bottles to assure consumers of high-quality production, content, varietal percentage, appellation, and vintage. Ontario and British Columbia are currently the only Canadian areas that produce wines meeting the VQA standard. If a specific appellation, such as Okanagan Valley, is used, it means that the wine is a minimum of 85 percent from Okanagan Valley, and only classic *vinifera* varieties have been used. An estate-bottled wine must be 100 percent from grapes owned or controlled by the winery specified. Wines designated by vineyard names must be 100 percent from grapes grown in the vineyard specified.

The Canadian wine industry is forecast to grow by 10 percent annually up to 2010

Wine Areas of Canada

With the exception of some small-scale producers in Nova Scotia and Quebec, virtually all Canadian premium wine is produced from grapes grown in the provinces of Ontario and British Columbia.

ONTARIO

Sandwiched between lakes Ontario, Huron, and Erie, Ontario has about 15,000 acres (6,000 ha) of vineyards, which lie on a similar latitude to Tuscany. It is only the snow-filled winters that stop Ontario from being as successful as California. Conversely, it is also the snow-filled winters that allow for the annual production of Ontario's celebrated icewine *(see p. 132)*, which is made from frozen grapes. The Great Lakes are largely responsible for Ontario's temperate climate, which allows several *vinifera* varieties to ripen successfully. There are three designated Viticultural Areas (VA).

Best Canadian Whites

1. **Lake Breeze: Pinot Blanc** Okanagan
2. **Mission Hill: Chardonnay** Okanagan
3. **Blue Mountain: Pinot Gris** Okanagan
4. **Jackson-Triggs: Viognier** Okanagan
5. **Quails' Gate: Chenin Blanc** Okanagan
6. **Sumac Ridge: Pinot Blanc** Okanagan
7. **Konzelmann: Chardonnay** Niagara
8. **Peninsula Ridge: Chardonnay** Niagara
9. **Cave Springs: Riesling** Niagara
10. **Malivoire: Moira Vineyard Gewürztraminer** Niagara

See pp. 132–3 for all

Niagara Peninsula

Bordered by Lake Ontario to the north and the Niagara River to the east, the Niagara Peninsula is the largest VA in Canada, accounting for 80 percent of the country's grape-growing volume. The vineyards here are protected by the famous Niagara Escarpment, a 1,100 ft- (335 m-) high ridge that creates a constant air flow over the vines. Lake Ontario acts as a sort of hot-water bottle, keeping air temperatures relatively warm across the region in winter, and preventing harsh frosts in spring when the vines are budding. Icewine is the flagship wine of the Niagara Peninsula, but some excellent wines are also produced from Riesling, and several other varieties are showing great promise. *sandy loam, gravel, sand-and-clay* *Cabernet Sauvignon, Cabernet Franc, Merlot, Gamay, Pinot Noir* *Chardonnay, Riesling, Auxerrois, Vidal, Gewürztraminer, Pinot Blanc* *red, white, sparkling, Icewine*

Lake Erie North Shore

About 500 acres (200 ha) of vines are situated along the north shore of Lake Erie. The southern exposure of the vineyards, and the warming effect of the lake, gives this VA interesting potential for the future. *sandy loam, gravel, clay* *Cabernet Franc* *Riesling, Vidal, Pinot Gris* *red, white*

Pelee Island

On approximately the same latitude as Rome, Pelee Island, 15 miles (25 km) off the shore in Lake Erie, is Canada's most southerly point. It has 500 acres (200 ha) under vine; *vitis vinifera* varieties were planted in 1980. *sandy loam to gravel* *Cabernet Franc* *Riesling, Chardonnay* *red, white*

BRITISH COLUMBIA

Four Viticultural Areas have been designated in British Columbia. The Okanagan and Similkameen valleys enjoy hot, dry summers because they are protected by the coastal mountain range. Heat during the day quickly builds up sugars in the grapes, while low temperatures at night allow the grapes to retain high acidity levels. Each VA has its own microclimate.

Okanagan Valley

Grapes were first grown in the Okanagan Valley in the mid-19th century. Today, the 100 mile- (160 km-) long valley is planted with 3,700 acres (1,500 ha) of premium varieties, making it British Columbia's largest and oldest grape-growing region. At the valley's southern end, near the US border, the red Bordeaux varieties such as Cabernet Sauvignon and Merlot are successful. Pinot Gris, Pinot Blanc, and Chardonnay thrive in the center. Farther north, the climate is cooler and more suited to German varieties such as Siegerrebe. *glacial stone, fine sand, silt, and clay in the north; sand and gravel in the south* *Pinot Noir, Cabernet Sauvignon, Cabernet France, Merlot* *Pinot Blanc, Pinot Gris, Chardonnay, Riesling, Siegerrebe, Sylvaner, Optima, Ortega* *red, white, sparkling, Icewine*

Similkameen Valley

Lying to the west of the Okanagan Valley, Similkameen follows the course of a river valley surrounded by steep hillsides. Only two wineries are located in this Viticultural Area. About 200 acres (80 ha) of vines are planted along the river's edge. *predominantly sand and gravel*

Vancouver Island

Situated off British Columbia's southwest coast, Vancouver Island is the province's newest wine region. The wet and windy climate might not seem conducive to growing wine grapes, but Vancouver Island already has more wineries than the Similkameen Valley and threatens to become British Columbia's second largest Viticultural Area in terms of vineyard area. *sandy loam or gravel* *Pinot Noir* *Pinot Blanc, Auxerrois, Ortega, Muller-Thurgau* *red, white, sparkling*

Fraser Valley

Lying east of Vancouver near the US border, Fraser Valley is British Columbia's most southerly wine region. Sylvaner, Optima, and Gewürztraminer are grown here, and there are trials with Pinot Noir. *sandy loam* *Pinot Noir* *Sylvaner, Optima, Gewürztraminer* *red, white*

Southern tip of Okanagan Valley, near the US border

Left **Burrowing Owl Winery** Right **Mission Hill Winery**

Major Canadian Producers

Cave Springs
Niagara

This large winery was founded in 1986. The vineyards are located on the Beamsville Bench, which is suited to aromatic *vinifera* varieties. *Jordan, Ontario • 905 562 3581 • www.cavespringcellars.com by appt. red, white ★ Riesling Off Dry, Indian Summer, Riesling Reserve*

Chateau des Charmes
Niagara

Established by Paul Bosc, who comes from a long line of Alsace winemakers, and run by his son, this winery excels with red wine styles and also makes a decent bubbly. *1025 York Rd., Niagara-on-the-Lake, Ontario • 905 262 5548 • www.chateaudescharmes.com by appt red, white, sparkling, dessert, icewine ★ St. David's Bench, Paul Bosc*

Icewine

Based on the German *Eiswein*, Canadian icewine is produced mainly from Vidal and Riesling. The harvest cannot take place until the temperature has dropped to at least 17°F (-8°C), usually in December and January. The grapes are allowed to freeze on the vine, then picked and pressed by hand. Because the water content of the grapes is frozen, it can be drawn out easily, leaving a concentrated mix of natural sugars and acidity. Riesling icewines are lusciously sweet with tropical flavors of guava and mango. Vidal icewines have honeysuckle, peach, and pear flavors.

Inniskillin
Niagara & Okanagan

On July 31, 1975, Karl Kaiser and Donald Ziraldo were granted the first winery license to be issued in Ontario since 1929. Since then, the pair have helped to bring the Canadian wine industry to the international wine stage. Their 1989 Icewine won the Grand Prix d'Honneur at Vinexpo in Bordeaux. Dozens of other labels include Inniskillin's Single Vineyard Series chosen from exceptional sites in the Okanagan Valley and Niagara Peninsula. *Niagara-on-the-Lake, Ontario • 905 468 2187 • www.inniskillin.com by appt. red, white, icewine ★ Silver Label Single Vineyards, Gold Label Founders' Reserves*

Jackson-Triggs
Niagara & Okanagan

Don Triggs and Allan Jackson are among the heavyweights of the Canadian wine industry, and their wines have won international acclaim. About 30 styles are produced from their estates in the Okanagan Valley and Niagara Peninsula. *2145 Regional Rd., Niagara-on-the-Lake, Ontario • 866 589 4637 • www.jacksontriggswinery.com red, white, rosé, sparkling, dessert, icewine ★ Propietors' Grand Reserve, Sun Rock Vineyard, Delaine Vineyard*

Blue Mountain
Okanagan

This winery released its debut vintage in 1991. The Pinot Gris was dull and toffeelike at first but now is one of BC's finest. The

In 1988, before the VQA was established, there were a dozen Okanagan wineries; now there are more than 50

sparkling wines have benefited from the guidance of Raphael Brisbois, formerly at Omar Khayyam in India and Iron Horse in California. There is also a fine Pinot Noir made by Blue Mountain. *Okanagan Falls, BC • 250 497 8244 • www.bluemountainwinery.com ☐ by appt. red, white, sparkling, rosé ★ Brut, Cream Label, Stripe Label*

Burrowing Owl
Okanagan

Located on the eastern side of the Okanagan Valley, Burrowing Owl's first wines were produced in 1997 by Jim Wyse with the help of Californian winemaker Bill Dyer. All of the varietals have won awards. *Oliver, BC • 877 498 0620 • www.burrowingowlwine.ca ☐ red, white ★ Meritage, Cabernet Franc, Chardonnay*

Mission Hill
Okanagan

Mission Hill started to win medals after New Zealander John Simes took over in 1992. Oculus is a Bordeaux-inspired blend; the SLC labels are the premium wines. *Westbank, Okanagan Valley, BC • 250 768 7611 • www.missionhillwinery.com ☐ by appt. red, white, icewine ★ Five Vineyards, Oculus, SLC Icewine*

Quails' Gate
Okanagan

The Stewart family planted their vineyards in the 1960s but it was only in the 1990s, after the arrival of Australian-born winemaker Jeff Martin, that the quality rapidly improved. The Family Reserve whites are among Canada's finest. *3303 Boucherie Rd, Kelowna, BC • 250 769 4451 • www.quailsgate.com ☐ by appt red, white, dessert, icewine ★ Family Reserve Chenin Blanc, Limited Release Cabernet Sauvignon, Allison Ranch Chardonnay, Riesling Icewine*

Icewine from Mission Hill

Sumac Ridge
Okanagan Valley

Sumac Ridge was the first Canadian winery to create Meritage wines—a blend of traditional Bordeaux varieties—and also the first in British Columbia to try the traditional, bottle-fermented method of sparkling wine, which is showing promise. The winery's Gewürztraminer Private Reserve is as good as those from Alsace. *Summerland, BC • 250 494 0451 • www.sumacridge.com ☐ by appt. red, white, rosé, dessert, sparkling, icewine ★ Black Sage Vineyard, Cellar Selection*

Other Canadian Producers

Cedar Creek *(Okanagan) Lakeshore Rd., Kelowna, BC • 800 730 9463 • wwwcedarcreek.bc.ca*

Henry of Pelham *(Niagara) Pelham Rd., St. Catherines, Ontario • 905 684 8444 • www.henryofpelham.com*

Konzelmann *(Niagara) Lakeshore Rd., Niagara-on-the-Lake, Ontario • 905 935 2866 • www.konzelmannwines.com*

Lake Breeze Vineyards *(Okanagan) Naramata, BC • 250 496 5659*

Malivoire *(Niagara) King St. East, Beamsville, Ontario • 866 644 2244 • www.malivoirewineco.com*

Nichol Vineyards *(Okanagan) Smethurst Rd., Naramata, BC • 250 496 5962*

Peller Estates *(Niagara) John St. East, Niagara-on-the-Lake, Ontario • 905 468 4678 • www.peller.com*

Peninsula Ridge *(Niagara) King Street West, Beamsville, Ontario • 905 563 0900 • www.peninsularidge.com*

Reif Estate *(Niagara) Niagara-on-the-Lake, Ontario • 905 468 7738 • www.reifwinery.com*

Stoney Ridge Cellars *(Niagara) King Street, Vineland, Ontario • 905 562 1324 • www.stoneyridge.com*

Thirty Bench *(Niagara) Mountainview Rd., Beamsville, Ontario • 905 564 1698 • www.thirtybench.com*

Inniskillin, Sumac Ridge, and Jackson-Triggs are owned by Vincor, the largest Canadian wine conglomerate

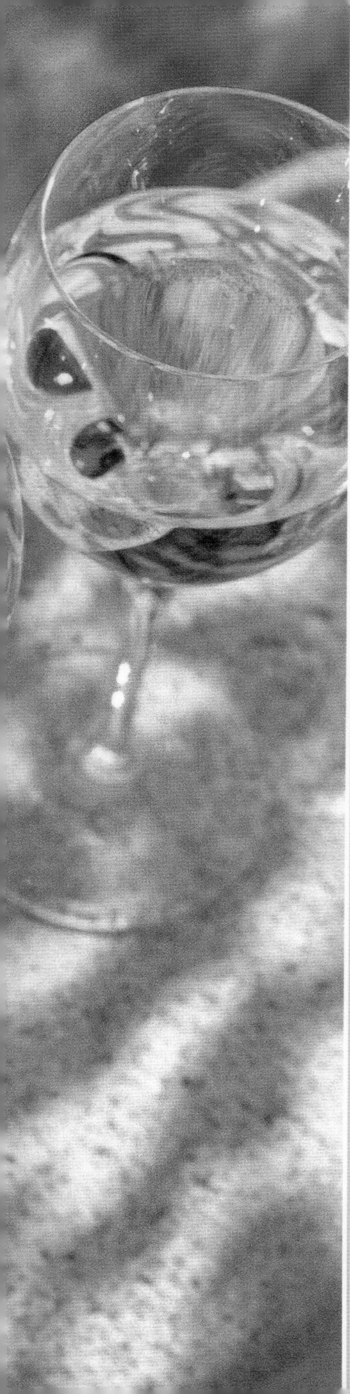

Wine Styles 136–137

Tasting Wine 138–141

Wine and Food Matching 142–144

Buying Wine 145

Storing and Serving Wine 146–147

Glossary 148–153

Index 154–159

Acknowledgments 160

Wine Styles

Obviously no two wines are ever exactly alike, but wine styles (excluding fortified wines such as port and sherry) can be broadly divided into the ten categories set out below. Examples from the United States and/or Canada are given for each style.

Sparkling

Sparkling wines run the gamut from light-as-air Italian prosecco and elegant, steely French Champagnes that mellow gently with age, to rich, heart-warming toasty bubblies from California and other warm New World vineyards and ripe-fruit red sparkling Shiraz from Australia. The classic blend for sparkling wine (Champagne in particular) is Chardonnay, Pinot Noir, and Pinot Meunier. This combination develops fruitiness with firmness and fragrance. The top sparkling wines also gain a certain complexity from the second fermentation in bottle and contact with the finished fermentation yeasts. Good Champagne should have complex toast, nut, butter, and biscuit flavors, and the bubbles should provide a tingling sensation to balance the flavor.

★ *"Traditional method" sparkling wines (California, especially Napa Valley)*

Crisp, dry, light-bodied whites

Expect pale, white, even green-tinged colors in the glass, and green apple, fresh-mown grass, wet stones, and even sometimes gooseberry on the nose. These wines will be light, with neutral aromas backed up by crisp acidity and tangy, refreshing fruit on the palate—with flavors of apples, pears, citrus fruits. Grapes to watch out for are Pinot Blanc, Pinot Gris, Sauvignon Blanc, Riesling, and lighter versions of Chardonnay. These wines are not widely found in the New World (except for Canada and the cooler parts of the United States and New Zealand); classic examples from the Old World include Vinho Verde from Portugal and Chablis and Muscadet from France. Oak-aging does a crisp, dry white no favors; it should be refreshing on the palate and is best consumed young.

★ *Ontario Riesling, New York State Riesling, Sauvignon Blanc*

Aromatic or flowery, dry to medium-sweet whites

Aromatic wines may have a strong color, but it is on the nose that they really make their mark. Expect anything from honey, diesel, and hay (Riesling), to smoky citrus notes (Pinot Gris), peaches (Viognier), to pure grape flavors (Muscat) and even roses, lychees, and Turkish delight from the most aromatic grape of all, Gewürztraminer. Most of these aromas will be backed up on the palate with similar flavors, but wines can vary from light and delicate (Germany, Greece) to robustly perfumed and weighty (Alsace, Australia). The powerfully aromatic character of these wines can integrate well with a touch of sugar, so some are made in an "off-dry" or medium-sweet style. No sensible producer will smother the lively character with oak.

★ *Gewürztraminer (US & Canada), California Viognier*

Tangy or steely, medium-bodied whites

Less flamboyant on the nose, but more assertive on the palate than aromatic wines, tangy/steely styles are some of the best to pair with food. Expect creamier, smoother aromas and allow time for these to open out in the glass as the wine warms up, and as it ages. Firm-fruited flavors tend to mellow as the wine gets older. Tangy wines suggest hazelnuts (Chardonnay), damp stones (Chenin Blanc), and beeswax (Semillon); steely ones lean toward flint and gooseberries (Sauvignon Blanc), and limes (Riesling). In general tangy wines respond better to oak-aging than steely ones, but not for long: oaky vanilla flavors have a tendency to overpower them.

★ *California Riesling*

Full-bodied, rich flavored whites

Full-on, bold, and golden in the glass, these wines look as luscious as they taste. Expect a waft of buttery, honeyed aromas, along with tropical fruit, peaches, nectarines, even pineapple. There will be a similar barrage of rich, mouth-filling flavor on the palate. Full-bodied whites often have higher alcohol, but the best of them still have a twang of acidity to keep them balanced. They all benefit from additional vanilla oak characters, but should not be overwhelmed by them.

Many gain complexity with age. Full-bodied whites hail mainly from warmer New World countries, but pockets of the Northern Rhône, Languedoc-Roussillon, and central Spain also produce powerful whites.
★ *Chardonnay (North Coast California and Central & Southern California))*

Rosé
Made from red grapes, but left only for a limited time with the color-giving grape skins, rosé can vary from palest powderpuff pink (California Zinfandel), to deep opaque red (Australian Grenache), depending on how long the grapes macerate. Many have the weight of a white wine on the palate, but the aromas of red fruits and hedgerow berries nearly always give away their red grape origins. Lighter wines—generally from Old World countries (Loire Valley and Provence in France, Navarra in Spain)—will be delicate, thirst-quenching, and tangy with a hint of red fruits. Heavier ones—from the Rhône Valley and Australia—have richer, deeper, almost red wine flavors, sometimes with a touch of tannin.
★ *Grenache, Zinfandel blush wines (California)*

Fresh, fruity, low tannin reds
This style is red wine at its simplest, freshest, and most juicy. These pinky reds are for drinking as young as possible, as they will greet you with pure, primary fruit aromas of raspberry, red apple, and cherry, backed up with cheery red-fruit characters which fill the palate. There will be no chalky tannins getting in the way of their satiny smoothness, and any acidity will be soft and supple. Fresh, fruity reds are as likely to come from the Old World as the New, from grapes low in tannin, such as Gamay, Grenache, and Barbera. In hotter countries where grapes will get riper in the sun, tannins are likely to be overtaken by full fruity flavors, so a usually robust grape like Merlot can exchange its tannin for plummy fruit. These reds trade on their fruity freshness, so are best without aging in oak.
★ *lighter Merlots (California), lighter Pinot Noirs (Canada)*

Medium to full-bodied reds
This group includes the world's classic red wines, which first and foremost have a firm structure and plenty of backbone. In medium- to full-bodied Old World wines—such as Burgundy, Bordeaux, and Barolo—aromas and flavors might not be very expressive at first, but with a year or two's age, the wines will open up to reveal wafts of bramble fruit, mulberry, plum, and violet. They develop in a similar way on the palate too: youthful hard tannins will soften, and as the wines mature, their range of fruit flavors will evolve to include cranberries, spice, truffles, and chocolate. Medium- and full-bodied reds call out for oak, which adds both structure and a touch of vanilla aroma. These wines match perfectly with meat dishes.
★ *Pinot Noir (Pacific Northwest, especially Willamette Valley, Oregon & Sonoma Coast, California), Cabernet Sauvignon-Merlot blends (California), Cabernet Sauvignon-Cabernet Franc blends (California)*

Full, powerful, often spicy reds
These are the most mouth-filling wines of all. Grapes such as Cabernet Sauvignon (black currant), Shiraz (spicy plum and liquorice), and Zinfandel (leather and strawberries) dominate this category. The wines are a rich, inky color in the glass, show intense, sweet dark fruit on the nose, then dense, velvety-smooth fruit on the palate. These wines are mainly from grapes tough enough to survive in the hot vineyards of the New World or the Rhône Valley. Many will develop in the cellar but their overwhelming ripeness also makes them fruity enough to drink young. They all require oak in order to balance their powerful fruit flavors.
★ *Cabernet Sauvignon (California, especially Napa Valley), Zinfandel (California)*

Sweet/Dessert
Sweet wines vary from light, delicate, grapey versions from the Muscat grape to full-on Australian liqueur wines (once again Muscats), which display all the golden sunshine of their origins. The former are aperitifs, the latter dessert wines, much too concentrated for drinking with a meal. In between are a host of sweet wines with richly honeyed aromas and buttery-smooth flavors. All sweet wines should have a crisp acidity to balance their sweet fruit, otherwise they become lifeless. Those from the Riesling grape are some of the zestiest; but Tokaji from Hungary has the tangiest, most lingering sweetness.
★ *late-harvest sweet wines (California & New York State), icewine (Niagara & Okanagan, Canada)*

For details on the practicalities of winetasting and a glossary of common terms used to describe wine **See pp. 138–141**

Tasting Wine

Wine can simply be consumed like any other beverage. Tasting wine, however, entails a more thoughtful, methodical approach. The following notes are designed to help you to maximize the pleasure you derive from every glass.

Practicalities

It is preferable to taste wine in a naturally lit, odorless room to allow its true color to be examined and to avoid other aromas interfering with the sense of smell. Avoid perfume, mints, and smoke. The most important factor when tasting is the shape and size of glass, as this can have a major impact on the taste of a wine *(See p. 146)*.

Look

Looking at a wine can provide valuable clues to its character. Note the color and check that the wine is clear—cloudiness can indicate a fault. For reds, tilt the glass away from you against a white background and inspect the rim of the liquid to see the true color. As a red wine ages, it changes from bright purple to tawny and then to brown. So if a red wine looks brown, it may be past its best (although brown would be normal in wines such as sherry and tawny port). A deep golden color in a white wine may suggest the wine has been aged in oak, but it can also indicate a sweet wine style or particularly ripe fruit.

Smell

Smelling wine will vastly improve your enjoyment and knowledge. First, gently sniff the wine. Make a note of any first impressions, as they are often the most revealing. Holding the glass by its stem, swirl the wine in order to help release its aromas. Then take another sniff. Note the fruit aromas you detect now. Are they intense or relatively subdued? Is there a range of suggested "flavors"? If so, this might indicate complexity, a sign of quality. Does it smell of the fruity flavors often found in a young wine, or does it boast more mature, developed aromas such as mushrooms, leather, and diesel? Is any one smell dominant, and do you like it? See *pp. 140–141* for help in identifying some aromas you may detect.

Taste

This stage often merely confirms the impression received on the nose. Take a small sip and allow the wine to linger on your tongue and mouth. You can enhance the flavors by pursing your lips and sucking a small amount of air into your mouth. This takes practice, but it is something professional tasters encourage as the presence of oxygen amplifies the flavors experienced. If you are tasting a lot of wines in one session, it is normally sensible to spit out each wine after noting the flavors and neutralize the palate by eating a cracker or taking a sip of water. Here are some further guidelines:

- Note the sweetness of the wine, detected on the tip of the tongue. Is it dry, medium, or sweet?
- Consider the acidity—the element of a wine that keeps it fresh—detected on the sides of the tongue. Is it in balance with the rest of the flavors?
- How heavy does the wine feel in your mouth? Do you think it is light-, medium- or full-bodied?
- Assess the wine's fruit qualities. Are they pure and fruity (as in a young wine), or mature and complex (as in an older one)?
- Can you recognize any individual flavors?
- With red wines, think about tannins—the drying, mouth-puckering elements picked up by your gums. Are they harsh and bitter, or in balance with the wine?

Finish

Consider how long the flavors last in your mouth after you spit or swallow. This is known as the "finish" and, in general, the longer it lasts, the better the wine.

Describing a Wine

It is virtually impossible to express in words the complexities and subtleties of even the most basic of wines. When it comes to identifying aromas and flavors, wine tasters borrow their vocabulary from all kinds of areas, including fruits, flowers, spices, nuts, and types of wood. Some of the flavor compounds actually exist in certain wines. For example, vanilla aromas come from vanillin, which occurs naturally in new oak barrels. However, others are mere impressions that wines create in the mind of the taster. Everyone's sense of smell and taste is, of course, different, as we all have our own memory bank of flavors.

For more details on US grape varieties **See p. 13**

Descriptive Terms

There are a large number of commonly used words and phrases for discussing the style and character of a wine. Definitions are not watertight and there is often a large margin of overlap between the various terms.

age-worthy Applied to wines that will benefit from further maturation in the bottle. Typical examples of age-worthy wines are young with either powerful tannins, good acidity, or some sweetness.
aromatic A wine with lots of perfumed, fruity aromas, which normally leap out of the glass. Aromatic grape varieties include Sauvignon Blanc, Riesling, Gewürztraminer, and Muscat.
austere A wine that lacks fruity flavors and displays harsh, bitter tannins and/or high acidity.
acidic All wines need acidity to keep them balanced, but too much is a fault. Acidity is detected on the sides of the tongue.
balanced A wine with all its components (mainly acidity, alcohol, fruit, tannins, sugar, and extract) in harmony, with no one element prominent.
big A full-bodied wine that leaves a major impression on the senses, typically containing high levels of fruit, tannins, and/or alcohol. Also used to mean plenty of flavor.
bitter Normally a negative term used to describe a wine with an excess of harsh tannins, which leaves a bitter taste in the mouth, detected at the back of the tongue. In some reds, however, a certain amount of bitterness is a desirable characteristic.
blockbuster Used to describe exceptionally "big" wines. Think large amounts of fruit, alcohol, tannins, or oaky flavors.
body The weight or feel of wine in the mouth, determined by its alcohol and extract. To work out whether a wine is light-, medium- or full-bodied, it may be useful to compare it to the feel of water.
clean Lacking faults in terms of aroma and flavor.
complex A wine with many layers of aroma and flavor—many different fruits, plus characteristics such as spice and vanilla. Complexity is one of the elements that separates an average wine from a good or great one. The most complex wines have typically gone through a period of aging, allowing more flavors to develop.
concentrated An intense taste, normally found in wines with high levels of tannin, sugar, and flavoring and coloring compounds.
crisp Noticeable acidity but in a positive, refreshing way. Usually used for white wines with clean, fresh flavors.
dry No obvious sugar or sweetness in the wine. Note that very ripe, fruity flavors and new oak flavors can sometimes give the impression of sweetness, although the wine itself can still be dry. "Dried-out" is a term given to red wines which have spent too long in barrel or bottle and have lost their fruit flavor.
easy-drinking A relatively simple wine that can be enjoyed without much thought. It will be fruity and, if red, low in tannin.
elegant A subjective term, used to describe a good quality, subtle, balanced wine which is not too fruity, and is extremely pleasant to drink.
extract All the solid matter in a wine such as tannins, sugars, and coloring and flavoring compounds. Extract is what gives a wine its body.
finesse Quality of a wine that displays elegance.
flabby A negative term used for a wine which has low acidity and is therefore unbalanced. It can make for a slightly cloying taste.
fleshy A wine which feels almost solid in texture when in the mouth, thanks to high levels of fruit and extract.
fresh Like crisp, noticeably acidic in an attractive, refreshing way. Normally used for young white wines.
fruity A wine with plenty of attractive fruit favors.
harsh Rough around the edges, lacking in subtlety.
heavy Normally refers to a full-bodied, tannic red wine, and means it is tough to drink or heavy going. It may indicate that the wine needs to spend further time in bottle.
mature Ready to drink. Generally used for quality wines that require time in bottle. Overmature is a euphemism for past its best.
oaky Normally a negative term to describe when oak flavors dominate other flavors in a wine. If the wine is young and good quality, it may lose some of its oakiness with a few years in bottle. Oak flavors can be desirable but only if they are balanced by fruit.
powerful A "big" wine with high levels of extract and/or alcohol. Can be used in a positive or negative sense.
racy Word similar in meaning to crisp and fresh, used to describe wines with noticeable levels of refreshing acidity. It is especially associated with Riesling.

For more details on Canadian grape varieties **See p. 129**

rich Like concentrated, implying deep, intense flavors in the mouth. Can also be used to mean slightly sweet.
ripe Wine made from ripe grapes and showing flavors of richer, warmer-climate fruits, such as pineapples (rather than apples). Ripe wine might also suggest a certain sweetness, even though it may not contain sugar.
simple Lacking complexity, with one-dimensional flavors. This is a fault in expensive wine, but it may not be a problem for everyday drinking wine.
soft A red wine with gentle tannins. Also known as smooth.
structured Normally refers to the tannins in a red wine, which support the other elements. In a "well-structured" wine the tannins are noticeable but still balanced. Sometimes used for acidity in white wines, for example a wine can be described as having a "good acidic structure."
subtle Normally linked to finesse, it means a wine contains a number of different nuances and tastes. It can also be a euphemism for a wine lacking in fruity flavors.
sweet A wine with noticeable levels of sugar, detected by the tip of the tongue. The phrase "sweet fruit flavors" may be used to describe an extremely ripe style of wine.
tannic An excess of tannins, the drying compounds that come from the skins, seeds, and stalks of grapes. Some tannic wines simply require further maturation in bottle. Tannins are not necessarily a bad thing, they just need to be balanced by fruity flavors.
up-front Used to describe an easy-drinking style of wine with straightforward, fruity flavors.
warm A wine with an excess of alcohol leaves a "warm" finish. Can be used to describe full-bodied, spicy red wines.

Aromas and flavors

There are obviously thousands of different identifiable aromas and flavors in wine, but here is a list of some of those most commonly detected. Certain flavors (such as black currant) speak for themselves, whereas others, such as "mineral" or "vegetal," require a little explanation. Entries include examples of grape varieties or wines where the flavor is usually encountered.

apple Often found in cooler-climate, dry white wines.
apricot Common in riper styles of white wine such as Viognier and oak-fermented Chardonnay.
black currant Widely associated with Cabernet Sauvignon and some other red grape varieties such as Merlot, Syrah/Shiraz, and Cabernet Franc. Occasionally a certain underripe black currant flavor can be detected in Sauvignon Blanc.
buttery A creamy texture reminiscent of butter (rather than a specific flavor) is commonly found in oak-fermented Chardonnay and other white wines. This is caused by malolactic fermentation in the barrel, particularly where lees stirring is used.
cherry Widely found in red wines, especially in cool-climate Pinot Noir.
citrus A character widely found in white wines, particularly fresh, aromatic styles. Can be further narrowed down to lemon, lime, orange, etc.
coconut A flavor commonly associated with both whites and reds when they have been fermented or matured in new American oak barrels. In excess it can indicate a fault.
creamy Used to indicate a smooth, quite full-bodied texture in a wine, or a smell of cream.
diesel Widely found in mature bottles of Riesling.
earthy A soil-like aroma commonly identified in older bottles of red Bordeaux.
farmyard A slightly dirty, earthy, manure-type aroma. In a young wine it may indicate poor (unclean) winemaking practices. In an older bottle of red Burgundy it can be a desirable, developed character.
floral A number of cool-climate whites display aromas vaguely reminiscent of flowers. Some are easy to identify, such as elderflower (aromatic whites), violets (mature Bordeaux or Californian Cabernet Sauvignon), and roses (Gewürztraminer).
game/gaminess A decaying, fleshy aroma commonly associated with older bottles of Pinot Noir, Syrah/Shiraz, and other mature red wines.
gooseberry A classic flavor of Sauvignon Blanc. Also found in other aromatic, zesty white wines.
grapey A term meaning smelling of grapes a vaguely "sweet" fruity aroma. The only variety for which this is true is Muscat (and all its various names and clones).
grass Widely found in fresh, aromatic wines from cooler climates from grapes such as Sauvignon Blanc, Sémillon, and Chenin Blanc.

honey Normally found in sweeter, late-harvest styles of whine wine made from Riesling or Muscat grapes. The flavor is especially strong when the grapes have been affected by botrytis.
jammy A slightly derogatory term for a red wine bursting with up-front flavors of black currant, raspberry, and other fruits, but lacking in structure.
It normally implies the wine lacks finesse.
lemon Widely found in white wines, particularly those from cooler climates.
licorice Commonly associated with full-bodied reds made from Syrah/Shiraz.
lychee An aroma widely found in wines made from Gewürztraminer.
mineral It is difficult to taste mineral but the term is usually used to describe a sharp, earthy character in cool-climate wines made from grape varieties such as Sauvignon Blanc.
mint Particularly associated with Cabernet Sauvignon grown in warm-climate countries.
mushroom An aroma displayed by Pinot Noir as it matures.
pepper (black) Commonly associated especially those made of the Syrah/Shiraz and Grenache grape varieties.
plum Apparent in many red wines but particularly those made from Merlot.
rose Found in Gewürztraminer and wines made from the Nebbiolo grape variety.
rubber Can indicate a wine fault caused by excessive sulfur, or is widely (and positively) associated with the Syrah/Shiraz grape variety.
spice Found in wines fermented and matured in new oak barrels. Also apparent in certain red grape varieties, such as Grenache (which often has a peppery flavor).
summer fruits Aromas such as strawberry, raspberry, and cherry. Especially associated with young Pinot Noir.
tangy Similar to zesty, but perhaps with more orange fruits. Mostly applies to whites but can also be used to describe reds such as fruity, crisp Cabernet Franc.
tobacco A mature, developed aroma found in older bottles of Cabernet Sauvignon, particularly red Bordeaux.
toast The word "toasty" is most frequently used to describe the aroma imparted by oak barrels, but "toastiness" is also a quality of mature Champagne, especially *blanc de blancs.* It may also be displayed by the best sparkling wines made by the "traditional method" in California's Napa Valley.
tropical fruits Ripe flavors such as banana, pineapple, and mango, often used to describe New World Chardonnay.
vanilla Derived directly from new oak barrels. The wood contains vanillin, the chemical compound that gives vanilla pods their distinctive aroma.
vegetal Rotting vegetable-type aromas found in older bottles of red and white wines, especially Burgundy (of both colors). It might sound unpleasant, but it is a desirable attribute in these styles of wine.
yeast Bread-type aroma widely associated with champagne (and the secondary fermentation process used to create it).
zesty Aromas of lemon, lime and, sometimes, orange. Normally found in crisp, refreshing dry white wines.

Common Faults

Wine today is much more reliable than ever before. With the exception of a corked bottle, seriously flawed wine is relatively rare. There are, however, a number of problems you may encounter, which would warrant returning a bottle of wine to the place of purchase.

corked This is the most common wine fault, found in 2 to 5 percent of all wines sold. It is caused by a mold found in some natural corks that can taint the wine, and has nothing to do with pieces of cork floating in your glass. Corked wine smells musty and lacks fruit flavors, but this may not become obvious until it has spent a few minutes in the glass. Plastic corks or screwcaps eliminate this problem.
oxidized Overexposure to oxygen harms wine, eventually turning it into vinegar. A winemay become oxidized if its seal is insufficiently airtight, if left too long in bottle before opening, or if left too longonce opened.
sulfur All wines are bottled with a dose of sulfur, which acts as a preservative. However, if too much sulfur is added, the wine acquires an astringent, rubbery smell. In large quantities, it can be dangerous for asthmatics.
poor winemaking If you taste a wine with excess acidity, tannins, or oak, or with an absence of fruity flavors, it may simply be the result of poor winemaking.

Wine and Food Matching

Wine and food have complemented each other for thousands of years. Wine comes into its own at the dinner table thanks to its moderate alcohol, refreshing acidity, and sheer range of flavors. It is worth knowing some successful pairings of food and wine that have stood the test of time.

Guidelines

Whether selecting a bottle to accompany carry out, or choosing different wines for each course at a dinner party, there are a number of basic guidelines

- Decide on the dominant taste and choose a wine to accompany it.
- Select a wine to match the weight and power of your food. Full-flavored foods require full-flavored, full-bodied wines. Delicate dishes are overpowered by heavily oaked or tannic styles, so they require light wines. Full-bodied whites have similar power and weight to lighter reds, so work equally well with dishes such as grilled tuna or roast turkey.
- Sweet food should be matched by a similarly sweet wine. Many Thai dishes, for example, contain a lot of sugar, which is why off-dry styles such as Gewürztraminer work so well.
- Tannins in a red wine taste softer when drunk with red meat. This is why classic combinations like beef with red Bordeaux are so effective.
- The more complicated the flavors in a dish, the more difficult it is to find a wine to pair with it, though some wines do work well with a range of flavors *(See In Restaurants p. 144)*.
- If serving top-quality wine, simply prepared dishes using the finest ingredients allow the wine to take center stage.
- Try to match regional dishes with the same region's wines.

Apéritifs

An apéritif should simply whet your appetite, leaving you ready to enjoy the food and wine to come, so never choose anything too heavy or overbearing.

- Dry, light, and refreshing white wine works well. Avoid oaked wine. Think unoaked Semillon or a dry Riesling.
- Champagne and traditional-method sparkling wines are ideal, particularly for special occasions. Their dryness and relative acidity stimulates the tastebuds.
- Do not serve the best wine of the evening as an apéritif. A well-made, basic bottle will allow true appreciation of the subtleties of the better wines to follow.

With Starters

Bear in mind the best order for serving wine when choosing your starter—white before red, dry before sweet, lighter-before fuller-bodied, and in ascending order of quality. If the choice of menu requires a full-bodied red for the starter, avoid serving a dish that needs a light white for the main.

Asparagus Sauvignon Blanc. If served in a creamy sauce, a fuller-bodied wine such as Semillon.

Foie gras A Sauternes-style botrytized wine, although serving a sweet wine this early in the meal could present problems later. Champagne and Gewürztraminer also work.

Gazpacho Relatively neutral, dry whites.

Pâtés and terrines A wine that works with the main ingredient in its cooked form *(See Fish and Meat sections)*.

Salad (no dressing) Sauvignon Blanc, Riesling, and unoaked Chardonnay are good options.

Salad (with creamy dressing) Chardonnay or Pinot Blanc.

Salad (with vinaigrette) A wine with high acidity like Sauvignon Blanc, or dry Riesling.

Soup (chicken) Medium-bodied Chardonnay or Pinot Blanc.

Soup (chunky, meaty) Inexpensive reds (Merlot or Cabernet-Merlot blends).

Soup (creamy and fishy) Fuller-flavored Napa Valley or Sonoma Valley Chardonnays work well, as can light rosés.

With Fish & Seafood

The dominant flavor in seafood dishes will often be the sauce. Creamy dishes demand a full-bodied white, whereas tomato-based ones require a medium-bodied red. Also consider the intensity of the cooking method, and the quality of the ingredients.

Bouillabaisse Inexpensive whites, reds, and rosés.

Chowder (creamy) Basic Chardonnay.

Chowder (tomato-based) Medium-bodied reds.

Cod (battered) Crisp, dry whites, such as Sauvignon Blanc or Chenin Blanc.

Cod and haddock (fresh) Unoaked Chardonnay.

Crab Sauvignon Blanc or a dry Riesling.

For more on wine styles **See pp. 136–137**

Lobster Good-quality Chardonnay.
Mackerel and sardines (fresh) Sauvignon Blanc or light rosé.
Mackerel (smoked) Pinot Gris or medium Riesling.
Mussels/Oysters A good Sauvignon Blanc or unoaked Chardonnay, or a crisp, dry Riesling.
Salmon (barbecued) Lighter cool-climate reds such as a Pinot Noir from Oregon.
Salmon (grilled) Unoaked Chardonnay, Semillon, or Pinot Blanc. Dry Riesling is also a decent match.
Salmon (poached) A delicate Chardonnay or good Semillon.
Salmon (smoked) Sauvignon Blanc or dry Riesling. Champagne-style sparkling wines also work well.
Sea bass (with butter sauce) A good-quality Chardonnay.
Sea bass (with tomato sauce) Light- or medium-bodied reds.
Trout (fresh) Pinot Blanc or unoaked Chardonnay.
Trout (smoked) A good Chardonnay.
Tuna (fresh) A fuller-bodied, dry white wine such as Semillon or a light to medium red such as a Pinot Noir from Oregon or Sonoma.
Turbot Top-quality Californian Chardonnay.

With White Meats

In general, white meat has a relatively neutral flavor. Take note of the recipe used when selecting a wine to show it off.
Chicken (barbecued) Chardonnay, Sauvignon Blanc, or light red wines.
Chicken (creamy sauce) Semillon, Riesling, or oaked Chenin Blanc.
Chicken (roast) Chardonnay or a light red wine such as a soft Merlot or Pinot Noir.
Coq au vin Good-quality Pinot Noir from Willamette Valley, Oregon.
Pork (roast) A range of wines from Chardonnay and Sauvignon Blanc through to lighter reds like basic Merlot or Pinot Noir.
Pork (spare ribs) A fruity Californian Shiraz or Shiraz-based blend.
Pork sausages Inexpensive reds.
Turkey (plain roast) Oaked Chardonnay or a light red wine like soft Merlot or Pinot Noir.
Turkey (with cranberry sauce/stuffing) Good Napa Valley Cabernet Sauvignon or a Cabernet-Merlot blend.
Veal Dry whites such as unoaked Chardonnay or a soft fruity red like Merlot.

With Red Meats, Barbecues & Game

These meats call for fuller-bodied styles of wine. Beef and lamb in particular tend to be complemented by tannic red wines. However, the sauces served also affect the choice.
Barbecues Powerful reds such as Shiraz or Zinfandel.
Beef (hamburgers, steak au poivre, or in pastry) Powerful, full-bodied Zinfandel from California.
Beef (roast beef or steak) Full-bodied Shiraz, Cabernet or Cabernet-Shiraz blend.
Beef (with wine sauce) A good-quality Oregon Pinot Noir.
Duck (roast) A good-quality Pinot Noir from Oregon or Sonoma.
Duck (with apple/orange sauce) Aromatic white such as Riesling from the Finger Lakes region.
Game A good-quality Cabernet Sauvignon.
Lamb (casseroles and stews) Spicy reds such as a peppery Shiraz or Shiraz-based blend.
Lamb (chops) Good Cabernet Sauvignon or Cabernet-Merlot blend.
Lamb (roast) Top-quality California Cabernet Sauvignon.

With Vegetarian Dishes

Vegetarians and vegans may find some wines unsuitable due to animal products used in them. Consult the back label or ask the retailer to pinpoint vegetarian- or vegan-friendly wine. It can be difficult to pair vegetarian food with top Chardonnay or full-bodied reds, but mushroom and pumpkin risotto stand up to the challenge.
Lentil- and vegetable-based casseroles Basic Californian reds.
Mushroom risotto Good Cabernet Sauvignon.
Pasta (creamy sauce) Unoaked Chardonnay, Pinot Blanc, or Semillon.
Pasta (tomato-based sauce) Light red such as Pinot Noir.
Pumpkin or butternut squash risotto Good-quality Chardonnay.
Quiches and omelettes Unoaked Chardonnay, Pinot Blanc, or light red like Pinot Noir.
Quorn and tofu Choose a wine according to the flavor of the ingredients with which they are cooked, as they tend to take on the same flavor.
Vegetarian chilli (with Quorn) Hearty reds such as a fruity Merlot.
Vegetarian lasagne (with tofu) Full-bodied whites such as Chardonnay or Pinot Gris.
Vegetable tarts, pies, and pasties Spicy reds such as a peppery Shiraz.
Veggie burgers and nut roast Full-bodied Shiraz or Cabernet-Shiraz blend as these dishes can taste quite "meaty."

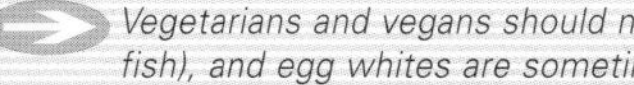
Vegetarians and vegans should note that gelatin, isinglass (made from fish), and egg whites are sometimes used to fine (clarify) wines

With Ethnic Dishes

Chinese Riesling, Gewürztraminer, Pinot Gris, or Sauvignon Blanc.
Indian With mild dishes an inexpensive Chardonnay. With medium-hot dishes, a soft, fruity red such as Merlot. With really hot and spicy dishes, avoid wine and choose beer, water, or lassi instead.
Japanese (sushi) A "rice wine" such as saké is traditional.
Japanese (teriyaki sauces) Fruity red such as Merlot.
Thai (curry) Inexpensive Sauvignon Blanc.
Thai (general) Off-dry white such as Riesling or Gewürztraminer.

With Desserts

Always try to select a wine that is sweeter than your dessert. You can also choose a wine with a slightly higher alcohol content here as it is the end of the meal. Intensely flavored desserts are well complemented by powerful, fortified styles.
Chocolate cake Select your wine depending on the richness of the chocolate. Certain Muscat dessert wines can work sensationally.
Crème brûlée Botrytized dessert wine makes a classic partnership.
Fruit A wide variety, such as sweeter styles of Riesling, Semillon, or Chenin Blanc.
Fruit tarts and pies Choose a wine based on the dominant flavor—normally the fruit itself.
Ice cream Thick, sticky dessert styles.

With Cheeses

Cheese and wine can be a wonderful combination, but pairing them is not as easy as many people think. The diverse flavors and textures of different cheeses mean that anything from a sweet white to a fortified red can be served successfully.
Blue cheeses A sweet wine is generally required. Roquefort and Sauternes-style dessert wine is a classic combination.
Brie Light, fruity reds.
Camembert Light and fruity reds, but can also be paired with whites such as Chardonnay.
Goat's cheese Sauvignon Blanc or a similar crisp, dry white.
Gruyère and Emmenthal Red wines such as Shiraz, Cabernet-Shiraz blends, or Merlot. However, Riesling can work well, too.
Mature Cheddar Good Napa Valley Cabernet Sauvignon or tawny port.
Mozzarella Unoaked Chardonnay.
Sheep's cheese Sweeter styles of white wine like Riesling and Muscat, as well as spicy reds.
Traditional hard cheeses Cool-climate, dry whites such as Sauvignon Blanc or Chenin Blanc.

Social Occasions

With food The general rules of wine and food matching still apply. It is often wise to select generally food-friendly wines *(see In Restaurants right)*, as guests are then able to enjoy one wine with all the canapés and different courses served.
Without food In general, wines to be enjoyed on their own should be light and unpretentious. For parties and social events where no food is offered, steer clear of anything too full-bodied and avoid high acidity or powerful tannins. Also take the time of year and weather into account.
In summer Choose crisp, refreshing wines like Riesling, Chenin Blanc, and other cool-climate, relatively low-alcohol whites. You could also go for light, fruity reds suitable for a brief chilling. Basic Merlot, and Pinot Noir are good choices.
In winter A medium-bodied wine, whether red or white, focusing on bright, fruity flavors and avoiding lots of oak. Good bets are Semillon, unoaked Chardonnay, and Pinot Blanc. Reds such as Cabernet-Shiraz or Cabernet-Merlot blends are also highly enjoyable at this time of year.
At celebrations Champagne and traditional-method sparkling wines are the classic choices. Champagne tends to be expensive, so is generally only an option for those with a bigger budget. Many California sparkling wines make excellent substitutes, however, and are normally a better choice to use in cocktails that require bubbly.

In Restaurants

Many top restaurants have a sommelier to offer diners advice on wine. If no sommelier is on hand, there are a few types of wine that are good with most foods. If you are all ordering different dishes, half bottles can help everyone get something to complement their particular meal.

- Opt for medium-bodied styles, avoiding extremes. For whites, unoaked Chardonnay, Semillon, Pinot Gris, or Sauvignon Blanc are the most versatile. Among the reds, Pinot Noir, inexpensive Merlot, or a fruity Cabernet-Merlot blend are excellent choices.
- If the restaurant focuses on a particular nationality or style of cooking, try and choose wines of the same nationality.

Buying Wine

There has never been so much choice when it comes to buying wine in the United States. However, due to controls implemented following the repeal of Prohibition, each state has its own laws as to how, when, and where alcohol can be sold. Therefore, selection, availability and price vary widely.

Supermarkets

Supermarkets are a reliable, if not especially adventurous, source of wine. In states where the sale of wine in supermarkets and grocery stores is legal, most major food chains have a selection designed to appeal to a broad range of tastes. While large supermarkets tend not to stock obscure styles or wine from boutique producers, some smaller specialty grocery stores offer a wider, more interesting selection.

Discount Stores

In states where they are allowed to sell wine, stores such as Sam's Club, Costco, and Target have a wide selection of basic brands at very reasonable prices. Although these types of stores lack a sales force able to answer wine-related questions, they offer excellent value. Costco and Sam's Club provide a good selection of high-end wines at very attractive prices, but bargain hunters should be aware that availability varies dramatically from week to week and popular wines are soon sold out .

Wine Merchants

The legal structure of selling wine in the United States means that there is no national chain that can sell wine in every state. As a result, there are hundreds of specialty wine merchants, each with a different selection and focus. This makes them the destination of choice for discerning wine lovers. They have much to offer in terms of advice and ranges of wines from small, high-quality producers. Owners and staff often have tasted most of the wines and are happy to share their knowledge. Take time to discuss your requirements and preferences: price, styles of wines you enjoy, and the food with which you plan to drink the wine.

Direct from the Winery

With wineries in 50 states, people can buy wine made in their own backyard. Although there may be little difference in price between the winery and a store, buying wine directly from a producer often means you can get hold of older vintages or wines not sold in stores. Depending on state laws it is possible to order wine directly from a winery and have it shipped to your home. To find out more about wine shipping laws vist the site of the Wine and Spirit Wholesalers of America *(www.wswa.org)*.

Auctions

It is not without risk, but buying at an auction or internet exchange can be an excellent way of acquiring cases of wine, particularly older, rarer vintages. Major auction houses such as Christie's *(www.christies.com)* and Sotheby's *(www.sothebys.com)* hold regular wine sales, as do smaller, local houses. Be aware of commission fees (10 to 15 percent on top of the price of the lot) and learn as much as possible about the condition and provenance of lots before bidding on them.

Wine on the Web

Many wine merchants and wineries sell on the internet, and there are also some virtual-only stores. Wine.com, the largest on-line retailer, offers a wide variety of wines, some that are difficult to find elsewhere. Shipping cost can be high and some states do not permit wine to be shipped directly to consumers.

Selected Retailers

BOSTON
Federal Wine & Spirits
(617) 367 8605
Marty's Liquors
(617) 782 3250

CHICAGO
Sam's Wine & Spirits
(312) 664 4394
Wine Discount Center
(312) 489 3454

LOS ANGELES
Wally's Wine & Spirits
(310) 475 0606
Woodland Hills Wine
(800) 678 9643

NEW YORK
Astor Wine & Spirits
(212) 674 7500
Zachys
(800) 723 0241

SEATTLE
McCarthy & Schiering
(206) 524 9500
Pike & Western Wine Shop
(206) 441 1307

WASHINGTON, D. C.
MacArthur Beverages
(202) 338 1433

Storing and Serving Wine

Over the years wine has become associated with a number of procedures, like cellaring, breathing, and decanting. While it is not strictly essential to know anything about these terms to enjoy wine, an understanding of these practices can maximize the pleasure gained from both buying and drinking it.

Storing Wine

The majority of wines sold today are designed to be enjoyed young. Almost all midpriced bottles will survive in a rack for around 12 months, but are likely to deteriorate if left for longer. Traditionally, most wines worth cellaring were from the Old World, but age-worthy bottles are now created by the finest producers elsewhere, too. If in any doubt, it is always better to drink a wine too young rather than too old.

Wine is best stored on its side, as constant contact between cork and liquid prevents the cork from drying out. Sparkling wines and wines with a screwcap can be stored upright because this problem does not arise. If you would like to cellar wine but lack the ideal conditions, alternatives exist: buying a wine fridge or cabinet that can hold bottles in perfect storage conditions; or paying a professional firm to arrange dedicated wine storage. Contact your local wine merchant for advice.

Cellars

A cellar can range from a humble, understairs closet to a gigantic underground labyrinth, as long as conditions are right for maturation. Key considerations when choosing the perfect "cellar" are as follows:

- A constant temperature between 50 and 60°F (10 and 15°C) is preferable. Slightly higher than this is not a major concern: the wine will mature more quickly, but slightly less favorably. It is temperature variation that causes most harm.
- Wine dislikes light, which is why many bottles are made of colored glass. Dark rooms or sealed boxes are best.
- A lack of moisture can cause corks to dry out, contract, and let air into the bottle, oxidizing the wine and eventually turning it into vinegar. Slightly damp cellars, on the other hand, will not harm the wine.
- Excess movement or vibration can damage wine so do not store next to fridges and washing machines, and also avoid handling or unnecessary transport.

Effects of Aging

As wines sit in the bottle, a series of chemical reactions changes relatively simple fruity flavors to more developed, complex tastes. In reds, the color becomes lighter, the tannins get softer, and the wine assumes aromas such as cedar, leather, or mushrooms. Whites, on the other hand, deepen in color, and become less sweet and more intense. Typical aromas of a mature white wine include nuts, wax, and even diesel. The effects of oak barrels—hints of vanilla, coconut, and spice—lessen in all wines as they mature.

Serving temperature

The correct temperature is extremely important to the taste of wine. White wines are often served too cold, and reds too warm. Some guidelines to follow:

- Sparkling wines: Cool temperatures of around 47°F (8°C).
- Light, aromatic whites: Quite cold—around 50°F (10°C) or a few hours in the fridge. Chilling emphasizes the crisp, fresh taste and does not dull the aromas.
- White Burgundy and other Chardonnays: These are less aromatic, so serve around 54°F (12°C).
- Light- and medium-bodied reds: Chill slightly to around 54 or 56°F (12 or 13°C) (half an hour in the fridge), particularly in summer.
- Full-bodied reds: Low temperatures emphasize the tannins in the wine, so serve these reasonably warm, around 59°F (15°C).

Serving Order

There are a number of generally accepted rules for serving wine:

- White before red—although a light-bodied red can be enjoyed before a full-bodied white.
- Dry before sweet whites—this keeps the wine from tasting excessively acidic.
- Light reds before heavy reds—lighter wines taste thin after heavier examples.
- Lower quality wines before more illustrious ones.

There is no clear consensus on whether young or old wines should be consumed first. Much depends on the individual wines in question.

Decanting

Certain high-quality wines (mostly reds), such as a 2000 Bordeaux, opened before their peak, can benefit greatly from exposure to oxygen in the air—or breathing—before drinking. Simply pulling the cork on a bottle and allowing it to stand open is unlikely to make much difference. Using a decanter, however, will. The shape of the vessel used makes very little difference, as long as it is made of glass and open-topped.

Another reason to use a decanter is to separate a wine from its sediment, especially if it is unfiltered. Wines that "throw" a sediment include vintage port, unfiltered or traditional LBV port, crusted port, and older vintages of full-bodied reds.

To decant a wine, stand the bottle upright for at least 24 hours to allow the sediment to fall to the bottom. Then, pull the cork and, with a source of light, either a lighted candle or a naked light bulb, behind the neck to allow you to see the contents, slowly pour the wine into the decanter. Stop when you see the sediment reach the neck of the bottle. Do not leave wine in a decanter for long, as prolonged exposure to oxygen will ruin it.

Opening Bubbly

The correct procedure for opening a sparkling wine or Champagne is as follows:

• Hold the bottle at an angle of approximately 55 degrees to the horizontal.
• Point the neck of the bottle away from other people and from breakables.
• Carefully remove the foil and wire muzzle.
• Holding the bottle in one hand and the cork in the other, gently twist the bottle (not the cork) until the cork eases with a satisfying pop.

Glasses

Using the correct wine glasses can influence the taste of a wine. Although you can buy individual glass designs for different wines, a good all-purpose wine glass will normally suffice. This should have a stem so that you do not have to handle the bowl; and the bowl should be large enough to hold a decent measure, yet still allow room for the wine to be swirled. The bowl should be narrower at the rim than at the base, directing the aromas toward your nose. Finally, clear glass—not cut, colored, or patterned—allows the color of the wine to show through. The only major styles that require a different shape of glass are Champagne and sparkling wines. Their tall, straight, thin glasses are specifically designed to show off and retain the bubbles.

How Much per Person?

Serving quantities depend on the occasion and, of course, the drinking capacities of your guests. At dinner parties estimate between half a bottle and a whole bottle of wine per person per evening. When ordering large amounts of wine for an event, remember that many retailers operate a sale or return policy, which allows you to return unopened bottles. In this instance always err on the generous side when ordering.

Leftover Wine

Leftover wine should be poured into the smallest appropriate bottle size, sealed with the original cork if possible, and kept in the fridge. It should be finished off within 24 to 48 hours, as deterioration will quickly set in.

Red and White Wines to Keep

Keeping times depend on the quality of the producer, vineyard site, and vintage. Bear in mind that only the finest wines can age for longer periods:

Whites

Chardonnay: 2 to 5 years for top-quality American examples.
Riesling: 2 years for low-priced wines; 5 to 20 years for the best German examples; up to 5 for the best American ones; sweeter styles keep longer than drier.
Semillon: 1 to 2 years for best American examples.
Sweet wine: 5 to 20 years for the finest examples from Sauternes and Germany; up to 10 years for the best from the US and Canada.

Reds

Cabernet Sauvignon-based wines: 5 to 20 years for the best Bordeaux; 3 to 10 years for the best US wines.
Merlot: 3 to 15 years for good quality Bordeaux; less time if from the US or elsewhere.
Pinot Noir: 2 to 5 years for the best examples from Oregon or California.
Syrah: 5 to 15 years for the best wines.

Glossary

Like any other specialized subject, wine has its own unique vocabulary. This glossary includes common terms originating in France and other Old World countries as well terms that are specific to winemaking in the US and Canada.

A

acid/acidity All wines contain various acids, including tartaric, malic, and citric. Acidity is an essential element in wine, helping to maintain freshness and balance—too much and it can taste unduly sharp, too little and a "flabby," cloying wine will result.

acidification The addition of chemical acids to the must during winemaking to compensate for a lack of natural acidity in the grapes.

aging Most wines are designed to be enjoyed as soon as they are released. However, a proportion will improve in bottle if stored in a cool, dark place. Full-bodied reds, sweet whites, and fortified wines can all benefit from aging.

American oak Wood originating from forests of the eastern US, used to make oak barrels. Popular in North and South America, Spain, and Australia, American oak barrels tend to impart a more powerful vanilla flavor than their European counterparts.

American Viticultural Area or **AVA** Wine-producing area in the US. An AVA is simply an indication of a wine's geographical origin and not a guarantee of quality.

appellation A legally defined area where grapes are grown and wine is produced, sometimes used as a shortened version of AOC or AC.

Appellation d'Origine Contrôlée or **AOC** (French) Also known as Appellation Contrôlée (AC). The highest quality classification for wines produced in France. It guarantees that a bottle has been made in a specific region, according to local regulations. Not all AOC or AC wines are good quality, but on average they should be better (though not necessarily better value) than wines with a lower classification such as *vin de pays* or *vin de table*.

B

barrel Barrels or casks can be used at several stages of winemaking. Better quality whites may be fermented in barrel to produce subtle and complex wood flavors. Maturation in barrel helps to soften the wine and, if the oak is new, pick up aromas such as cedar or vanilla. "Barrel select" may imply quality, but has no legal definition. *See also* **American oak** and **French oak**.

barrel-aged The process of maturing wine in oak barrels, softening its taste and possibly adding oak flavors.

barrel-fermented This indicates a wine has been fermented in an oak barrel. Normally applicable to white wines, the process helps to integrate oak flavors.

barrique (French) Originally a small oak cask or barrel holding 225 liters of wine. Now often used to describe any small oak cask.

base wine The still wine used to create champagne and other sparkling wine.

bin Originally a collection or stack of wine bottles. It is commonly found on wine labels, to signify different brands of wine.

biodynamism An extreme form of organic viticulture that emphasizes the health of the soil. Some of its methods may sound bizarre, but a number of world-class wines are produced using this approach.

blanc de blancs (French) White wine made entirely from white grapes. The term is commonly used for Champagne and other sparkling wines.

blanc de noirs (French) White wine made entirely from red grapes, usually applied to Champagne and other sparkling wines.

blend A mixture of wines of different grape varieties, styles, origin, or age, contrived to improve the balance of the wine or maintain a constant style.

blush A term used in the US for a pale pink wine.

bodega (Spanish) Winery or cellar.

Bordeaux A wine from the Bordeaux region of France made using the grape varieties and/or techniques common in this area. Bordeaux is a famously full-bodied red wine made from a blend of Cabernet Sauvignon, Merlot, Cabernet Franc, Malbec, and Petit Verdot. Often matured in oak barrels, it can age for decades.

botrytis A vine disease, also known as noble rot, responsible for some of the world's greatest dessert wines. In the correct conditions, the fungus *(Botrytis cinerea)* produces shriveled, sugar-rich grapes that can be fermented into a naturally sweet and intensely flavored wine.

bottle fermentation The technique that gives champagne its "fizz." After a normal fermentation, still wine is placed into a bottle with sugar and yeast. A secondary fermentation begins, producing carbon dioxide gas inside the bottle and creating a sparkling

For terms commonly used in winetasting **See pp. 138–141**

wine. The term is normally used by sparkling wine producers outside the Champagne region.
Bourgogne The French word for Burgundy.
brut (French) Means dry. Normally used to describe Champagne and other sparkling white wines.
Burgundy A wine from the Burgundy region of France, made using the grape varieties and/or the techniques common in this region. Burgundy is world famous for its dry whites made from Chardonnay and medium-bodied reds from Pinot Noir.

C

canopy All parts of the vine that are visible above ground including the trunk, leaves, shoots, stems, and grapes.
canopy management The practice of manipulating the vine and its canopy to ensure the grapes and leaves are correctly exposed to the sun. It also aims to ensure a good circulation of air through the vine, helping to prevent fungal diseases. Canopy management includes training and pruning.
carbonic maceration Winemaking technique associated with Beaujolais in France. The grapes are fermented as whole berries, producing a deep colored, fruity wine, light in tannin.
chaptalization The practice of increasing alcohol levels through the addition of sugar during winemaking. Common in cooler wine regions where the climate may struggle to produce sufficient natural sugar in the grapes.
château (French) Used to denote a French wine-growing/producing estate. The term is widely used in Bordeaux.
clairet (French) A dark pink style of wine between a rosé and a light red.
claret A uniquely English term for red Bordeaux.
clone A group of vines all descended from a single parent vine using cuttings or buds. They are genetically identical to the parent plant and are usually selected for characteristics such as fine flavor or good color.
cold fermentation A slow fermentation at low temperatures to extract freshness and fruit flavor from the grapes.
cooperative Organization collectively owned by its members. Typically wine cooperatives consist of a number of growers who join together for winemaking and marketing purposes. Quality can vary from good to extremely poor.
corked Wine that has been affected by a moldy, musty taint from a defective natural cork. The wine may be stripped of its normal fruit flavors and can have a slightly bitter taste. It is believed that around six percent of wines using natural corks are corked, and many producers and retailers have changed to screwcaps and synthetic stoppers.
côte(s)/coteaux (French) Hill or hillside.
crémant (French) Indicates a sparkling wine produced outside the Champagne region, but using the same methods as Champagne.
cru (French) Literally "growth" or "vineyard." Hence *cru classé* means classified vineyard. *Cru bourgeois* is a classification for estates in Bordeaux's Médoc appellation. *See also* ***premier cru*** and ***grand cru***.
cuvée (French) Normally used to mean blend. Wine labels that say *cuvée de prestige* or *tête de cuvée* are no guarantee of exceptional quality. In Champagne, *cuvée* denotes the first and finest juice to come from the press.
cuvée de prestige (French) Term normally associated with Champagne, referring to a top quality, luxury wine from the best vineyards and matured for many years before release. Examples include Dom Pérignon from Moët & Chandon and La Grande Dame from Veuve Clicquot Ponsardin.

Key Climatic Terms

continental climate A climate characterized by extreme temperature variations across the year. Usually found in regions far away from the influence of water (sea or lakes). Cold winters and hot summers are the norm.
degree days A unit devised to measure the suitability of climates for viticulture.
macroclimate The overall climate within a region.
maritime climate A climate which is influenced by a large body of water, typically a sea or lake. Temperatures will tend to remain relatively stable across the year with mild winters and warm summers.
marginal climate A climate that is barely sufficient to permit viticulture. Normally applied to weather that is too cold rather than too warm. Expect regions with a marginal climate to have wide variations in quality between vintages.
mesoclimate The climate in a small district or even an individual vineyard.
microclimate A specific climate within a very small area.
moderate climate A climate with only minimal temperature variation over the course of the year. Most commonly found near to a large body of water. *See* maritime climate.

D

decanting The process of pouring wine from its original bottle into another vessel or decanter. The technique is normally used for old or unfiltered wines to separate the liquid from the sediment deposited in the bottle. It can also be used for younger wines, to allow them to be exposed to air, or "breathe."
dessert/sweet wine Wine containing large amounts of sugar. It tastes sweet and is traditionally used to accompany dessert.
disgorgement The process by which sediment is removed from a Champagne bottle following the second fermentation.
domaine (French) Estate.
dosage This is the term given to the replenishment of the small amount of wine lost during disgorgement in the process of making Champagne. Sugar is also normally added at this stage.
dry-farmed Vines grown without the use of irrigation, thus relying entirely on natural rainfall.

E

Eiswein (German) Sweet wine made in Germany in tiny quantities from grapes that have naturally frozen on the vine. The berries are pressed immediately, leaving the moisture behind as ice and producing a luscious, intensely flavored liquid.
enology (or oenology) The study of wine. The term is principally associated with winemaking.
en primeur (French) Wine sold by a producer before it has been bottled. Typically customers pay for the wine six months after the harvest, then wait a further 18 months to receive it. This is the best way to secure a wine limited in quantity, but is no guarantee of a cheaper price.
estate bottled/grown Today, most quality producers bottle on site. It is no guarantee of quality, but is generally a good indicator. In the US, estate bottled wine must also come from the producer's own vineyards or those on a long-term lease. The equivalent in France is *mise en bouteille à la propriété/au domaine/au château*; in Italy it is *imbottigliato all'origine*.

F

fermentation The process that turns the juice of crushed, pressed, or whole grapes into wine. The natural sugars within the berries are converted into alcohol and carbon dioxide using yeast. Fermentation generally takes place in stainless-steel, lined concrete, or large wooden vats, or in oak barrels. *See also* **malolactic fermentation**.
filtration A technique that removes the tiny solid particles from a wine before bottling, leaving it clear and bright. Some producers believe that filtration can strip a wine of its flavor and will avoid the technique—often including words such as unfiltered or *non-filtré* on their label. Wines which have not been filtered will generally require decanting.
fining A process used to remove suspended deposits in wine. When a fining agent such as egg white or bentonite clay is added, it binds with the deposits and causes them to fall to the bottom of the cask.
first growth *See* ***premier cru***.
flying winemaker An individual who produces wine in a number of locations around the world. The term was originally coined when highly trained New World winemakers were brought in to revitalize old fashioned, traditional estates in Europe.
fortified A wine bolstered by the addition of a spirit—usually grape spirit—such as port, sherry, or madeira.
French oak A type of wood originating from forests in France such as Allier and Vosges. French oak is widely considered to make the finest barrels for fermenting and maturing wine.
fruit set This is when the fertilized vine flowers become grape berries—not all flowers will actually turn into berries.
fungal diseases Collective term for a number of diseases such as powdery mildew, downy mildew, and black rot. The fungi attack grapes or foliage and, without preventative measures, can cause considerable damage. The benevolent disease *Botrytis cinerea* is also included in this category.
futures The American term for *en primeur*.

G

garage wine A relatively recent term given to the tiny quantities of top quality (and often very expensive) wine made by small-scale producers. Equipment and facilities are generally extremely basic and production may even take place in a garage, hence the name.
grand cru (French) Literally "great vineyard." In Burgundy the term *grand cru* is applied to the finest vineyards in the region. In the St.-Émilion area of Bordeaux, the best châteaux are classified as *grand cru classé*, with the top tier known as *premier grand cru classé*. *See also* ***premier cru***.
grand vin (French) Often seen on French AOC labels, this literally means "great wine" and is often used to indicate that this is the top wine of a particular estate.
green harvesting The practice of removing and discarding grapes in the buildup to the (conventional)

harvest. The idea is to allow the vine to concentrate its energies on ripening the grapes that remain.

H

hybrid A plant created from parents which belong to different species of vine. An example is the Baco Noir grape variety, made by crossing Folle Blanche of the *Vitis vinifera* species with a variety of *Vitis riparia*, a native American species of vine. In the EU, quality wine can only be made entirely from *Vitis vinifera* plants.

I

icewine The name given to *Eiswein* when it is produced outside Germany, for example, in Canada.
Indicazione Geografica Tipica or **IGT** (Italian) A relatively recent classification for Italian wines, similar to *vin de pays* in France.

J

jeroboam A bottle size containing three liters or four conventional (75cl) bottles.

KL

late harvest *See* ***vendange tardive***.
lees Known as *lie* in France, lees are the remains of yeast, grape seeds, and other sediment that settle in a wine after fermentation. Extended contact with the lees plays an important role in wines such as Muscadet and Champagne. Lees stirring (*bâtonnage* in French) in cask helps to accentuate this process.
limited release A term used by marketing people on wine labels. It may indicate additional quality, but there is no guarantee.
long-lived This term describes a wine able to develop and improve in bottle over years or decades. Only a small proportion of wines are capable of this. *See also* **aging**.

M

maceration The practice of soaking grape skins in their juice or must. This gives red wines their color, tannins, and flavors.
madeira A fortified wine produced on the Portuguese island of Madeira.
maderized A wine which has been exposed to oxygen and/or heated to make it taste like madeira. The term is also used occasionally to describe a wine which has been oxidized.
magnum A 1.5 liter bottle (equivalent to two conventional bottles). Wine in a magnum tends to mature more slowly and elegantly than in 75cl bottles and this is believed to be the ideal size for Champagne.
malolactic fermentation A process which converts tart malic acids (as found in apples) into softer lactic acids (as found in milk). It occurs shortly after the first (conventional) fermentation. Most red wines undergo malolactic fermentation; in whites the decision largely depends on the style of wine the producer is trying to achieve.
Master of Wine or **MW** An extremely demanding wine qualification developed by the Institute of Masters of Wine in London. It covers winemaking, distribution, tasting, and commercial aspects of the industry. There are currently fewer than 250 MWs worldwide.
maturation The process of aging or maturing a wine in cask or bottle, normally at the winery. Once the wine is released it may be matured further by the purchaser, but this is more commonly referred to as cellaring or laying down.
Meritage A wine made from the same blend of grape varieties as Bordeaux (Cabernet Sauvignon, Merlot, Cabernet Franc, Malbec, and Petit Verdot for reds; Sauvignon Blanc and Sémillon for whites) but from an alternative origin, usually California or South Africa.
méthode champenoise/ classique Alternative terms for *méthode traditionnelle*.
méthode traditionnelle (French) Sparkling wine made using the same techniques as Champagne. In particular it indicates the wine has undergone a secondary fermentation in bottle.
monopoly or ***monopole*** (French) A term used for a vineyard completely owned by one individual or organization.
must The mass of grape juice, skins, seeds, stems, and other matter before fermentation begins.
mutage A French word to describe the process of halting fermentation before it has naturally finished, normally through the addition of a spirit. The technique is used to create port or *vin doux naturel*.

N

négociant (French) Literally merchant; a person or organization that buys grapes, must, or wine from growers to bottle under its own label. Particularly important in areas with large numbers of small vineyard holdings such as Burgundy. The quality of *négociant* wines can range from poor to excellent.
noble rot *See* **botrytis**.
nonvintage (NV) A blend of wines from different years. Although "vintage" is often used to imply high quality, there is nothing inherently wrong with nonvintage wine—in fact, most Champagnes are nonvintage.

O

oak The wood favored by winemakers to ferment and mature wines. Many cheaper wines receive their oaky taste from oak chips or oak staves submerged in the

tanks. *See also* **American oak**, **French oak**.
oaked A wine made in a deliberately creamy, oaky style through the use of oak barrels, oak chips, or oak staves. *See also* **unoaked**.
old vines *see* ***vieilles vignes***.
organic It is very difficult to produce a completely organic wine since certain chemicals are virtually essential during winemaking. Many wines advertised as such are simply grown without the use of chemical fertilizers, fungicides, and pesticides.

PQ

Pierce's disease A potentially devastating bacterial disease for which there is no known cure. The disease is spread by small insects, known as sharpshooters, and attacks the leaves of the vine. It is most common in the southern part of the US and South America.
phylloxera A vine disease which devastated the vineyards of Europe at the end of the 19th century. Phylloxera is a small insect or aphid that feeds on the roots of grapevines and ultimately kills the plant. Even today there is no cure for the pest—instead almost all European vines are grafted onto rootstocks from American species, which are phylloxera-resistant.
port A sweet, fortified wine produced in the Douro Valley in northern Portugal.
premier cru (French) First growth or first vineyard. In the Médoc region of Bordeaux, the finest châteaux are classified as *premier cru*. In St.-Émilion just across the river, the top producers are known as *premier grand cru classé*. Confusingly, in Burgundy *premier cru* vineyards lie just below *grand cru* in the classification hierarchy.

R

racking The process of separating a wine from its sediment in the winery. The sediment is normally allowed or encouraged to fall to the bottom of the barrel. The liquid is then drained or pumped into a clean vessel.
raisining The practice of drying grapes either on the vine or after picking. Raisined grapes are normally concentrated with sugar, making excellent sweet wines.
reserve A term seen regularly on wine labels to denote a special bottling or release. Unless the wine comes from a reputable producer, however, it is no guarantee of special quality.
residual sugar Sugar that remains in a wine after fermentation. High levels of residual sugar make a wine taste sweet.
rootstock The root system of a vine. Today almost all vines consist of an American rootstock grafted onto a fruiting European variety to protect against phylloxera.
rosé (French) Wine with a pink color, a halfway house between a red and a white wine. The only region allowed to produce rosés by mixing red and white wines is Champagne; the vast majority of other rosés are made using red grapes and a short period of maceration.
ruby port The youngest and fruitiest style of port.

S

sec (French) Dry.
sediment Solid matter found in wine. Sediment may come from yeasts, fragments of grape skin and pulp during winemaking, or it may form naturally in the wine. Certain wines "throw" a sediment when matured in bottle for a long period. Such wines will need to be decanted.
sherry A fortified wine from the Jerez region of Spain.
single vineyard Wine made using grapes from just one vineyard.
stabilization The processes in the winery designed to ensure a wine undergoes no further fermentation or reaction once it is bottled. These include fining and filtration.
structure A tasting term used primarily for red wines to describe the weight of fruit and tannins on the palate. Full-bodied wines such as high quality red Bordeaux should have a "good structure."

T

table wine In theory, this is the lowest wine classification in the European Union. In general, table wines are cheap and not especially good. However, some of Europe's finest wines are labeled "table wine." Price is a good guide to quality here—finer wines in this category tend to cost significantly more than basic table wine.
tannins The astringent, mouth-drying compounds found when a teabag is soaked in water too long. Tannins in grapes are found in the skins, seeds, and stalks, and are particularly important in the composition of a red wine. They provide the wine with its structure and weight and also act as a preservative, helping it to mature in bottle. A wine with excessive tannins is described as "tannic."
tawny port A style of port characterized by its distinctive tawny color. Better examples achieve their appearance and soft, mellow taste through extended maturation in cask.
terroir A French word used to describe the overall growing environment of a vineyard, covering its climate, soil, slope, and exposure, among other factors. Advocates of terroir

believe that a wine should not simply taste of fermented grape juice, but rather it should express a sense of the place where the grapes are grown.
traditional method *See* ***méthode traditionnelle***.

U

unfiltered/***non-filtré*** *See* **filtration**.
unoaked A wine deliberately made without oak barrels to emphasize its fresh fruit flavors.

V

varietal A wine that has been labeled on the basis of its principal grape variety. It can also be used as another word for "grape variety."
vendange tardive (French) A French term meaning late harvest. Grapes which have been harvested later tend to be riper and more concentrated, producing sweeter styles of wine. In Alsace the term carries a legal definition, elsewhere it can be used simply at the discretion of the producer.
vieilles vignes (French) Literally "old vines." As a vine gets older it tends to produce fewer, but better quality grapes. It is no guarantee of a superior wine, as there is no legal definition of what constitutes old.
vin de pays (French) Often excellent value, "country wines" sit between table wines and *appellation contrôlée* wines in the classification hierarchy.
vin de table (French) *See* **table wine**.
vin nouveau (French) *See* ***vin primeur***.
vin primeur (French) Young wine made to be drunk in the same year that it is produced, the best-known example being Beaujolais Nouveau.
vine density The number of vines planted in a specified area in a vineyard. High density planting (3,200 vines per acre/8,000 per hectare) is practiced in many European vineyards, as the competition between plants is believed to help lower yields and produce better quality grapes.
vine pull The removal of vines. In parts of Europe where overproduction is a problem, governments pay growers to pull up their vines in vine pull programs.
vinification Essentially, "winemaking," the process that converts grape juice into finished wine.
vino da tavola (Italian) *See* **table wine**.
vintage Can be used to mean either "harvest" or the year in which the grapes were grown to produce a wine. A vintage wine must come from a single year. Vintage Champagne is only produced in exceptional years and must be matured for at least three years on its lees. *See also* **nonvintage**.
vintage port The very best port made from a single fine harvest and aged in wood for around two years. It is "declared" or released by producers only in the best vintages, on average three times a decade.
viticulture Vine growing – the science, techniques, and skills required to produce commercial-quality grapes.
Vitis vinifera The species of vine responsible for the majority of the world's wine.

W

wooded/unwooded *See* **oaked** and **unoaked**.

XYZ

yeast A single-cell fungus that converts sugar into alcohol during fermentation. In many regions yeasts occur naturally on the skins of grapes and in the air. Many local winemakers prefer these "wild" strains, although cultured yeasts are often more reliable.
yield The total amount of wine produced by a vine or vineyard in a particular vintage. In general, lower yields will produce better quality grapes, and in European appellations the maximum yields are prescribed by law. These range from about 400 gallons per acre (38 hectoliters per hectare) for *grand cru* red Burgundy to more than 1,050 gal/acre (100 hl/ha) for less illustrious classifications.

Index

A

Abacela Vineyards 109
Abreu Vineyard 45
Acacia Winery 45
Alban Vineyards 82
alcohol consumption 18
Alexander Valley AVA, Sonoma 48
Alexander Valley Vineyards 55
Alexander, Cyrus 52
Allen, Greg 38
Allied-Domecq 13
Altmira, José, Padre 52
Am Rhein Wine Cellars 123
American as a general wine appellation 19
American Viticultural Areas (AVAs) 18
Amity Vineyards 106
Anderson Valley AVA, Mendocino 58
Andrew Murray Vineyards 84
appellations 18–19
Applegate Valley, Pacific Northwest 97
Araujo 31, 33, 36
Arcadian Winery 84
Archery Summit Winery 106
Argyle Winery 106
Arrowood 50
Arroyo Grande Valley AVA, Central & Southern California 73
Artist Series Wines *see Bedell Cellars*
Associated Vintners *see Columbia Winery*
Atalon Vineyard 45
Atlas Peak AVA, Napa Valley 31, 32–3
Atlantic Northeast & other regions 112–25
  Great Lakes 113
  introduction 112–13
  map 114–15
  New York State 112, 114–123
  other wine states 124–5
  producers 120–3
  regional information at a glance 115
  Virginia 113
  wine areas 116–18
Au Bon Climat Winery 84
AVAs (American Viticultural Areas) 18

B

Baldwin, Justin 82
Baron, Christophe 104–5
Barrett, Bo 37
Beaulieu Vineyard 16, 30, 33, 36
Beaux Freres 106
Becker Vineyards 125
Bedell Cellars 120
Bennett, Ted 62
Bergström Winery 106–7
Beringer 26–7, 31, 36–7
Beringer Blass 13, 36
best-kept secrets of California wine 39
big producers 13
Bixler, Mark 54
Blackjack Ranch 85
Blue Mountain 132–3
blush (rosé) wine 15
  blush wines (Top 10) 72
Boeger Winery 87
Bonny Doon Vineyard 17, 75, 81
Bosc, Paul 132
branded wines 6
Breaux Vineyards 123
British Columbia wine areas, Canada 131
Broman, Bob 63
Brotherhood Winery 117
Brown, Ken 85
Buena Vista Winery 22, 52
Bunnell, Ron 102
burgundy, semigeneric appellation 19
Burrowing Owl 133
Bursick, George 51
Byron 85

C

Cabernet Franc grape variety 15
Cabernet Sauvignon
  grape variety 14–15, 30–1, 32
  California Cabernet Sauvignons (Top 10) 43
Cahn, Deborah 62
Cain 33
Cakebread Cellars 45
Cakebread, Rosemary 44
Calaveras County, Central & Southern California 76
Calera Wine Company 72, 82
California 22–87
  Central & Southern California 66–87
  introduction 22–3
  Lake County 59
  Mendocino 58–63
  Napa Valley 30–45
  North Coast California 26–63
  Sonoma 48–55
  wine areas 23
  wine history 22
  wine maps 28–9, 68–9
California Cabernet Sauvignons (Top 10) 43
California Chardonnays (Top 10) 36
California fortified wines and Muscats 76
California Rhône Rangers 17, 75
California Syrahs (Top 10) 77
California wine, best-kept secrets of (Top 10) 39
Calistoga AVA, Napa Valley 31, 35
Campbell, Joe & Pat 107
Canada
  introduction 128–9
  producers 132–3
  wine areas 130–31
  Top 10 red wines 128
  Top 10 white wines 130
Canadian icewine 132
Canadian red wines (Top 10) 128
Canadian white wines (Top 10) 130
Canandaigua Industries Co. *see Constellation Brands*
Canoe Ridge Vineyard 104
Carmel Valley AVA, Central & Southern California 71
Carmenet 55
Carneros AVA, Napa Valley 33, 36
Carneros, Domaine 38
Carroll, Deborah & Peter 120–21
Cave Springs 132
Caymus Vineyards 37
Cayuse Vineyards 104–5
Cedar Creek 133
Cedar Mountains 87
celebration wines (Top 10) 66

Centerra Wine Company 43, 121 *see also Constellation Brands*
Central & Southern California 66–87
map 68–9
producers 80–87
regional information at a glance 69
wine areas 70–77
winemaking history 66–7
Central Coast AVA, San Benito County, Central & Southern California 72
Central New York State, Atlantic Northeast 118
Central Valley, Central & Southern California 77
chablis semigeneric appellation 19
Chalk Hill 55
Chalk Hill AVA, Sonoma 48–9
Chalone AVA, Central & Southern California 71
Chalone Vineyard 81
Chalone Wine Group 104
champagne semigeneric appellation 19
Chandon, Domaine 38–9
Chardonnay grape variety 15, 30–31
California Chardonnays (Top 10) 36
Charles Krug 26, 31
Chateau des Charmes 132
Chateau Grand Traverse Winery 123
Chateau LaFayette Reneau 118, 122
Chateau Montelena 31, 33, 37, 44
Chateau St. Jean 49–50
Chateau Ste. Michelle 102
Chautauqua Vineyards 125
Chehalem Mountains, Pacific Northwest 98
chianti semigeneric appellation 19
Chiles Valley AVA, Napa Valley 33
Claiborne & Churchill 87
claret semigeneric appellation 19
classic European grape varieties 15
Clear Lake AVA, Lake County 59
Clendenen, Jim 84
Cline 50–51
Clore, Dr. Walter (Grandpa Grape) 90, 95
Clos du Bois 51
Clos du Val 45
Clos Pegase 35, 38
Codorníu 33
Cohn, Jeff 80
Colgin 37
Columbia Crest *see Ste. Michelle Wine Estates*
Columbia Valley AVA, Pacific Northwest 95
Columbia Winery 102–3
Constellation Brands 13–14, 43, 67
cool–climate viticulture in the Pacific Northwest 99
Cooper Vineyards 123
Copia Center, Napa Valley 34, 43
Coppola, Francis Ford 34, 38
Coturri 55
county appellation 19
Croser, Brian 106
Cucamonga Valley AVA, Central & Southern California 77
cult wines 30
Cuvaison 38

D
Davis Bynum 55
Davis, Joseph 84
DeLeuze, Norman 45
DeLille Cellars 103
Dervin, Ludovic 42
dessert wines (Top 10) 80
Devaux, Guy 42
Diageo 13, 36
Diel, Armin 104
Dolce Vineyard 38, 40
Domaine Carneros 38
Domaine Chandon 38–9
Domaine de la Terre Rouge 86–7
Domaine Drouhin 106–7
Dominus 31, 33, 39
Dr. Konstantin Frank 112, 122
Draper, Paul 17, 80
Drouhin, Domaine 106–7
Dry Creek Valley AVA, Sonoma 48
Duckhorn Vineyards 27, 33, 39
Dumol 55
Dundee Hills AVA, Pacific Northwest 98
Dunn Vineyard 45
Duval, John 105
Dyer, Bill 133

E
Eberle Winery 87
Ecole No. 41, L' 105
Edna Valley AVA, Central & Southern California 73
El Dorado AVA, Central & Southern California 76
Elk Cove Vineyards 107
Eola Hills, Pacific Northwest 98
Ernest & Julio Gallo 13, 83
Eroica Washington Riesling 104
estate wines 6
Etude 45
Etzel, Michael 106
everyday drinking wines (Top 10) 53
Eyrie Vineyards 99

F
Far Niente 38, 40
Farrell, Gary 52
Ferrari-Carano 51
Fetzer 60
Fiddletown AVA, Central & Southern California 76
Finger Lakes, Atlantic Northeast 117–8
Firestone Vineyard 85
Flat Creek Estate 125
Flora Springs 45
Florida Orange Groves 125
Florida wine region 124
Flowers 49, 55
fortified wines (Top 10) 109
Foster's Group 13
fox grape *see vitis labrusca*
Fox Run Vineyards 122, 123
Frank, Dr. Konstantin 112–13
Franks, Alec 86
Fraser Valley, British Columbia 131
Freemark Abbey 31
Frog's Leap 40, 63
Fumé Blanc grape variety *see Sauvignon Blanc*

G
Gainey Vineyard 87
Gallo 13, 52, 66, 83
Gallo of Sonoma 52
Ernest Gallo 66
Julio Gallo 66
Gamay grape variety 15

Gary Farrell 52
Gasnier, Vincent, Top 10 lists 7
generic appellations 19
geology of the Pacific Northwest 102
Georges de Latour Private Reserve 16
Georis Winery 71, 87
Geyser Peak 55
Glenora Wine Cellars 121, 123
Gloria Ferrer 52
glossary 148–53
Gobbi, Daniel 59
Graf, Mary Ann 54
Graff, Dick 71
Grahm, Randall 17, 75, 81 *see also Bonny Doon Vineyard*
grape varieties 14–15
Graves, Michael 35
Graziano, Greg 62
Great Lakes, Atlantic Northeast 113
Green Valley AVA, Sonoma 48–9
Green, Allan 60–1
Green, Russell 27, 54
Greenwood Ridge 60–61
Grenache grape variety 15
Griffin Creek *see Willamette Valley Vineyards*
Guenoc Estate 63

H

Haas, Robert 82
Hacienda 55
Hamptons, The, Atlantic Northeast 117
Handley Cellars 61
Hargrave, Alex & Louisa 116
Harlan Estate 40
Hartford Winery 53, 55
Havens Wine Cellars 45
Hedges Cellars 104
Heitz 31, 40
Heller Estate 87
Hendry 41
Henry of Pelham 133
Hermann J. Wiemer Vineyard 121, 123
Hess Collection, Napa Valley 34
Hill, William 52
history of US wine industry 10–11
Howell Mountain AVA, Napa Valley 31, 32
Hudson River Valley, Atlantic Northeast 117

I

icewine 132
Icon Estates *see Constellation Brands*
Idaho, Pacific Northwest 91
Illinois River Valley, Pacific Northwest 97
influential winemakers 16–17
Inglenook 26, 30
Inniskillin 132
Iron Horse 49, 52–3
Italian influence on Mendocino wine 59

J

Jack London Ranch 53
Jackson Wine Estate 13
Jackson, Allan 132
Jackson, Jess 53
Jackson-Triggs 132
J. C. Cellars 80
Jensen, Diana 80
Jensen, Josh 72, 82
Jensen, Rob 80
Johnson Estate 118, 123
Joseph Drouhin 99
Joseph Filippi 87
Joseph Phelps 33, 41
Joullian 87
Judgment of Paris, legendary blind tasting 17, 22–3, 32, 44
Justin Vineyards & Winery 82

K

Kaiser, Karl 132
Ken Wright Cellars 107
Kendall-Jackson 53, 71
Kennan 33
Kenwood 49, 53
Keswick Vineyards 123
Kistler 54
Knights Valley AVA, Sonoma 48
Kongsgaard 41
Konzelmann 133
Kunde Estate 55

L

La Crema 53
La Jota Winery 45
Lacroute, Bernie 109
Laetitia Estate 87
LaFayette Reneau, Chateau 118, 122
Lake Breeze Vineyards 133
Lake County, North Coast California 27
Lake Erie AVA, Atlantic Northeast 118
Lake Erie North Shore, Ontario 130
Lake, David 102
Landmark 49, 55
Langtry, Lillie 63
Latour, Georges de 36
Laurel Glen 49, 55
Lefranc, Charles 66
Lemelson Vineyards 108
Lenz Winery 117, 120–21
Lett, David 17, 90, 99
Levenerg, John Irving 120
Levy, Bob 40
Lewis Cellars 45
Livermore Valley, Central & Southern California 70
Llano Estacado Winery 125
Lokoya Winery 45
Long Island, Atlantic Northeast 116
Long Shadows Vintners 105
Long, Zelma 54
Loosen, Dr. Ernst 103–4
Lynne, Michael 120

M

Macinski, Marti & Tom 123
madeira semigeneric appellation 19
malaga semigeneric appellation 19
Malibu-Newton Canyon AVA, Central & Southern California 77
Malivoire 133
maps
  Central & Southern California 68–9
  New York State 114–15
  North Coast California 28–9
  Pacific Northwest 92–3
  US (general wine regions) 13
Marimar Torres 54
Marin County, North Coast California 27
marsala semigeneric appellation 19
Martha's Vineyard 31
Martin, Jeff 133
Martinelli 55

Masson, Paul 66–7
Massoud, Charles & Ursula 120
Matanzas Creek 53
Mayacamas Mountains, Napa Valley 31
McCrea Cellars 103
McDowell Valley Vineyards 59, 61
McMinnville AVA, Pacific Northwest 98
Mendocino 58–63
  introduction 27
  major producers 60–63
  sparkling wines 61
  wine areas 58–9
  wine map 28–9
Mendocino Ridges AVA 58
Mendocino Wine Co. 59
Meridian Vineyards 82
Merlot grape variety 14–15, 30
  Merlots (Top 10) 41
Merritt Estate 118
Merryvale 41
méthode champenoise 61
Michael, Sir Peter 54
Millbrook Vineyards & Winery 117, 121, 123
Miller, Tim 122
Minnesota wine region 124–5
Mission Hill 133
Mission Mountain Winery 125
Mokesa, Agoston Haraszthy de 22, 52, 125
Mondavi, Robert 13, 16–17, 22, 43
Montana wine region 125
Monte Volpe 62
Montelena Chateau 31, 33, 37, 44
Monterey AVA, Central & Southern California 70–71
Moraga Vineyards 87
Morgan Winery 87
moselle semigeneric appellation 19
Mount Harlan AVA, Central & Southern California 72
Mount Veeder AVA, Napa Valley 33
multicounty appellations 19
multistate appellations 19
Mumm Napa 42
Murray, Andrew & James 84
Muscadine grape variety *see Vitis rotundifolia*

N
Nalle Winery 55
Napa Valley 30–45
  California history 22–3
  cult wines 30
  introduction 26
  George Yount 42
  Judgment of Paris 44
  map 28–29
  producers 36–45
  producers (Top 10) 33
  wine areas 30–33
  wine tour 34–5
Napa Valley Vintners (trade organization) 26
Napa Wine Train 34
Navarro 62
Nevada wine region 125
New Mexico wine region 125
New World wines versus Old World wines 6
New York State, Atlantic Northeast 112–13
  map 114–15
  producers 120–23
  wine areas 116–18
Newton 33
Neyers Vineyards 45
Niagara Peninsula, Ontario 130
Nichol Vineyards 133
North Coast California 26–63
  introduction 26–7
  Lake County 59
  map 28–9
  Mendocino 58–63
  Napa Valley 30–45
  producers 36–45, 50–55, 58–9, 60–63
  regional information at a glance 29
  Sonoma 48–55
  wine areas 30–33, 48–9, 58–9
North Fork, Atlantic Northeast 116–7
North Lake Wines *see Constellation Brands*
North Lake Wines 122
North Yuba AVA, Central & Southern California 77
Northern Sonoma AVA, Sonoma 49
Northern Vineyards Winery 125

O
O'Reilly, Jerry 108
Oakville AVA, Napa Valley 31
Ojai Vineyard 86
Okanagan Valley, British Columbia 131
Old Inglenook Museum 34
Old World wines 6
Olsen, Erik 51, 102
Ontario wine areas 130
Opus One 31, 33, 38, 42
Oregon wine region, Pacific Northwest 90, 92–3, 97–9, 106–9
organic viticulture 63
organic wines (Top 10) 62
Ortman, Chuck 82
other wine regions of the US 124–5
Owen Roe Winery 108
Owen, Jerry 108

P
Pacific Northwest 90–109
  introduction 90–1
  Oregon 97–8
  producers 102–9
  regional information at a glance 93
  Washington 94–6
  wine areas 94–8
  wine map 92–3
  wineries (Top 10) 96
Palmer Vineyards 120
Panther Creek Cellars 108
Paraiso Springs Vineyards 81
Paso Robles, Central & Southern California 73
Patz & Hall 42–3
Paumanok Vineyards 120
Pelee Island, Ontario 130
Pellegrini Vineyards 121, 123
Peller Estates 133
Peninsula Ridge 133
Perrin family 82
Peter Michael 48, 54
Peterson, Joel 54
Pfeiffer, Harold 86
Phelps, Joseph 41
Philippe-Lorraine Vineyard 45
phylloxera 10–11, 22

Pindar Vineyards 121, 123
Pinot Gris grape variety 15
Pinot Noir grape variety 14–15, 33
Pinot Noir wines (Top 10) 103
pioneering winemakers 12, 16–17
Ponzi Vineyards 109
port appellation 19
Potter Valley AVA, Mendocino 59
Prohibition 11, 22, 26, 119
Prosser research station 12, 90
Putnam, Stephanie 40

Q
Quady Winery 76, 87
Quails' Gate 133
Qupé 87

R
Rancho Sisquoc Winery 86
Ravenswood 54–5
Ray, Martin 16
reading a US wine label 19
red grape varieties 14
Red Mountain sub-AVA, Pacific Northwest 96
Red Newt Cellars 118, 122–3
red wines of the US (Top 10) 27
Redwood Valley AVA, Mendocino 59
Reeder, Steve 50, 54
Reif Estate 133
Reno, Betty & Dick 122
Rhône Rangers 17, 75
Ribbon Edge, Pacific Northwest 98
Ridge Vineyards 17, 80
Riesling grape variety 15
Riesling makers (Top 10) 85
Robert Mondavi 11, 16–17, 26–7, 31, 34, 38, 43
Rochioli Vineyard 55
Roederer Estate 58, 63–4
Rogstad, Steven 38
Rogue Valley AVA, Pacific Northwest 97
Rolland, Michel 41, 105
rosé (blush) wines (Top 10) 72
Roth, Roman 121
Roussanne grape variety 15
Rubicon Estate 38
Russian River Valley AVA, Sonoma 48–9
Rutherford AVA, Napa Valley 30–1

S
San Benito County, Central & Southern California 72
San Francisco Bay, Central & Southern California 70
San Luis Obispo, Central & Southern California 72–3
San Pasqual Valley AVA, Central & Southern California 77
San Sebastian Winery 125
Sanford Winery 86
Santa Barbara County, Central & Southern California 74
Santa Clara Valley, Central & Southern California 70
Santa Cruz Mountains AVA, Central & Southern California 70
Santa Lucia Highlands AVA, Central & Southern California 71
Santa Maria Valley AVA, Central & Southern California 74
Santa Rita Hills AVA, Central & Southern California 75
Santa Ynez Valley, Central & Southern California 74–5
sauterne(s) semigeneric appellation 19
Sauvignon Blanc grape variety 15
Sawyer, Tex 63
Sbragia, Ed 36
Scharffenberger Cellars 61, 63
Schneider Vineyards 122–3
Schramsberg 26
Schuppert, Jay 38
Scuppernong grape variety *see Vitis rotundifolia*
Sea Breeze Winery 125
Seghesio Family Vineyards 55
semigeneric appellations 19
Serra, Father Junípero 23
Shady Lane Cellars 123
Shafer 33, 44
Shalestone Vineyards 122–3
Shenandoah Valley AVA, Central & Southern California 76
sherry semigeneric appellation 19
Shoup, Allen 104–5
Shrem, Jan 35
Silver Thread Vineyard 118, 122
Silverado Trail, Napa Valley 35
Simes, John 133
Simi Winery 27, 54
Similkameen Valley, British Columbia 131
Small, Rick 105
Smith, Rich 81
Solano County, North Coast California 27
Sommer, Richard 90, 99
Sonoma 48–55
introduction 27
producers 52–5
wine areas 48–51
wine map 28–29
Sonoma Coast AVA 49
Sonoma Mountain AVA 49
Sonoma Valley AVA 49
Southern California wine area, Central & Southern California 77
sparkling wine houses (Top 10) 60
Spottswoode 33, 34, 44
Spring Mountain AVA, Napa Valley 33
Spurrier, Steven 44 *see also Judgment of Paris*
sustainably farmed grapes 62
St. Helena AVA, Napa Valley 31
St. Julian Wine Company 123
St. Francis 49, 55
Stag's Leap Wine Cellars 26, 32–3, 44–5
Stags Leap AVA, Napa Valley 32
Standing Stone Vineyards 118, 122–3
state appellations 19
Ste. Chapelle 91
Ste. Genevieve Winery/ Cordier Estates 125
Ste. Michelle Wine Estates 103
Ste. Michelle, Chateau 102
Stemmler, Robert 54

Sterling Vineyards 35, 38
Sterling, Audrey & Barry 52
Stevenson, Michael 108
Stevenson, Robert Louis 35
Stimson Lane Estates 104
see also Ste. Michelle Wine Estates
Stonestreet 53
Stoney Ridge Cellars 133
Stony Hill 33
Storybook Mountain Vineyards 45
Sumac Ridge 133
Switchback Ridge 45
Syrah grape variety 14–15, 30
California Syrahs (Top 10) 77

T

Tablas Creek Vineyard 82
Taittinger 33
Taittinger, Claude 38
Tancer, Forrest 52
tasting terms 138–41
Tchelitscheff, André 11, 16, 36, 54
Temperance Movement 119
Terre Rouge, Domaine de la 86–7
terroir 5
Testarossa 80–81
Texas wine region 124
The Hamptons, Atlantic Northeast 117
The Wine Group 13
Thée, Etienne 66
Thirty Bench 133
Thornton Winery 87
Togni 33
To-Kalon 31
Torres, Marimar 49, 54
tour of Napa Valley 34–5
Tra Vigne Restaurant, Napa Valley 35
Triggs, Don 132
Turley Wine Cellars 45
Turley, Helen 17

U

Ukiah Valley 59
Umpqua Valley AVA, Pacific Northwest 98
University of California Davis 12, 23
US appellation 19

V

V. Sattui Vineyards 45
Vancouver Island, British Columbia 131
Verdad 87
Viader Vineyards 45
Vignis, Jean-Louis 22
Vincent Gasnier's Top 10 lists 7
Vincor Group 13
Viognier grape variety 15
Virginia, Atlantic Northeast 113
viticulture and vinification in the US 12
Vitis labrusca grape varieties 10–11, 14, 112
Vitis riparia grape variety 14
Vitis rotundifolia grape variety 14
Vitis vinifera grape varieties 10
Vlossak Mark 108
Vogué, Count Robert Jean de 38–9
Volk, Ken 84

W

Wagner Vineyards 118, 121, 123
Walla Walla AVA, Pacific Northwest 96
Walter Hansel 87
Washington State 91–6, 102–5
Washington Hills Cellars 104
Wente Vineyards 81
Weyrich, Arnaud 63
white wines of the US (Top 10) 70
Wild Horse 84
WillaKenzie Estate 109
Willamette Valley, Pacific Northwest 98
Willamette Valley Vineyards 109
Williams Selyem 55
Williams, Craig 41
Williams, John 40
Windsor Vineyards 55
wine buying 145
wine & food matching 142–44
Wine Group, The 13
wine introduction 4–6
wine laws (US) 18
wine regions
Atlantic Northeast 112–13
California 28–9, 68–9
Canada 130–31
other regions 124–5
Pacific Northwest 92–3
US 13
wine serving 146–7
wine storing 146–7
wine styles 136–7
Winiarski, Warren 17, 44–5
Wisconsin wine region 125
Wisted, Roger 85
Wölffer Estate 117, 121
Woodward Canyon Winery 105
Wright, Ken 107–8
Wyse, Jim 133

Y

Yakima Valley AVA, Pacific Northwest 96
Yamhill Carlton AVA, Pacific Northwest 98
York Mountain AVA, Central & Southern California 73
Yorkville Highlands AVA, Mendocino 58
Yount, George 22, 26, 42
Yountville AVA, Napa Valley 31

Z

ZD Wines 45
Zepponi, Gino 45
Zinfandel grape variety 14–5, 30, 51
Zinfandels (Top 10) 50
Ziraldo, Donald 132

Acknowledgments

AUTHORS
Top 10 lists by Vincent Gasnier *(see p7)*; other text by Ruth Arnold, Julie Besonen, Stephen Brook, Paul Hines, Richard Jones, Susan Keevil, Dr. Paul White

BLUE ISLAND PUBLISHING

Editorial Director
Rosalyn Thiro

Art Director
Stephen Bere

Senior Editor
Ferdie McDonald

Associate Editor
Michael Ellis

Designer
Ian Midson

Editorial Researcher
Paul Hines

Picture Researcher
Helen Stallion

DORLING KINDERSLEY

Senior Editor
Janet Mohun

US Senior Editor
Jennifer Williams

Americanization Editor
Margaret Parrish

Senior Art Editor
Helen Spencer

DTP Designer
Traci Salter

Picture Researcher
Romaine Werblow

Production Controller
Mandy Inness

Executive Managing Editor
Adèle Hayward

Managing Art Editor
Karla Jennings

PICTURE CREDITS
The publishers would like to thank all the wine producers and picture libraries for their kind permission to reproduce their photographs.

CEPHAS: Jerry Alexander 24–5, 50, 56–7; Kevin Judd 12, 20–21, 27, 46–7, 126–7; R&K Muschenetz 8–9, 23, 32, 36, 64–5, 67, 68, 74, 78–9; Fred. R. Palmer 113; Mick Rock 71, 72, 80, 83 (top and bottom), 93, 94, 96, 99, 100–101, 110–11, 115; Ted Stefanski 32.

CORBIS: Bettmann 119 (bottom); Robert Holmes 35 (bottom); K. J. Historical 199 (top); Phil Schermeister 34 (top); Jim Sugar 49.

PARAISO: Doug Steakley 4–5.

Left **Panther Creek Cellars, Oregon** Right **Duckhorn, Napa Valley**

LONDON, NEW YORK,
MELBOURNE, MUNICH AND DELHI
www.dk.com

First American Edition, 2006

Produced by Blue Island Publishing,
Studio 218, 30 Great Guildford Street, London SE1 0HS, UK

First published in the United States by
DK Publishing, 375 Hudson Street
New York, NY 10014

06 07 08 09 10 10 9 8 7 6 5 4 3 2 1

Based on Wines of the World, first published by Dorling Kindersley 2004

A Cataloging-in-Publication record for this book is available from the Library of Congress.

ISBN-10: 0-7566-2255-7
ISBN-13: 978-0-7566-2255-8

Color reproduction by Colourscan, Singapore
Printed and bound in China by Leo

Discover more at www.dk.com

TOP 10 WINES USA

INCLUDING CANADIAN WINES

TOP 10 WINE SELECTIONS BY VINCENT GASNIER